LIFE ALONG THE SOUTH MANCHURIAN RAILWAY

THE MEMOIRS OF ITŌ TAKEO

Itō Takeo

LIFE ALONG THE SOUTH MANCHURIAN RAILWAY

THE MEMOIRS OF ITŌ TAKEO

Translated with an Introduction by **JOSHUA A. FOGEL**

An East Gate Book

M. E. Sharpe, Inc.

Armonk, New York/London

East Gate Books are edited by Douglas Merwin

Copyright © 1988 by M. E. Sharpe, Inc.
80 Business Park Drive, Armonk, New York 10504

Available in the United Kingdom and Europe from M. E. Sharpe,
Publishers, 3 Henrietta Street, London WC2E 8LU.

Library of Congress Cataloging-in-Publication Data

Itō, Takeo, 1895-
    Life along the South Manchurian Railway.

    Translation of: Mantetsu ni ikite.
    Includes bibliographical references and index.
    1. Minami Manshū Tetsudō Kabushiki Kaisha.
Chōsabu—History. 2. China—Research—China—
Manchuria—History. 3. Itō, Takeo, 1895-   .
4. Railroads—China—Manchuria—Employees—Biography.
5. Manchuria (China)—Biography. 6. Minami Manshū
Tetsudō Kabushiki Kaisha—Biography. I. Fogel,
Joshua A., 1950-   . II. Title.
HE3290.M5I7613   1988   385′.065′518   87-322030
ISBN 0-87332-465-X

Printed in the United States of America

Contents

Introduction:
Itō Takeo and the Research Work of the
South Manchurian Railway Company
    Joshua A. Fogel   vii

1. The Origins of the South Manchurian
Railway Company
The South Manchurian Railway and the
    Management of Manchuria   3
The Earliest Array of Research
    and Study Agencies   16

2. I Enter the Company
My First Encounter with China   29
The Shinjinkai and My Position   34
The Research Organs at the Time
    I Joined the SMR   43

3. My Years in Peking—Japan in China
Peking Friends and Acquaintances   60
In the History of China's Struggle
    for Liberation (1)   71
The Peking Institute   79
In the History of China's Struggle
    for Liberation (2)   87

4. The Study of China and the
Invasion of China
Modern China Studies at the SMR   102
The Research Section and Intelligence
    Agencies   114

5. The Manchurian Incident and the Reorganization of the South Manchurian Railway Company

The SMR Is Outwitted   121

The Fantasy of a State in Manchuria:
The Ideology of Ethnic Harmony   133

Behind the Scenes at the Economic
Research Association   151

6. The Sino-Japanese War Begins

In North China   160

Head of the Shanghai Office (1):
War and the Enlarged Research Department   170

Head of the Shanghai Office (2):
The Inside Story of Shanghai During the War   180

7. The SMR Incident: The Assault on Science

Point of Departure   186

The Second Series of Arrests   191

Arrested for Suspicion of a Scientific Approach   198

8. Defeat and the Dissolution of the Enlarged SMR: Structure Destroyed but Personnel Remain

Defeat   204

Final Scene of the Enlarged SMR   208

9. Conclusion:

A Statement of Introspection   216

Postscript   224

Addendum to the New Edition   225

Index   227

Joshua A. Fogel

Introduction: Itō Takeo and the Research Work of the South Manchurian Railway Company

In November 1906, following the Russo-Japanese War, Japan acquired the South Manchurian Railway (SMR). Gotō Shimpei was named its first president, and he immediately made plans for inaugurating a Research Department. "Research" was something Gotō considered utterly essential to colonial management. Tokutomi Sohō once said of Gotō: "Everyone has his own peculiarities. 'Research' is something that always hung close to Gotō like a briefcase."[1] The Research Department began in April 1907 as a small agency and changed its name many times, at its height, around 1940, encompassing a total of 2,354 employees. It lasted for thirty-eight years, before the arrest of many of its main operatives by the Kwantung Army and Japan's defeat in World War II spelled its demise. Who came to work for it and why? How did they see themselves? To what use was their research put, and what did they think about that? These are a few of the questions to be addressed in this introduction.

With Japan as the major force in Manchuria after 1906, Gotō Shimpei proceeded with his master plan for colonial development through research. The SMR received a huge quantity of capital, 200 million yen, half from the government and half in a public offering. It was never simply a for-profit company, for the SMR had a sense of immense responsibility, of mission. Among other things, Gotō wanted to be sure Manchuria never ceased to be under Japanese control, and that necessitated the immigration of

500,000 Japanese to the area.[2]

The slogan he devised for his conception of colonial control has been the object of considerable discussion: *bunsō teki bubi*, or "military preparedness in civil garb." Itō records Gotō's words on the subject:

> In short, colonial policy is military preparedness in civil garb; it is carrying out the hegemon's strategies under the flag of the kingly way. Such a colonial policy is inescapable in our time. What facilities, then, are necessary to see it through?
>
> We have to implement a cultural invasion with a Central Laboratory, popular education for the resident populace, and forge other academic and economic links. Invasion may not be an agreeable expression, but [language] aside we can generally call our policy one of invasion in civil garb. . . . Certain scholars have said that the secret of administration lies in taking advantage of the people's weaknesses. . . . Insofar as the secret to administration does hang on the weak points of mankind's way of life and in fact has throughout history, it is that much more so with colonial policy.[3]

No mincing of words here. A main research office was established in Dairen, a branch in Tokyo for the first project in January 1908, and the East Asian Economic Investigation Bureau (EEB) later that year. Both the human and natural sciences were to be researched, and a massive network of facilities took form in Manchuria and later in China proper. Gotō had been trained as a medical doctor in Germany, and the methodical, clinical approach to research problems became a hallmark of SMR research.

Gotō asked Professor Okamatsu Santarō of Kyoto University, an expert in Chinese law, to head the Research Department. Okamatsu had led the team that researched the "old customs" of Taiwan when Gotō had been colonial civil governor there. But, Okamatsu had never run the kind of Research Department now envisioned for Manchuria, so Gotō sent him to Europe to study the operations of such an outfit. Manchuria was many, many times the size of Taiwan; it was not yet an outright colony of Japan; and the Research Department had not yet acquired the kind of staff needed for a comparable study of Manchuria. Nonetheless, Gotō regarded it as absolutely indispensable to colonial management to have detailed research on the "Old Customs of Manchuria," for without this background knowledge, transforming and protecting the region would be difficult.[4]

The next major project, begun in response to a suggestion of Shiratori Kurakichi (founder of the Tokyo University School of Sinology), was a research facility for the study of Manchurian and Korean history and geography. Only an age of imperialism could have brought together two such different personalities as Shiratori and Gotō. Shiratori was the quintessential scholar, whose only thoughts about contemporary China were scornful and condescending.[5] With the Japanese now ruling the roost in Manchuria as well as in Korea (which would be officially annexed in a few years), Shiratori saw a prime opportunity (with Japanese military and financial support) to get his hands on previously unseen quantities of documents lying dormant throughout the region. Gotō had another vision altogether, but that would not become apparent until their three reports were published in 1913–1914. Shiratori had mobilized the cream of Tōdai Sinology, all of whom were his students, to compile this work: five volumes with a total of about 2,250 pages. Considering the short time they had to prepare this research, Shiratori's young men produced a magnificent piece of pioneering scholarship, a major inspiration to subsequent generations of Japanese, Chinese, and Western scholars.[6]

Gotō and subsequent SMR heads were not pleased, and the facility was immediately closed in 1914. Shiratori removed the materials to the Faculty of Letters at Tōdai and continued work for the next twenty years, producing another thirteen volumes of research. Gotō's displeasure was with the lack of colonial drive on the part of the pedants who had collected the documents with his money. Whatever scholarship their work may have achieved, he found little worth in it for Japanese colonization of the region under study. This mix of scholarship and colonial policy, *bunsō teki bubi* in Gotō's words, became the main research tradition at the SMR. Even though many of the researchers forgot this fact at times, the leaders never did. As Hara Kakuten has accurately noted, "research" organs were not established for the sake of scholarship, but to facilitate the management of Manchuria and the operations of the SMR.

In the late 1910s, the Research Department (or Research Section, as it was called after late 1908) began slowly to expand its staff, principally through its EEB, to 51 employees in 1918. By 1926, the number reached 167, and after the Manchurian Incident of 18 September 1931 it began to mushroom. The post-World War I era witnessed a boom in research institutes in the private industrial sector in Japan, and a competition developed for staff from university graduates. Only around 1920 did the SMR begin to consider hiring youngsters fresh out of college.[7] Itō Takeo, who completed school that year, recalls seeing an SMR recruitment poster on the Tōdai campus and going to sign up for a test.

Why would a liberal-minded young man run off to join a colonial company in a foreign country? From the time he graduated from Tokyo University in 1920 until the end of the war, Itō Takeo's life was consumed by SMR research on China. His autobiography is a fascinating document in the history of that immense Japanese colonial enterprise, its collection of invaluable materials on China, and the tragedy of those idealistic young men who went to work for the SMR and were broken by the Kwantung Army. As an undergraduate, Itō and his school buddies had become aware of large social issues of the day. Henry Smith has shown how these confused but concerned young men looked to themselves for standards the nation could no longer supply. Finally they formed the Shinjinkai (New Man Society), a liberal group of boys facing real problems in Japan and the world and posing timeless, imponderable questions about mankind. Ozaki Hotsumi, who later joined the SMR as a consultant, was one of Itō's classmates also in the Shinjinkai. "The typical member of the Shinjinkai," writes Chalmers Johnson, "adopted this socially tolerated method of student protest but took care not to go so far to the left as to endanger his chances for bureaucratic employment."[8]

But why the SMR? Itō explains that through the Shinjinkai he and his friends met men they admired like Sano Manabu, who was active in social movements in Japan and was also working for the EEB. They had already been introduced to China and the Chi-

nese revolution through the lectures of one of their heroes, Professor Yoshino Sakuzō, the patron saint of Taishō democracy.[9]
There was an excitement after World War I, when the Western
powers were no longer so powerful in East Asia, about the possi-
bilities for social reform, not just in Japan but all over East Asia.
Manchuria was sparsely populated; Japan was feeling a population and job crunch; and peaceful expansion for economic development became a popular notion of Japan's role in forging the new,
postwar international order. It is worth reiterating that Japanese
liberalism and reformism have never been strictly separated from
something known generically as "Japanese imperialism." Young
men like Itō Takeo were not thinking about the conquest of Asia
when they joined the SMR, and under their leadership many
other like-minded young men came to the research agencies of the
SMR.

There were, however, other men associated with SMR research who had radically different ideas about the future of
Northeast Asia. Take, by way of example, the case of Ōkawa
Shūmei. A believer in Indian Buddhism, he made a sharp transition to radical pan-Asianism when he learned of British imperialism and its deleterious effect on the real India. Two years later, in
1918, he joined the EEB. In China he made contact with Kita
Ikki, the noted fascist and former friend of Chinese revolutionary
Sung Chiao-jen, and got to know others who would later form the
extreme right wing. He attracted a good number of followers in
Manchuria in the 1930s.

Another group of right-wing SMR researchers who worked
intimately with the Kwantung Army would include first and foremost Miyazaki Masayoshi. Miyazaki had studied in Moscow before World War I, and he was there at the time of the Bolshevik
Revolution. He became the leading figure among SMR Russian
specialists, particularly in economic matters. He later forged
close ties with Ishiwara Kanji and the Kwantung Army, respond-
ing to their call for researchers to take a more active role in the
military's planning. He was there for the Kwantung Army at the
time of the Manchurian Incident.[10]

It is much less difficult to understand why men like Ōkawa,

Miyazaki, and those associated with such groups as the Manchurian Youth League went to work for the SMR. Nonetheless, the atmosphere among researchers was decidedly liberal and antimilitary. Every memoirist and every critic who has written about SMR research institutions, regardless of their political views, recalls the vibrantly open and free atmosphere there. That atmosphere made it possible for such different types to mix and work together. It also made research at the SMR and in Manchuria generally a much freer place than Japanese institutions or Japan.[11] As the political climate moved to the right at home, the SMR would become a haven for many leftists under great pressures in the mother country.

The Kwantung Army had high hopes for the research, but it was still unhappy at what it perceived to be a lack of direction on the part of the Research Section. For all their antimilitary feelings, the researchers could hardly fight the Kwantung Army; in fact, they often needed military protection in the field. This mutual need was satisfied when Sada Kōjirō became head of the Research Section in the mid–1920s. Sada worked hard to convince the Kwantung Army that by creating an anti-Japanese incident out of Chinese nationalism in Manchuria, the military could strengthen its hold in the region.[12] It may not be too far-fetched to say that the Manchurian Incident was the result.

After the Incident, it became increasingly apparent to many SMR researchers that they had no choice but to go along with the Kwantung Army. The volte-face of SMR President Uchida Kōsai illustrates this shift. Although initially antimilitary, after September 1931 he began proposing Manchurian independence, and he earned the disgust of many of his employees. By contrast, Vice-President Eguchi Teijō abruptly resigned, saying: "This [Incident] is Napoleon's Moscow. It will end in dismal failure." But, despite its harsher stance, the military still needed the research resources of the SMR to carry out its plans for construction in Manchuria/Manchukuo. It was able easily to entice Miyazaki Masayoshi and several others to plan the creation of an agency that would prepare policy for a new regime in Manchuria. Ultimately, they formed the Economic Research Association (ERA) within the SMR in January 1932, shortly before the establishment of the puppet state of Manchukuo was announced. Miyazaki and his co-workers then moved en masse over to the ERA to help facilitate the passage of research information to the Kwantung Army.[13]

Loyal research staffers began to fear for their autonomy, one of the cherished traditions at the Research Section. Their leaders could no longer be trusted, for everyone knew that SMR presidents came and went as a function of party politics back home, and now the head of research, Sada Kōjirō, was demonstrating more fidelity to the military than to his own men. Word got out in mid-1933 that, at the Kwantung Army's instigation, the Secretariat for Manchurian Affairs was planning a massive reorganization of the SMR to place it directly under the control of the military. Unified military control in the region, it was hoped, would facilitate economic and industrial development.

The SMR employees association, under the leadership of Itō Takeo, decided to confront the army. They issued a manifesto which began with the words: "The SMR is an inheritance bequeathed by the Meiji Emperor, and it will permit no arbitrary violations." As he vividly describes below, Itō immediately fell under a shadow, suspected by the military police and criticized openly by the Manchurian Youth League, but he persevered. The association decided to send representatives to the SMR stockholders' meeting in Tokyo with the authority to speak on behalf of the entire SMR staff. Even the SMR board of directors tried to stop this "unthinkable" opposition to the Kwantung Army—unsuccessfully. Ultimately, Itō realized that the only sane solution was for the employees association to devise its own reorganization plan, which the military eventually accepted.[14] Although ostensibly a victory, this was the last gasp of overt research independence. The Kwantung Army now had high hopes for research to be prepared by the ERA.

It was one of the fascinating ironies of this whole subject that the man hired to head the ERA's "agricultural economy" desk, a position of considerable importance and responsibility, was a well-known Marxist from Kyoto University, Ōgami Suehiro, a

man much influenced by Japan's first Marxist economist, Kawakami Hajime. Ōgami came to the SMR on the recommendation of
his senior classmate from Kyōdai, Amano Motonosuke, perhaps
the most famous scholar of Chinese agriculture in the postwar
period and also a Marxist. From the mid-1930s, they and others
brought numerous left-wing scholars onto the research staff.
ERA research still served the needs of the military, and this fact
no one denies. ERA staffers prepared enormous quantities of
reports, surveys, and document collections on every aspect of the
economy, natural resources, local industry, and agriculture of
Manchuria and North China. Research for the strategic needs of
the army was carried out in six areas—agriculture, the general
economy, timber, livestock, marine produce, and transport.[15]

Although researchers could no longer oppose the military in
their reports, there were several other means by which they
might express their own views. For example, the 101 members of
the ERA staff sent to study agriculture and water utilization
based their examination on the unit of the village. After a thorough analysis of the contemporary state of village life, their reports often stressed rural poverty in China and the ill it boded for
public order. Indeed, it could lead to banditry or rebellion, code
words for anti-Japanese or Communist uprisings. The implication
was clearly that unless conditions were improved, the Japanese
Army would have monumental problems on its hands. Independent views might also see the light of day in one of the SMR serial
publications. Tremendous debates transpired on such things as
the nature of the Chinese economy, and the lingua franca of these
debates was always Marxism. In addition there were private
ways to retain one's integrity, such as the study groups of SMR
researchers on Marx's *Capital* or Wittfogel's work.[16]

In 1935 Itō Takeo was transferred to the SMR office in Tientsin, near the Chi-tung (Kitō, in Japanese) area recently demilitarized by the Japanese Army. He used his time to devise a rural
investigation scheme for twenty-five villages in Chi-tung, to
which the military promptly and unexpectedly consented. Itō was
an avid student of the work of Liudvig I. Mad'iar, and he used the
theories of this Hungarian refugee in the Soviet Union to frame

the overall questions asked about the nature of Chinese villages, water control, and the like. Concern at this time with the Chinese village was not just an ERA phenomenon. Many scholars—John Lossing Buck, Wilhelm Wagner, Karl A. Wittfogel, and Mad'iar, among others—focused on it as holding the secret to the Chinese economy, and the works of all these foreign scholars were translated by SMR organs in the 1930s. Itō hoped that his fourteen teams (thirty-one researchers in all) would be able to apply "scientific" (namely, social scientific) methods and come up with "scientific" results. Although the reports were criticized then and Itō felt that they fell somewhat short of "science," we are nonetheless indebted to these researchers for bequeathing us a wealth of data not otherwise available anywhere, even though it may have served the military's needs. In actual fact, as Hara Kakuten has shown, some of the research findings did not accord with the military's wishes, and this led to distrust and eventual tragedy for some of the researchers.[17]

After the outbreak of the Sino-Japanese War in July 1937, the short-lived Industrial Department, which had replaced the ERA, was renamed the Research Department again (the Research Section having been dissolved shortly after the founding of the ERA). The military was becoming desperate, as it now needed large-scale integrated research for long-term planning. To that end, the Research Department underwent an enormous expansion from early 1939. The scholars brought onto the staff in the late 1930s were largely left-wing, socialists and Communists. This was precisely at the time when Marxism was all but banned in Japan, when (as Yamada Gōichi put it) if the expression *shakai* (social) appeared in the title of a book, it was usually confiscated. As Itō notes, and many have followed him in this regard, Japanese leftists were prepared to come to Manchuria for three reasons: their political movements in Japan had been crushed; they had been arrested and made *tenkō* (true or false); or their pasts were known and they were unable to find work at home.

The SMR research organs welcomed them with open arms, especially because the SMR was expanding and because these people, politics aside, were trained in research and had a "scientific" approach. Hama Masao put it well: "Between Japan and Manchuria there was an 'intellectual time-zone change.'" Among the many leftists who joined the SMR in the late 1930s were Ishihama Tomoyuki, Hosokawa Karoku, Itō Ritsu, Gushima Kenzaburō, and Ozaki Hotsumi. Some of these fellows then helped others, and some came with letters of introduction from former members of the Shinjinkai to the SMR's Shanghai office where Itō Takeo was now in charge. This body of leftists then proceeded, ironically, to aid the main players in Japan's pursuance of total war.[18]

The Kwantung Army must have been aware of all the thinkers of dangerous thoughts who were coming to work for the SMR. Staffer Yamaguchi Susumu recalls that when he left the Research Department in 1942 to return to Japan, he was given a party at a Shanghai restaurant, and the "Internationale" was sung by way of send-off.[19] This would have been unimaginable in Japan, and the army must have known about such things. I have no definitive answer to this puzzle, just a few suggestions. Perhaps the army believed these *tenkōsha* had truly reformed. More likely the military's need for overall large-scale research by a large number of well-trained social scientists, knowledgeable in the latest methodologies, outweighed immediate political interests. Men like Ōgami Suehiro were indeed Marxists, but only as intellectuals or theorists, not as movement activists. Might an otherwise obtuse military have been aware of such subtle distinctions? Might it have been willing to accept the value of Marxist analysis while keeping close wraps on any spread of a social (or socialist) movement in Manchuria or North China?

Indeed, many left-wing researchers had managed to conceive of the role of Japanese imperialism as ultimately progressive as far as Manchuria's and China's social development were concerned. In 1937 Ōgami wrote an essay arguing that the perspective of class was appropriate to historical research but that, in the final analysis, the state took precedence over class. Most researchers buried themselves in the institutes of the SMR to wait out the war.

Among the major "integrated" studies were the famous village investigations of North China, which have been used by Ramon Myers, Philip Huang, and most recently Prasenjit Duara. The SMR now had considerable experience with field work in Chinese villages (throughout Manchuria and Chi-tung), and a more thorough, long-term investigation was launched in 1940, completed in 1942. The fascinating background to this cycle of research has never been discussed in English. Although space precludes a detailed analysis here, one should at least note that, beyond the many volumes of research reports, an additional eighty or more articles were published in the SMR journal *Mantetsu chōsa geppō* by these very researchers on Chinese agriculture and village society.[20] This represents an untapped gold mine. The subjects of several other massive, "integrated" studies can only be mentioned: Chinese property laws, the textile industry, financial structures and practices, inflation, rice markets and brokers, wartime economic conditions, and much more.[21]

A remarkable story surrounds perhaps the most interesting of the "integrated" projects of SMR research, discussed briefly by Itō: "The Investigation of the Resistance Capacity of the Chinese" (Shina kōsenryoku chōsa). The implications of such a study for military needs are self-explanatory. In mid–1938 a base office in Dairen was set up, and research began out of the Research Department branch offices in Nanking, Hankow, Canton, Tokyo, Hong Kong, and elsewhere, with the center of operations under Itō's auspices in Shanghai. There were thirty researchers in all, including Ozaki Hotsumi. Nakanishi Tsutomu (Kō) had responsibility for writing up the group's findings.

Unbeknownst to all but a tiny handful of his co-workers was the fact that Nakanishi was all the time an operative of the Japan Communist Party (JCP). He had entered the Tō-A dōbun shoin (East Asian Common Culture Academy) in Shanghai in 1929, a common route into the SMR, and there he acquired a mastery of the Chinese language. During his time in school in China, he and several schoolmates developed overwhelming sympathies for the Chinese revolution, and they felt part of an international workers' movement. When he was finally expelled from school for his activities, he returned to Japan to take guidance from the JCP.

He returned to China to enter the SMR (presumably under a JCP directive) in April 1934. Hidden away as a small cog in a mammoth machine, he made his own studies of the workers' movement and general economic conditions in Manchuria, which were published in SMR journals in 1934-1935 and were completely in the analytical Marxist vein.[22]

By 1937 Nakanishi had developed the commonplace Communist depiction of the Chinese economy as "semifeudal and semicolonial." Manchuria was different, however, and he broke with the party line and disagreed with Ōgami's designation of "semifeudal" for the Northeast. In Manchuria, according to Nakanishi, one could clearly see the development of capitalism underway. The debate evolved in SMR serials, entirely in the language of Marxism, although it was not entirely a theoretical exercise. Nakanishi had been one of Itō Takeo's Chi-tung village investigators, and he had spent fifty-five days in four villages (one in each of four counties), questioning locals about land practices and the like. His analysis of the "ruthless feudal exploitation" of landlords in China, backed up by large quantities of data, provided the background for several more research essays in SMR journals. He also travelled extensively in China on his own or to make political contacts.[23]

Throughout his years in China, Nakanishi was establishing and retaining contact with a small circle of JCP and CCP agents. What these contacts ultimately amounted to is difficult to surmise; for it is precisely in this extremely intriguing aspect of his activities in China that Nakanishi combines a large dose of boasting with little real information. The result is a combination of frustration and infuriation on the part of the reader of his memoirs, for even the names of his Chinese Communist contacts are usually only pseudonyms. Two words he repeats endlessly throughout his memoirs are *undo* (the movement) and *soshiki* (the organization).[24]

For some reason Nakanishi, a low-level SMR employee and a sub rosa Communist, received major responsibility in this project, most likely because he, of all people, was on good terms with the military. He had served for a time in the Shanghai office of the special services unit of the Kwantung Army. He threw himself into this new work with a supreme sense of confidence that could only have been supported by complete methodological certainty. His assessment of the resistance capacity of the Chinese was not simply going to be a comparison of Chinese and Japanese troop strength or abstract economic might. One had to analyze the specific nature of the formation under wartime conditions of China's capacity to resist Japan materially, politically, and economically. The five basic elements to be studied in the formative process of Chinese resistance were: its weaknesses as a semi-colonial, semifeudal state; its national development over the previous century, especially the previous two decades; its backward rural economy; international conditions; and, finally, the Japanese occupation of China and the consequences of a guerrilla war.[25]

Two years after the commencement of research, a huge report was drawn up for submission to the Kwantung Army. It stressed the importance of political rather than purely economic factors in the mobilization of China's capacity to resist. Although Nakanishi was attacked by a more devoted Marxist on his staff for not giving sufficient weight to economics, he took the blame for this and stressed that for him "politics" encompassed "revolution." He argued that the political and economic realms had been inextricably united over the previous century of rapid modernization in China. And now the Japanese invasion had forced an alliance between the CCP and the KMT.[26]

China was an immense agrarian society, the report argued, and Japanese forces could occupy all of its major cities while the hinterland would become the bases of anti-Japanese resistance. For, and here Nakanishi injected results of his earlier research, the city and the village were not organically linked by economic ties as was the case in modern states. The links, such as existed, were extraeconomic. Researchers examined eleven places of Chinese resistance, especially in the countryside, and studied rural reconstruction, peasant mobilization, and the flow of goods to the resistance bases from foreign countries. They concluded that the Chinese could resist from the rural areas for an exceedingly long time in what would become a war of attrition, and that they would continue to receive military hardware from the USSR. In other words, Japan could not win militarily in China without stretching supply lines so far as to be unable to protect them.

The report went on the compare the roles of the CCP and the KMT in mobilizing resistance. It found the key in the CCP's superior political organization and military leadership. The Communists had been successful because they were implementing land reform programs to gain peasant support. The report emphasized that, because of the conditions of the United Front, these land policies were no longer aimed at eliminating private property in land or wiping out landlords as a class. By contrast, the KMT sought to preserve the landlord system; once trapped by the masses, such landlord-KMT types often realized they were better off with the Japanese, and Wang Ching-wei provided the perfect example. The fall of Hankow had made many Chinese landlords fear that support for Chiang Kai-shek would only insure their destruction, and that they now had to throw in their lot with the Japanese. But the real bases of resistance were in the rural hinterland, primarily under Communist control. Whereas the countryside could carry on economically without the urban areas, the reverse was not true. Thus, conquest of China's coastal cities did not imply control over China and the end of resistance; in addition, without the flow of goods from the countryside it ultimately would be impossible even to hold these areas. After all, even after the fall of Hankow and Canton, unoccupied China was still larger than the continental United States.[27]

Even from this brief, skeletal description of an extraordinaily rich study, it should be clear that Nakanishi was right in almost every way. Japan could not defeat China militarily. When Mao Tse-tung's "On Protracted War" became known shortly after this report was completed, it made many of the same points. Nakanishi now had to present his report to its sponsors, the Kwantung Army. He persuaded the commanding officer of Japan's Nanking Army that what he had to say was important, and he and Gushima Kenzaburō, a collaborator on the study, travelled by military transport to Tokyo to make the same report to General Staff Headquarters. There they argued on the basis of their findings for a political end to the war in China. When they were finished there was silence; finally a young staff officer asked: "So, then, what sites would it best for us to bomb? I'd like to know the key points." It is impossible to know if he was being sarcastic, if he was hiding something, or if he was just an idiot. They lectured elsewhere in Japan, before returning to China for engagements before military and civilian audiences in Peking, Chang-chia-k'ou, and elsewhere.[28]

As it became clear that the essential points of this study were in actuality taking place for all to see and defeat loomed large on the horizon, the military responded by "killing the messengers."

The first sign of trouble was the arrest in November 1941 by the Kempeitai (military police of the Kwantung Army) of Suzuki Kohei, Satō Daishirō, and about fifty other organizers of a peasant cooperative movement in northern Manchuria. Suzuki had been a member of the Shinjinkai at Tōdai, became involved in left-wing politics in the 1920s, was arrested three times in Japan, and was a well-known theorist and author of *Manshū no nōgyō kikō* (The Structure of Manchurian Agriculture). At the invitation of Ōgami Suehiro, he joined the Research Department, although he later broke with Ōgami theoretically, stressing (with Nakanishi) that developing capitalism characterized Manchurian agriculture. He left the RD in July 1940 to devote himself to organizing peasants in Manchuria. For their part, the authorities saw the agricultural collective movement, and its founder Satō Daishirō in particular, as organizing peasants in the interest of the rural areas, not working for the greater glory of the Japanese Empire.[29]

In June 1942, Nakanishi was arrested. He had expected the ax to fall at any moment, especially after the arrest of his friend Ozaki Hotsumi, and had packed his bags in preparation for departure to Yenan where fellow JCP member Nozaka Sanzō spent the entire war. Nakanishi claims to have known that Ozaki was a JCP member, but nothing at all about the Sorge spy ring. The Kempeitai had been following him for some time, apparently having begun to suspect his Communist sympathies after hearing his report on the resistance capacity of the Chinese. Apprehended with him in this sweep were his long-time friends, classmates at the East Asian Common Culture Academy, and fellow sub rosa Communists Anzai Kuraji, Ozaki Shōtarō, and Nishizato Tatsuo.[30]

The Kempeitai became convinced that what linked all these groups—the peasants organizers, the Ozaki circle, and Nakanishi and other members of the JCP—was the SMR's Research Department. No one was especially surprised then when the arrests moved over directly into the research staff. A Kempeitai order dated 17 September 1942 read in part:

> (1) The complete picture of the Communist movement among those associated with the SMR has now become clear as a result of the 28 January operation [arrests in the agricultural cooperative movement]. (2) The Kempeitai of the Kwantung Army will move to extract and remove it. (3) The heads of the Kempeitai in the cities of Hsinking, Dairen, Harbin, Fengtien, and Chin-chou are responsible for the arrest and detention of suspects according to item one of the enclosure. Arrests will begin on 21 September.[31]

Roughly fifty researchers were rounded up late that September. Among them Ōgami was arrested in Kyoto, where he was back teaching economics at Kyoto University. A second group of SMR employees, including Itō Takeo, was arrested in June and July 1943. There he was reunited with former members of the Shinjinkai, apparently one of the sufficient conditions for arrest. Ōgami and four others died of typhoid fever contracted in Manchurian prisons.[32]

The Kwantung Army had also begun a massive confiscation of books and periodicals in an effort to substantiate the existence of an intricate Communist plot among Japanese in Manchuria. The result was an 850-page tome, completed in 1944, entitled *Zai-Man Nikkei kyō sanshugi undō* (The Communist Movement of Japanese in Manchuria). It analyzed hundreds of books and articles principally from SMR publications for the political bent of the argument, and it described the background and activities of numerous SMR staffers.

In spite of their expectation of being apprehended after others' arrests, most SMR employees and subsequent commentators

seem genuinely surprised that the "SMR Incident" took place.
Weren't these researchers, whatever their theoretical views, aiding and abetting the Kwantung Army's conquest of Asia? Hadn't
they been providing the military with reams of research? The
answer to both questions is, of course, yes. In fact, many lived out
their lives with a profound sense of guilt. Ishidō Kiyotomo, a
former Shinjinkai member from Tōdai and an SMR researcher,
threw a wet blanket on this whole discussion several years ago
when he argued that the SMR Incident has to be understood
purely as an army operation. *Zai-Man Nikkei kyōsanshugi undō*,
he argues, is a tissue of pure fiction, proof of nothing. If the SMR
was packed with actively engaged Communists, why were those
arrested charged as individual violators of the peace preservation
law, and only a few charged as conspirators? The whole mess was
an elaborate excuse for the military's failures in China, he claims,
and this helps explain why many arrested researchers languished
in prison for several years before even being indicted.[33] The authorities were unable to get their stories straight. With the exception of Nakanishi Tsutomu and a tiny handful of others, all talk
of "Mantetsu Marxism" (the term is Yamada Gōichi's, but the
idea is widespread), he argues, is utter nonsense.

Except for the five who died of fever, arrested researchers did
not suffer excessively in prison, certainly not as much as apprehended Chinese Communist guerrillas. Itō Takeo recalls their
screams from regular torture sessions every evening, although
he himself was scarcely ever questioned. Nakanishi says not a
word about his prison experiences, interrogations, or torture;
and he welcomes 15 August 1945 as a glorious event, a "May
Fourth for East Asia." Released from prison that November, he
stayed in Tokyo to take his marching orders for the new postwar
movement rather than return home to his certainly anxious family.[34]

At one point in his memoirs, Nakanishi, who became a celebri-
ty in the postwar Communist movement in Japan, says of SMR
field work:

Our immensely detailed research in no way served the cause of
Japanese imperialism. Just before the 7 July [1937] invasion and war

in China, the Japanese military authorities in North China requested of the research organs of the SMR a study of whether they could
manage the five provinces of North China severed from South and
Central China. The conclusion reached by the SMR study was *no*.

Itō Takeo similarly suggests that the military attacked the SMR
as part of an irrational, antiscientific bias.

> From the very beginning the military welcomed and made use of the
> results of our research activities, but as defeat in the war became
> more clearly ominous, the situation changed. They compelled intel-
> lectuals to provide all sorts of materials and to study them, but when
> the results of all this research pointed to defeat, it was extremely
> undesirable to them. Although the military realized that it would be
> defeated, they had to continue to fight, and in order to cover over
> this complex they abused their final authority and the Research
> Department of the SMR was liquidated.
>
> The dissolution of the Research Department did not have to wait
> for the 15th of August—it had occurred in the arrests of 1942–43.
> The real significance of the SMR Incident lay in *the fascist assault
> and repression by the military of our scientific work*.[35]

There is more than a kernel of truth in both these assessments.
The Japanese military had some of the finest minds at their disposal to carry out the most detailed theoretical and field work
studies that have ever been done by anyone in China. None of the
researchers really fooled themselves into thinking that they were
not collaborating with the army; many actually felt that, although
they disagreed fundamentally with the military, in the final analysis they had the best interests of Japan and the Japanese at heart.
The army listened closely to what SMR researchers said and
wrote.

The problem is that when an SMR report conflicted with what
the army really wanted to do, as startlingly apparent in its response to Nakanishi's report on China's resistance capacity, the
army simply ignored it. A comparison with the American military
and the war in Vietnam suggests itself here. The United States
was similarly fighting a limited war against a guerrilla foe with
principal support in the villages (not the cities); and one can

imagine General Westmoreland's commissioning an American Nakanishi to prepare a report of the Vietnamese resistance and receiving exactly the same conclusions the Kwantung Army got. The interesting thing is that the U.S. Army, of course, had no such research operation as the SMR, and the U.S. government was often criticized in the 1960s for being colossally ignorant of Vietnamese realities; for, if it knew anything about its enemy and that enemy's history, the argument went, it never would have waged such a land war in Southeast Asia. The Kwantung Army had the largest research institute in the world at its beck and call. When it commissioned just such a report, it simply ignored the conclusions, arrested the authors, and pressed on with a calamitous and brutal war.

This experience should make us all pause and reflect. The simple fact that after 1932 the SMR researchers were not exercising free rein over the topics of their research is important. The vanity that one reads in the memoirs of those whose lives were linked to SMR research, vanity in the sense that their work, because of its "scientific" pretensions, was somehow beyond reproach, is startling. The army ran the whole show. The only freedom that researchers had was within parameters prescribed by the army. When the army needed a scapegoat, it blamed the researchers for reports full of Communist influence. The army did what it wanted.

I think that the questions often raised about the utility of this immense volume of research bequeathed by the SMR may be meaningless. Philip Huang and others caution that however valuable the village studies may seem, they were ultimately the product of an aggressive occupying force. First of all, the village field work in Manchuria and China proper was but one tiny part of the SMR's total research accomplishment. Second, researchers were clearly aware at the time of the extraordinary situation in which they found themselves. Third, if bias is imputed to researchers because of natural sympathies for their Japanese army sponsors (something, in any event, that is patently false for the most part), then would they not have striven to make their reports as accurate as possible? Finally, if there is any systemic prejudice in SMR research that postwar scholars using this material should be aware of, it is ironically the general intellectual Marxist inclination of all the research, especially the village studies and the numerous articles published separately in SMR journals.

In the postwar period many former SMR researchers found jobs without much difficulty in Japanese institutions of higher learning, something that had been virtually impossible for people of their general intellectual persuasion in the 1930s. Others became involved in leftist postwar politics. They lived with a mixture of guilt and pride: guilt for their service to Japanese imperialism; pride for their accomplishments as free-thinking scholars, a fact attested to by their arrest by the real perpetuators of aggression. Itō Takeo, Kazami Akira, and several others came together shortly after the war to organize a Sino-Japanese Friendship Association, which, like comparable associations elsewhere in the world, combined an uncritical respect for the People's Republic of China with criticism for the policies of the Japanese government vis-à-vis China. When their delegations returned from trips to China, they reported on a new, liberated country, something rapidly approaching heaven on earth.[36]

A number of SMR researchers decided to stay in China after the collapse of Japan and the SMR. Some of these men wanted to facilitate the transfer of the SMR's immense holdings to the Chinese. Although many returned to Japan after a period of five to ten years, they were instrumental in negotiating Sino-Japanese normalization. Yokogawa Jirō, an SMR sociologist arrested in 1943, remained in China for many years after 1945. Sarakura Masao, an employee in the Ore Deposit Geological Research Division of the SMR, chose to stay in the Northeast after the arrival of the Eighth Route Army. He worked for years with Chinese technicians to pass along the technological advances in Manchurian energy resources to the Chinese. Blamed for an accident and arrested as a "counterrevolutionary element," he eventually was repatriated to Japan where he wrote his memoirs, *Jinmin fuku nikki* (A Diary of Serving the People). In it he explained that he felt the SMR had a responsibility that its nearly forty years of research not go for naught.

Many of the SMR researchers who obtained university positions after the war became major figures in postwar East Asian studies. Village investigators Niida Noboru, Amano Motonosuke, and Hatada Takashi are just three of the most prominent names in three different fields. They have all gone to pains in the decades since the war's end to assume some measure of guilt, albeit unconscious, for Japanese imperialism, while retaining a sense of pride in their truly formidable accomplishments. This was also the only opportunity any of them would ever have to do field work in China.

Itō Takeo first published his memoirs in 1964, long before the more recent spate of books on the SMR, the Research Department, and Manchuria itself. His book has become a minor classic in this area of research and remembrance in Japan, in part because he was able to bridge many ideological gulfs that otherwise separated Japanese connected to these events in China and Japan. The integrity of his position has reached a position that has now become virtually unassailable. His memoirs were the starting point for Yamada Gōichi's study of the Research Department in 1977 and the most often quoted secondary source in Hara Kakuten's mammoth study of the Research Department published a few years ago.

When I first decided to translate *Mantetsu ni ikite* in 1984, I discussed it with Mr. Sakatani Yoshinao in Tokyo. It turned out that Mr. Sakatani was a close personal friend of Itō, and when he communicated the news Itō was overjoyed. He died shortly thereafter. I sent my draft translations of chapters to Sakatani as I completed them, and his corrections and comments amount to over one hundred pages. Was a translator ever so fortunate? Particular difficulty arose with a number of names of Germans who were invited to Japan as consultants in the early days of the SMR. All the biographical information supplied by Itō concerning Messrs. Thiess, Wiedfeldt, and others was simply copied uncritically by subsequent scholars (Yamada, Hara, and others) into their accounts, despite the fact (as I recently discovered) that this information is not completely correct. I have amended the translation in those few places where Itō introduced extraneous and incorrect material.

Notes

1. Cited in Yamada Gōichi, *Mantetsu chōsabu, eikō to zasetsu no yonjūnen* (The Research Department of the SMR, Forty Years of Glory and Frustration) (Tokyo: Nihon keizai shimbun sha, 1977), p. 9.

2. Hara Kakuten, "Mantetsu chōsabu no rekishi to Ajia kenkyū" (A History of the Research Department of the SMR and Asian Studies), part I, *Ajia keizai* 20, 4 (April 1979): 48, 60; and Yamada, *Mantetsu chōsabu*, pp. 12, 29–30.

3. Cited in Itō Takeo, *Mantetsu ni ikite* (Life Along the SMR) (Tokyo: Keisō shobō, 1964), pp. 16–17.

4. There has been considerable scholarly criticism of the massive volumes that this research produced: *Manshū kyūkan chōsa hōkoku* (Report on the Investigation into the Old Customs of Manchuria), 9 vols. Nonetheless, this research did uncover lots of historical materials unknown or thought lost. See Hara, "Mantetsu chōsabu no rekishi," part 3, *Ajia keizai* 20, 6 (June 1979): 58–68; and Yamada, *Mantetsu chōsabu*, p. 36. See also "Chūgoku kyūkan no chōsa ni tsuite: Amagai Kenzaburō shi o meguru zadankai" (On Research into the Old Customs of China: Roundtable Discussion with Amagai Kenzaburō), *Tōyō bunka* 25 (March 1958): 50–123; and Fukushima Masao, "Okamatsu Santarō hakushi no Taiwan kyūkan chōsa to, Kahoku nōson kankō chōsa ni okeru Suehiro Gentarō hakushi" (Professor Okamatsu Santarō's Research into the Old Customs of Taiwan and Professor Suehiro Gentarō in the Village Studies of North China), *Tōyō bunka* 25 (March 1958): 22–49.

5. On Shiratori, see Tsuda Sōkichi, "Shiratori hakushi shōden" (Short Biography of Professor Shiratori), in *Tsuda Sōkichi zenshū* (Collected Works of Tsuda Sōkichi), vol. 24 (Tokyo: Iwanami shoten, 1976): 107–61; and Joshua A. Fogel, *Politics and Sinology: The Case of Naitō Konan (1866–1934)* (Cambridge: Council on East Asian Studies, Harvard University, 1984), pp. 119–20.

6. Hara, "Mantetsu chōsabu no rekishi," part 14, *Ajia keizai* 21, 7 (July 1980): 111, 113–14, 116–18. The volumes are: (a) *Manshū rekishi chiri*, vol. 1 (459 pp.); vol. 2 (686 pp.), publ. 1913, comp. Shiratori Kurakichi, Yanai Wataru, Matsui Hitoshi, and Inaba Iwakichi. (b) *Chōsen rekishi chiri*, vol. 1 (366 pp.); vol. 2 (394 pp.), publ. 1913, comp. Ikeuchi Hiroshi and Tsuda Sōkichi. (c) *Bunroku keichō no eki* (360 pp.), publ. 1914, comp. Ikeuchi Hiroshi and Tsuda Sōkichi.

7. Andō Hikotarō, *Mantetsu: Nihon teikokushugi to Chūgoku* (The SMR: Japanese Imperialism and China) (Tokyo: Ochanomizu shobō, 1965), p. 236; Hara, "Mantetsu chōsabu no rekishi," part 2, *Ajia keizai* 20, 5 (May 1979): 63–67; and Harada Katsumasa, *Mantetsu* (The SMR) (Tokyo: Iwanami shoten, 1984), pp. 138–39.

8. Henry Dewitt Smith, *Japan's First Student Radicals* (Cambridge:

Harvard University Press, 1972), p. xii, *passim*; Chalmers Johnson, *An Instance of Treason: Ozaki Hotsumi and the Sorge Spy Ring* (Stanford: Stanford University Press, 1964), pp. 29–30; and Hara, "Mantetsu chōsabu no rekishi," part 9, *Ajia keizai* 21, 1 (January 1980):69–70.

9. Itō, *Mantetsu ni ikite*, pp. 43–50.

10. Hara, "Mantetsu chōsabu no rekishi," part 10, *Ajia keizai* 21, 2 (February 1980): 71–78; Yamada, *Mantetsu chōsabu*, pp. 61–63; Takeuchi Yoshimi, "Profile of Asian-Minded Man: Ōkawa Shūmei," *The Developing Economies* 7, 3 (1969): 367–79; Hara, "Mantetsu chōsabu no rekishi," part 3, pp. 61–62; and Mark R. Peattie, *Ishiwara Kanji and Japan's Confrontation with the West* (Princeton: Princeton University Press, 1975), pp. 109–10, 208.

11. Noma Kiyoshi, "Mantetsu keizai chōsakai setchi zengo" (The Establishment of the ERA of the SMR), *Rekishi hyōron* 169 (September 1964): 69, 72; Andō, *Mantetsu*, p. 236; Yamada, *Mantetsu chōsabu*, p. 142; and Nakanishi Tsutomu, *Chūgoku kakumei no arashi no naka de* (In the Tempest of the Chinese Revolution) (Tokyo: Aoki shoten, 1974), pp. 78, 81.

12. Yamada, *Mantetsu chōsabu*, pp. 88–95; Hara, "Mantetsu chōsabu no rekishi," part 3, pp. 60–61.

13. Itō, *Mantetsu ni ikite*, pp. 154–55; Yamada, *Mantetsu chōsabu*, pp. 97–102; Hara, "Mantetsu chōsabu no rekishi," part 19, *Ajia keizai* 22, 1 (January 1981): 78–79; and Noma, "Mantetsu keizai," pp. 72–74.

14. Itō, *Mantetsu ni ikite*, pp. 156–64; Hara, "Mantetsu chōsabu no rekishi," part 4, *Ajia keizai* 20, 7 (July 1979): 52–54.

15. Yamada, *Mantetsu chōsabu*, pp. 132–33; Ishidō Kiyotomo, "Mantetsu chōsabu to Marukusushugi" (The Research Department of the SMR and Marxism), vol. 2 in *Undō shi kenkyū* (Studies in the History of the Movement), ed. Undō shi kenkyūkai (Tokyo: San'ichi shobō, 1978), pp. 8, 10–11; Kusayanagi Daizō, *Jitsuroku Mantetsu chōsabu* (The True Story of the Research Department of the SMR), vol. 1 (Tokyo: Asahi shimbun sha, 1979), p. 121; Hara, "Mantetsu chōsabu no rekishi," part 19, pp. 84–87; part 20, *Ajia keizai* 22, 2 (February 1981): 87–90; part 21, *Ajia keizai* 22, 3 (March 1981): 89; part 25, *Ajia keizai* 22, 7 (July 1981): 91–95, 97–98; part 18, *Ajia keizai* 21, 12 (December 1980): 56–67; and part 29, *Ajia keizai* 23, 2 (February 1982): 74–75, 79.

16. Hara, "Mantetsu chōsabu no rekishi," part 30, *Ajia keizai* 23, 3 (March 1982): 71–74; Yamada, *Mantetsu chōsabu*, p. 129; and Ishidō, "Mantetsu chōsabu to Marukusushugi," p. 10.

17. Hara, "Mantetsu chōsabu no rekishi," part 32, *Ajia keizai* 23, 10 (October 1982): 58–61; part 31, *Ajia keizai* 23, 8 (August 1982): 77, 80, 82–86; and the details of the reports of the various research teams summarized in part 33, *Ajia keizai* 23, 12 (December 1982): 85–88.

18. Ibid., part 5, *Ajia keizai* 20, 8 (August 1979): 99, 102–103; Itō, *Mantetsu ni ikite*, pp. 217–19; citation from Kusayanagi, *Jitsuroku Mantetsu chōsabu* 1:25.

19. Kusayanagi, *Jitsuroku Mantetsu chōsabu* 1:25.

20. Ibid., pp. 122–25; Hara, "Mantetsu chōsabu no rekishi," part 34, *Ajia keizai* 24, 1 (January 1983): 60–66; part 35, *Ajia keizai* 24, 2 (February 1983): 80–84; and part 36, *Ajia keizai* 24, 3 (March 1983): 56–57, 60–62. Niida Noboru makes three important points about these village studies: (1) While they were surely part of Japan's colonial aims, the researchers themselves

were just scholars, without any political motives. (2) The aim of the research was not to come up with a "definitive thesis" (*teisetsu*) but to find, insofar as they could, the "living laws" (*ikeru hō*) that operated within Chinese society, replete with all their contradictions. (3) The research was carried out in the latter half of the Sino-Japanese War, and the researchers were unable to see the internal changes underway in Chinese villages at the time, new elements emerging and to be found in post-1949 society. See Noma Kiyoshi, "Chūgoku nōson kankō chōsa no kikaku to jisseki" (The Planning and Execution of the Village Studies in China), *Rekishi hyōron* 170 (October 1964): 9; and Hara, "Mantetsu chōsabu no rekishi," part 35, pp. 80–81.

21. Analyzed in much detail in Hara, "Mantetsu chōsabu no rekishi," part 37, *Ajia keizai* 24, 4 (April 1983): 61–63, 67–78; part 38, *Ajia keizai* 24, 5 (May 1983): 42–50; and part 39, *Ajia keizai* 24, 6 (June 1983): 74–80.

22. Nakanishi, *Chūgoku kakumei no arashi no naka de*, pp. 35–37, 47–48, 77–78, 81–83. On the Tō-A dōbun shoin, see Douglas R. Reynolds, "Chinese Area Studies in Prewar China: Japan's Tōa Dōbun Shoin in Shanghai, 1900–1945," *Journal of Asian Studies* 45, 4 (November 1986): 945–70.

23. Yamada, *Mantetsu chōsabu*, pp. 139, 150–52; Nakanishi, *Chūgoku kakumei no arashi no naka de*, pp. 96–101, 112–15.

24. See, for example, Nakanishi, *Chūgoku kakumei no arashi no naka de*, pp. 142–45, 166, 177, *passim*, especially the very last lines of his book, p. 275.

25. Shina kōsenryoku chōsa iinkai, *Shina kōsenryoku chōsa hōkoku* (Investigative Report into the Resistance Capacity of the Chinese) (Tokyo: San'ichi shobō, 1970); Nakanishi, *Chūgoku kakumei no arashi no naka de*, pp. 220–21; and Hara, "Mantetsu chōsabu no rekishi," part 41, *Ajia keizai* 24, 8 (August 1983): 83–84.

26. Miyanishi Yoshio, *Mantetsu chōsabu to Ozaki Hotsumi* (The Research Department of the SMR and Ozaki Hotsumi) (Tokyo: Aki shoten, 1983), pp. 56–57, 60, 65; and Hara, "Mantetsu chōsabu no rekishi," part 41, pp. 85–86.

27. Hara, "Mantetsu chōsabu no rekishi," part 41, pp. 86–87, 89–91; part 42, *Ajia keizai* 24, 9 (September 1983): 82–91; Kusayanagi, *Jitsuroku Mantetsu chōsabu* 1: 20–21; and Nakanishi, *Chūgoku kakumei no arashi no naka de*, p. 222.

28. Citation from Kusayanagi, *Jitsuroku Mantetsu chōsabu* 1:22; Nakanishi, *Chūgoku kakumei no arashi no naka de*, pp. 224, 242; and Itō, *Mantetsu ni ikite*, pp. 219–21.

29. Tanaka Takeo, *Tachibana Shiraki to Satō Daishirō: Gassakusha jiken Satō Daishirō no shōgai* (Tachibana Shiraki and Satō Daishirō: The Agricultural Cooperative Incident and the Career of Satō Daishirō) (Tokyo: Ryōkei shosha, 1975), pp. 1–5; Yamada, *Mantetsu chōsabu*, pp. 150–52; and Kodama Taizō, "Hiroku: Mantetsu chōsabu" (Memoir: The Research Department of the SMR), *Chūō kōron* 75, 13 (December 1960): 201, 203–204.

30. Nakanishi, *Chūgoku kakumei no arashi no naka de*, pp. 263–65, 269–74; and Itō, *Mantetsu ni ikite*, pp. 237–39.

31. Cited in Yamada, *Mantetsu chōsabu*, p. 162.

32. Nakanishi, *Chūgoku kakumei no arashi no naka de*, pp. 266–67; Itō, *Mantetsu ni ikite*, pp. 239–43; and Yamada, *Mantetsu chōsabu*, pp. 155, 158–60, 163–65.

33. Itō, *Mantetsu ni ikite*, pp. 243–51; Yamada, *Mantetsu chōsabu*, pp. 154–55; and Ishidō, "Mantetsu chōsabu to Marukusushugi," pp. 11–12, 16–18.

34. Itō, *Mantetsu ni ikite*, p. 244; Nakanishi, *Chūgoku kakumei no arashi no naka de*, p. 275.

35. Nakanishi, *Chūgoku kakumei no arashi no naka de*, p. 115; Itō, *Mantetsu ni ikite*, pp. 256–57, emphasis Itō's.

36. Itō, *Mantetsu ni ikite*, pp. 272–74, 277–78.

37. Ibid., 271–72; Yamada, *Mantetsu chōsabu*, pp. 182–83.

LIFE ALONG THE SOUTH MANCHURIAN RAILWAY

SOUTH MANCHURIAN

RAILWAY THE MEMOIRS OF ITŌ TAKEO

1

The Origins of the South Manchurian Railway Company

The South Manchurian Railway Company and the Management of Manchuria

The SMR and I

When I graduated from college in 1920, I entered the South Manchurian Railway Company (SMR), and for the next twenty-five years, ending just prior to the dismantling of the company with Japan's defeat in 1945, my life became a part of the SMR During that period I was away from China for a short time when the company sent me to study in Europe and America. Be that as it may, half of my career was consumed by the quarter century that I lived in China.

The South Manchurian Railway Company was a railroad company just as its name indicates. My life with the SMR, however, was spent without knowing a thing about the railroad business. I spent my entire tenure there with the research division. As everyone knows, the SMR was a mammoth company. Just before it was dissolved, it embraced a staff that claimed over 200,000 persons, including Chinese and Korean employees.

Our personnel could be divided into a wide variety of categories, but we can distinguish three types along occupational lines. The first were people who worked in the business department for railways, ports, coal mining, and the like, which were run by the

SMR. The second were people in the areas of administration, public welfare, education, and cultural affairs. The SMR had "railroad affiliate sites" that retained their own administrative powers along the lines of the railway. The third group of employees was involved with research and study, and I was a member of this division of the company.

We can also divide the employees along lines of nationality. Five different national groups worked for the SMR: Japanese, Chinese, Koreans, Russians, and Mongolians. The Japanese numbered about 140,000 just prior to its dissolution. We used the so-called personnel system of dividing the staff into white-collar workers, blue-collar workers, clerical workers, and part-time employees. The SMR was involved in all sorts of business, research, and intelligence matters, and it employed numerous consulting staff. These included retired military officers, a swarm of journalists, dopesters, and a wide assortment of others. Scholars and writers—such as the famous Nakae Ushikichi, Suzue Gen'ichi, Ozaki Hotsumi, Hosokawa Karoku, and Tachibana Shiraki—all worked for the SMR in a part-time consulting capacity. The majority of foreign intellectuals—Chinese, Korean, and Russian—were similarly attached to the SMR under this system. Incidentally, the people on part-time salary numbered about 2,000 at one time, and the research and study agencies supported a little less than 2,000 men, including consultants, in the Research Department's heyday around the time of the beginning of the Pacific War.

The scope of my contacts within the SMR concerned its research facilities because my life within the company was limited to matters of research. This all began when I entered the company in 1920. Although my story should begin at that point, I would like to start with an overview of the SMR Company. So, let me describe my thoughts about the "nature" of the SMR and then detail my experiences within it as they occurred.

The SMR Company

If I were to sum up the role of the SMR Company in a few words, I think it fair to say that as Japan embarked on the management of

Manchuria in the aftermath of its victory over Russia in 1905, the SMR served as an agency of the state. The first president, Gotō Shimpei, expressed the SMR's position as follows: "Insofar as the management of Manchuria is an affair of the 'railroad,' in name this is extraneous business but in fact this constitutes the main business we undertake. Thus, while the conduct of the entire military administration should in theory regulate the railroad business, in practice it has to be regulated by the railroad business." As Gotō described, Japanese imperialism in its advance into Manchuria, which comprised one part of China, chose to assume the form of a railroad company. To understand this, it is necessary to take into account a variety of factors, such as the international conditions facing Japan and its own physical might at that time.

The Portsmouth Treaty, signed between Japan and Imperial Russia after the Russo-Japanese War, consisted of two parts: recognition of Japan's occupation in Korea and a settlement regarding Japanese and Russian spheres of influence in Manchuria. It was a widespread opinion in and out of governmental circles in Japan after the war that Manchuria was territory *regained*. The temperament of the Japanese people aside, though, all that the treaty provided for with respect to Manchuria was the transfer from Russia of the southern branch (from Ch'ang-ch'un south) of the Chinese Eastern Railway and the Kwantung Leased Territory. Generally speaking, Japanese rights in Manchuria ended here, and anything further was recognized neither by China (the country concerned), nor by the imperialist Powers led by England and the United States, nor for that matter by Imperial Russia.

While Japan recognized that Chinese sovereignty extended to Manchuria, it sought through control over Manchuria to gain the same commercial and industrial privileges granted the Western Powers elsewhere in China as well as to strengthen its position there. To this was added the need to prepare for another war with Russia. Strengthening its position meant, in the final analysis, turning Manchuria into an occupied colony of Japan. And this transpired before the very eyes of the Chinese and the Powers. Here then was what Japan's "management of Manchuria" amounted to in the period following the Russo-Japanese War.

For Japan at this time, this was an extremely difficult business.

However, there was a remunerative item attached to the attainment of this goal: the Kwantung Leased Territory and the Chinese Eastern Railway both became Japanese. Control over the railroad appeared particularly conducive to the attainment of the goal of the management of Manchuria. Gotō Shimpei's remarks concerning the railroad and Manchuria, cited above, make this point explicitly. These were the very words the company used to explain to us what the role of the SMR was.

The Company's Beginnings

In actual fact, the SMR Company faced all sorts of problems before it began management in Manchuria, and numerous difficulties were to arise in the process. The first obstacle was the capital procurement necessary for the establishment of the company. This was related to the cause of the Harriman incident, an international "act of bad faith." The problem arose from a decision by the authorities that because of the state of national finances at the time—depleted by expenditures from the Russo-Japanese War and dependent on huge foreign loans—the goal of commencing control over Manchuria could not be carried through.

Furthermore, there was a pessimistic outlook regarding management of the railroad itself in Manchuria. Running a railroad that ran through a vast wilderness poor in resources as well as sparsely populated was not considered something that would yield much of a profit. Although management began, the losses incurred there were regarded as one more heavy burden on an already suffering national treasury.

Granting that Japanese nationalism was fanned after the victory over Russia and that control over Manchuria was regarded and pursued as new territory for the Empire, this adventuristic view of the management of Manchuria became rampant in Japan. Side by side with this development grew up an extremely fainthearted, opportunistic conception concerning Japanese control over Manchuria.

The SMR Company held its inaugural meeting on 26 November 1905. It had authorized capital to the order of 200 million yen and at that time it was called the largest joint-stock company ever in Japan. Half of the initial capital (100 million yen) was invested by the Japanese government in the form of capital in kind, namely existing railways that were turned over to Japan from the Chinese Eastern Railway, together with their rolling stock and other railway property, as well as the coal mines of Fu-shun and Yen-t'ai. The remaining 100 million yen was to be collected from the Japanese public. At the time of the company's founding, however, the amount collected was one-tenth of the total capital amount or 20 million yen, and the amount paid out at that time was 10 percent of that figure. Thus, the SMR Company began with 2 million yen in cash. The property of the existing railways given the SMR by the government had been destroyed by the ravages of the war over a two-year period, and the railroad had been shut down or demolished at many sites. Because in areas occupied by the Japanese Army the rails were used for wartime transport, for a time they were made narrow gauge. Thus, the rail lines were newly broken down, the rolling stock was in bad shape, and the coal mines had just been opened.

To restore the railroad and set the company's business on the right track, where was the huge amount of needed capital to be procured? This difficulty spawned a plan to dispose of any "faint-hearted conception of management" as well as to sell the management rights of the railroad to the American railway czar, Harriman.

Procurement of the initial capital, in the final analysis, was again supplied by foreign loans from the London market, just as expenses for the Russo-Japanese War had been offset earlier. In two flotations of 1907–1908, a total of 6 million pounds, the equivalent of 60 million yen, was raised. And, with this money the SMR Company of Japan commenced its management of Manchuria.

Gotō Shimpei

Amidst the fears and hopes that aroused the entire Japanese nation, Gotō Shimpei assumed office as the first president of the newly established SMR Company. He allegedly received the unanimous endorsement of the *genro* and other senior statesmen.

The circumstances surrounding this affair are detailed in his own "letter describing the reasons for [my] installation into the position of president of the Manchurian railways, offering to circulate it to your excellencies General Yamagata, Prime Minister Saionji, and Foreign Minister Hayashi, and soliciting the views of the foreign minister." Gotō had stated in this letter that at the time he assumed the position of president he had, in response to the opposition of the military authorities and the foreign ministry, given up his wish for the governor-general system which would preserve integrally all Japanese rights and privileges, a point of view he had long advocated. In any event, as its first president he was charged with bringing organization to the SMR, and the principle he adopted for running the company became the great power of control which he exercised not only over the company itself but over its entire personnel as well. His influence remained enormous to the end.

A wide variety of evaluations have been offered concerning Gotō Shimpei, differing according to commentator and time. More than anything, though, Gotō was a leader on a grand scale, a great man with the sort of character to which modern Japan gave birth. Under the auspices of the governor-general of Taiwan, Kodama Gentarō, Gotō had served as civil governor and accrued an impressive administrative record. This experience was esteemed highly when he assumed the task of managing Manchuria. Perhaps also he was the only experienced colonial manager in Japan at that time.

What, then, was his policy for running Manchuria? To avoid a long-winded explanation, let me quote Gotō himself, albeit at some length.

> The Russo-Japanese war will probably not conclude this situation in Manchuria with a single war. Will a second war actually come at some point in the future? If our prospects for victory are indeed to be anticipated, we must forestall our rival. If the chances for victory are not yet firm, we must devote ourselves to preparation and wait for the right time. Even if we are beaten in a second war, we must reserve for ourselves sufficient strength for effective

countermeasures. In short, we must occupy a position in Manchuria wherein we are far in the lead and, full of vigor and vitality, confront our rival with fatigue. The necessity of doing things in this way primarily involves the sort of skills needed for running a railroad. . . . Our plan for reaching this end is: (1) management over the railroad; (2) opening of the coal mines; (3) bringing over settlers; and (4) creating facilities for cattle-raising. Among these points, settlers [from Japan] must be seen as our most vital task. We fought a victorious war in vain to gain the superficial appearance today of having sovereignty over Korea, and although our diplomacy met with good results, in fact there is no success with such simple and rapid results. The attainment of sovereignty originated in the earlier emigration of Japanese settlers to Korean soil. The [European] Powers retained a superior position and we proved unable to contest them with words. Furthermore, we can resolve the Manchurian issue by moving people there. . . . If within ten years by managing the present railroad we are able to induce 500,000 Japanese to emigrate to Manchuria, we will not have to commence hostilities recklessly despite Russian strength. Control over the tempo toward war or peace will fall firmly into our hands. Even were Russia to defeat us in battle, we would still not lose the foundation to recover our successes.

Although the main point of this document was to demonstrate how to resist Imperial Russia in Manchuria effectively, pay heed to the method suggested by Gotō: Manchuria would become Japanified by bring in large numbers of Japanese immigrants by the railroad. Thus, his objective of managing Manchuria with the SMR was an effort at colonization, just as had been the case in Korea.

Gotō's Policy for the Management of Manchuria

A scientific mind was Gotō Shimpei's most distinctive trait. He had studied medical science in Germany, and he actively used the scientific perspective this training had given him in his work as the first president of the SMR. This point distinguished him from later presidents whose origins were in politics, and this "scientific" quality he possessed permeated the SMR till its very end.

When we entered the SMR, we were immediately informed that the company had this character. It was a colonial company but different from England's East India Company. It was also different from the Chinese Eastern Railway run by Imperial Russia. One SMR employee who later became a leader of the right wing, Ōkawa Shūmei, wrote as his doctoral thesis "A Study of the East India Company" with the intention of clearly noting the difference in character between the SMR and the East India Company. He produced it to meet the precise requirements of the company in clarifying the above distinction.

How, then, did the two differ? I think all of the SMR employees, or at least most of the intellectuals, understood the following. They were managing a company, the SMR, in Manchuria—and, through the continuity of such management, they were colonizing the region. In contemporary language we call this "indirect invasion." This course of action suggested that one learn from the example of England, which had adopted the approach of a single commercial company (the East India Company) to colonize India. The SMR was not to imitate the English plundering of India but observe a casual plan of encroachment. According to Gotō, this was where the two companies diverged.

This distinction is further emphasized by the difference from czarist Russia's Chinese Eastern Railway. Russia used the railway as a vehicle of military advance into the region. Unlike Russia, Japan cleared and developed the land in Manchuria. We were told that the SMR Company was a pioneering railway concern aimed at these goals for Japan. SMR employee Nagao Sakurō actually received his university degree with a thesis entitled "On the Colonial Railway as Seen from the Perspective of International Policy." The SMR stressed this rationale of "pioneering railway" not only, of course, to the outside world but also strongly within the company. Thus, employees were presented with the notion that the SMR, in addition to the colonial advantages for Japan, served the populace living in Manchuria. From this conception of things was born the idea that SMR personnel were supposed to cooperate and act in harmony with the local populace. Later something known as ethnic harmony was born of this.

Three Lines of Thought Within the SMR

Speaking in rather broad terms, we can divide SMR personnel along three ideological lines. The main stream of thought included people who saw Manchuria as Japan's lifeline. This was Matsuoka Yōsuke's favorite expression, but to put it another way, this might be called the vanguard of imperialism. Most of the Japanese members of the staff fell into this category. That is just what you would expect. The second group comprised people who believed in ethnic harmony among the different Asian peoples living in the region. Clearly not many people embraced this ideology, but as a mood it permeated the entire staff.

In its articles of incorporation the SMR specified that both Chinese and Koreans could own stock. Although there were very few who did, a number of Chinese became shareholders. These articles of incorporation were in effect until the beginning of the second Sino-Japanese War. Thus, the SMR and, hence, the management of Manchuria were not solely in the hands of Japanese. This fact may be seen as an expression of the second ideology I have cited, for the people who advocated ethnic harmony were representative of such a mood. A number of young intellectuals on the SMR staff in Manchuria began publishing a magazine entitled *Shin tenchi* (New Universe), and the harmonizers who had assembled around it were purged after World War II because they encouraged imperialism. Also, an official organ of the SMR staff association was created, and it was given the name *Kyōwa* (Harmony). I think we can get a glimpse of this second line of thought from this publication as well.

One individual representative of this ideology was Kasagi Yoshiaki, and I shall introduce him in more detail later. For a time he worked for the East Asian Economic Investigation Bureau and at the same time became a member of the Kōchisha (Society to Practice the Way of Heaven on Earth) of Ōkawa Shūmei of the imperialist faction. Later, he split with Ōkawa and formed an organization in Manchuria known as the Yūhōkai (or Daiyūhōkai, Majestic Peak Society). The young group of SMR staff members who gathered here believed firmly in the philosophy of ethnic harmony and Asian republicanism.

Gotō Shimpei's policy for the management of Manchuria, a plan that involved 500,000 Japanese settlers within a ten-year period, never did see fruition. Yet, as if in its place, Chinese settlers rushed into Manchuria after the SMR operations began. In this sense the SMR was a railroad company primarily in contact with Chinese. Thus, since it had to have their cooperation to run its affairs, there arose harmonizers who emphasized concord and ethnic harmony with the people living in the region. I think their position on the principle of harmony—that is, anticolonialism—was thoroughly conceptual, but insofar as they were themselves exceedingly earnest, they typified one aspect of the nature of the SMR.

When the state of Manchukuo was established [in 1932] and Kasagi Yoshiaki's group confronted actual realities, it became quite active for a time. Soon, however, they were suppressed by the military. I shall return to this topic later. The fact that later only the name, Kyōwakai (Concordia Society), remained indicates the vestiges of a conceptual anticolonialism.

Finally, the third school of thought was anticolonialist, although subjectively. This position emerged after men who had experienced the intellectual trends of Taishō democracy and believed in liberalism entered the research organs of the SMR. Anticolonialists may be ill-suited to a colonial company. However, a liberal tradition of sorts was preserved within the Research Department until the Pacific War began, and these anticolonialists were completely trapped and oppressed at the time of the SMR Incident, described below. If the company expected excellent investigative research, it had no choice but to employ in this very department men learned in the social sciences who were liberal of mind. While they were not necessarily warmly welcomed for this inclination by their superiors, they nonetheless remained in the SMR Company for this reason. I would like to recount in due time my own experiences in this regard.

Thus, within the SMR there were three lines of thought. The second group I mentioned, the ethnic harmonizers, argued that the SMR should cooperate cordially with the resident population in the field, but while conforming to the real demands of a colonial company—cordial exploitation—this group stressed the cordiality side of things. They were strongly opposed to the first group I mentioned, the imperialists, who placed more accent on the exploitation side. Both of these groups supported control over Manchuria and Japanese advancement into Manchuria and Mongolia. In this regard both originated in Gotō Shimpei's conception of colonial rule: "military preparedness in civil garb." This notion gave rise to the differentiation of these two groups in the actual development of the management over Manchuria. From this perspective, even the third line of thought, the liberal tradition of anticolonialism, was rooted in Gotō's scientific rationalism.

"Military Preparedness in Civil Garb"

My story may digress a bit now. I would like to go back and pick it up from the point where the SMR made known the fact that it was a pioneering railway.

It was often pointed out that, unlike Russia's Chinese Eastern Railway, the SMR did not simply provide military transport. In fact, a great deal of its energy was devoted to agricultural development and cultural facilities in Manchuria. Much effort was invested in agricultural development by setting up experimentation stations at various places, building nurseries, and increasing the productivity of the land. A Geological Research Institute was established, and the company worked to develop mineral resources. It also created the Central Laboratory on a massive scale, incomparably larger than the laboratories at specific sites in Japan or any of the research organs, and the arrangements were completed for the processing and industrialization of Manchuria's natural resources.

Furthermore, cultural institutions such as schools, hospitals, and environmental sanitation plants were established. The South Manchurian Medical College of Fengtien—initially known as the South Manchurian Medical Academy—was built by the SMR with the intention of training Chinese doctors. In the hospitals created by the SMR, medical treatment was offered to Chinese without any serious discrimination between them and Japanese nationals. This particular point was stressed.

In the educational field, the SMR established facilities for the Chinese people—public schools, middle schools, and normal schools—in cities along the railway lines. The major responsibility for putting these cultural-educational installations in order followed SMR plans. Gotō Shimpei called this "indirect preparation to serve as the basis for colonial policy." He defined his vision of colonial management that laid such preparations as "military preparedness in civil garb" (*bunsō teki bubi*). He had the following to say concerning the secret to this policy:

> In short, colonial policy is military preparedness in civil garb; it is carrying out the hegemon's strategies under the flag of the kingly way. Such a colonial policy is inescapable in our time. What facilities, then, are necessary to see it through?
>
> We have to implement a cultural invasion with a Central Laboratory, popular education for the resident populace, and forge other academic and economic links. Invasion may not be an agreeable expression, but [language] aside we can generally call our policy one of invasion in civil garb. . . . Certain scholars have said that the secret of administration lies in taking advantage of the people's weaknesses. . . . Insofar as the secret to administration does hang on the weak points of mankind's way of life and in fact has throughout history, it is that much more so with colonial policy.

Gotō went on to say that Manchuria was certain to be transformed into a Japanese-occupied colony if "the people who are night and day taking these matters into consideration for effective use come to work as the governor-general or as top executives of the company" and gain control over Manchuria with a thorough spirit of military preparedness in civil garb.

This conception of "military preparedness in civil garb" was opposed to one of military preparedness in military garb. In other words, it contradicted the notion of holding Manchuria with military might in preparation for a second Russo-Japanese war. These were the two directions for the colonization of Manchuria to take: through a hazardous military policy or through the gradual investment of capital. It is fair to say that on this point Gotō opted for the latter.

His ideas for emphasizing capital export were expressed in the colonial management policies constructed around the railway. Yet we should note that at the basis of this colonial policy lay agencies for "indirect preparedness," which were to lure native Japanese capital—the Geological Research Institute, the Central Laboratory, Agricultural Experiment Stations, schools, hospitals, and the like. Furthermore, the benefits from these cultural facilities were said to hit at the weaknesses of the colonized people, seduce them, and make them dependent on the home country. By capturing the minds of the colonized, one was said to have attained the secret to complete control over the colony.

Gotō's conception of things, as he put it himself, was a colonial policy for this century. In other words, it partially paralleled the normal course of a colonial management corresponding to the new imperialist age of the twentieth century. This is the crucial point to keep in mind when we evaluate Japanese imperialism at the time, colonialist statesmen, and, in particular, Gotō Shimpei.

As president of the SMR, and afterward as well, Gotō offered numerous innovative plans and visions. Politicians and journalists ridiculed all of these as his "huge cloth wrapper" (*furoshiki*). Gotō's ideas, however, were on a wholly different plane from the braggadocio of the later president of the enlarged SMR, Matsuoka Yōsuke, with whom he is often compared. Matsuoka's plan for a "3-P" railway line from Peking to Paotou to the Persian Gulf was an illusion pure and simple. In the case of Gotō's plans, though, even if they never saw fruition, we should pay attention to the fact that they were supported by a pragmatic rationalism that emerged during a wave of unfolding imperialism.

The Earliest Array of Research and Study Agencies

Research Agencies and the Management of Manchuria

Gotō Shimpei established the research and study facilities as one link in his conception of the management of Manchuria, "military preparedness in civil garb." At the time of its founding the SMR Company was divided structurally into three major divisions: field work organs for railways, harbors, and mines; local bureaus in charge of subsidiary administrations as well as cultural matters; and the Research Department. The following year the Research Department was reorganized and renamed the Research Section. The three divisions were now called, respectively, the Railway Section, the Local Section, and the Research Section— known collectively as the Three Section system. Thus, at the time of its founding one of the three legs supporting this immense company, the SMR, unprecedented for Japan in size, was its research agencies. I think one can see from the creation of this structure the immensity of Gotō's hopes and aspirations.

What attracted Gotō to research was rooted, as I mentioned above, in his scientific and rationalistic nature. Yet, on top of all this, the enthusiasm and ambition that went into the creation of the Research Section at the main office in Dairen, the East Asian Economic Investigation Bureau in Tokyo, the Research Bureau for the Study of the Geography and History of Manchuria and Korea as well as the Central Laboratory, the Geological Research Institute, and the Agricultural Experiment Stations of the Natural Sciences Agency—this massive array of research and study organs—occurred in the last years of the Meiji era, which was a tribute to his foresight. "I cannot exaggerate the essentiality to the management of Manchuria of research into the economic conditions of Manchuria as well as study of popular and commercial customs," he explained in the context of the objective of establishing research institutions. "For only after we have completed research in our hands can we undertake specific policies." While it was only natural that he would explain the necessity to the management of Manchuria of these research institutes, there would still be difficulties in seeing this through to completion.

Investigation into the Old Customs of Taiwan and Manchuria

The establishment of the SMR, and the founding of its research organs, mark a major epoch in the history of Japanese Sinology. The cornerstone of research concerning China was laid here in the form of colonial studies. Bearing this point in mind, let me now describe the creation of each of the various research institutions.

When he had been the civil governor of Taiwan, Gotō Shimpei mobilized the scholars Okamatsu Santarō and Oda Yorozu to carry out, respectively, a massive investigation of the old customs of Taiwan and the editing of the Ch'ing administrative code. In particular, the study of Taiwanese customs later proved useful in effectively implementing the colonial administration in Taiwan, and his accomplishments as civil governor were attributed in large measure to the success of this investigation.

The research on the "old customs" of Taiwan was understood generally to indicate Gotō Shimpei's cultural sense, although the man who actually proposed such a study was Ouchi Ushinosuke. Just before the start of the first Sino-Japanese War, Ōuchi had been a student in Germany. He studied German colonial policy, and in order to penetrate its mysteries he entered a colonial business organ and gained the experience of actually participating in colonial affairs. After returning to Japan, in 1898 he sought a meeting with Gotō Shimpei, who was then about to leave to take up his post as civil governor of Taiwan. For several hours he spoke to Gotō about what a colonial policy ought to include, and apparently Gotō had Ōuchi accompany him to Taiwan. He completed the writing of his views on board ship, entitled the piece "Views on Colonial Administration," and presented it to Gotō. He listed in great detail all the reasons why an investigation of indigenous customs was indispensable to colonial rule, and he went so far as to list concrete methods to carry out such an investigation.

Following this scheme, Gotō decided upon arrival in Taiwan to call on Kyoto University Professor Okamatsu Santarō and entrust him with just such an investigation in Taiwan, before even a land survey commenced. "The most essential tasks in ruling a colony," as Okamatsu put it later, "are to study the old customs and institutions of the colony, different in human feelings and practices [from our own], and to make laws that will conform best to them." This is now considered common knowledge in colonial rule.

Making the most of this experience in Taiwan, Gotō again quickly summoned Professor Okamatsu from Kyoto University when the SMR project began and appointed him executive director of the Research Department. Thus, an investigation of the "old customs" of Manchuria became the first task for the SMR's Research Department [soon to be renamed the Research Section]. At this time, Mr. Ōuchi moved with Gotō from Taiwan to Manchuria and took up the new post of civil counselor to the office of the Kwantung governor-general. Gotō Shimpei simultaneously assumed the positions of SMR president and adviser to the office of the Kwantung Governor-General. Accordingly, Ōuchi performed tasks under Gotō's command. And, needless to say, Ōuchi at the same time provided assistance to the work on the investigation into the old customs of Manchuria.

The Style of the Early Period

Mr. Kawamura Chūjirō, who served as head of the Research Section in the early years, from late 1908 through 1917, also had had actual experience in the investigation of Taiwanese customs. Before that, during the single year of the existence of the Research Department, Director Okamatsu Santarō was directly in charge. Kawamura later became a director of the SMR. Among the main members of the staff of the Research Section involved in this investigation beneath him were Mori Mikage, a master of the Russian language and later head of the Harbin Museum; Mori

Shigeru, a long-time Chinese-language expert; and Nomura Kiyoki, also involved in Chinese matters and later head of the Foreign Affairs Section of the SMR. In addition, among the staff of the Research Section in the early years were Kamebuchi Ryūchō and Amakai Kenzaburō, in charge of and authorities on land law and government land systems, and Isaka Hideo and Miura Yoshitomi, who were in charge of monetary and financial matters. According to the records, the Research Section staff in 1909 numbered forty-two, and six of them were dismissed the following year.

I heard from Miura, the only one among them who is still alive today [in 1964] and who was until recently the mayor of the city of Usuki, that as head of the Research Section Kawamura was extremely austere in his plans, demanded innovative research from each member of the staff, examined every detailed item one by one, and repeatedly asked questions until he personally understood everything. Without this procedure he would not allow a report to be written. For the documents and materials used for preparing reports, Miura said that Kawamura demanded substantiation based on research in the field insofar as it then was possible. As a result, no time limits were attached to the preparation of written reports.

In another story, one I heard from Amakai, who recently passed away, in his first three years after joining the Research Section he did not have to write a single report. He had to spend this time exclusively poring over documents and studying. He said he felt humiliated in the office, but in matters of salary and bonuses he was no different from the other staff members. Such leniency remained a feature of the Research Section in my years there; it was one aspect of the magnanimity of the SMR.

The staff was trained in this way, and in actual investigative work the SMR was never sparing of time or money for document searches or field work. Thus, in matters of management, staff members were trained as specialized authorities. Each of the Research Section staff was allowed and encouraged to display his capacities freely. This style eventually became a tradition at the Research Section of the SMR.

The Policy of "Affecting a Scholarly Manner"

The fact that the style of not restraining the research and study agencies with rules and regulations became a tradition of sorts might be called the founder Gotō Shimpei's policy on scholarship. His notion was that study and learning originated in colonial management, which led to investigative activities, which in turn led to scholarship. Let me now introduce his views on "affecting a scholarly manner."

The time was when Gotō again chose Okamatsu Santarō, dean of the Law Faculty at Kyoto University, to be executive director in charge of both the SMR's Research Department and legal matters. Kyoto University, in compliance with the concerns of the Ministry of Education, opposed him, saying: "To give an educational official on the job such a concurrent post is to make him an employee of a commercial company, and that is exceedingly inexcusable." Gotō responded with a critique of the state of scholarship at the imperial universities then and of the relationship between scholarship, reality, and politics.

> Nowadays . . . learning as provided by education in our schools is no more than training in accepted views and fixed opinions. . . . As a result, it used to be that many scholars educated in their own traditions became biased, idiotic purveyors of abstract theories. Statesmen think highly of these scholars as wise men and establish laws and legal institutions based upon their investigations which are only desk plans. Hence, although excessively literary, their actual utility is inordinately wanting, and each and every law and ordinance is apt to prove to be an obstacle in actual society. Therefore, the voices of opposition to such laws and ordinances were many. *The vulgar opinion is wrong that reveres scholarship for standing outside actual affairs and institutions for serving scholars. They simply do not understand that scholarship is worthwhile only when it is consistent with reality and that institutions have value only because they derive from actual society.* For this reason, these "scholars" with their vulgar opinions nowadays are not the scholars for whom we are looking. The Manchurian issue cannot be resolved simply on the basis of written arguments. [Emphasis Gotō's]

Then, in concrete terms, scholars and scholarship of what sort corresponded to the actual needs of colonial rule? What sort of scholarship would take shape in the field and bring about what kinds of benefit to colonial policy? After discussing these questions, Gotō continued:

It is my wish that we be rid of the vice of rendering university lectures empty talk and that we implement my notion of affecting a scholarly manner. The Professor [i.e., Okamatsu Santarō] will thus gain actual experience in the civil and commercial activities of the colony; this will supply material for his research which will be transported to the classroom, and we can expect great success by passing this on down to posterity for the use of the nation.

The hopes Gotō invested in the research and study institutes were not merely that they would prove useful to policy planning for colonial management. He had dreams beyond these. It is clear at the same time just what a pragmatist he was. Whether or not Japanese scholars could fulfill his hopes was another problem. In considering this point we can in part anticipate the fate that the research facilities would meet.

Dr. Shiratori Kurakichi and the Research Bureau for the Study of the Geography and History of Manchuria and Korea

We can see an excellent example of this in the case of Professor Shiratori Kurakichi, who founded the Research Bureau for the Study of the Geography and History of Manchuria and Korea within the SMR. At the time Shiratori was professor at Tokyo Imperial University and was energetically active in establishing East Asian historical studies in Japan. One day he paid Gotō a visit and spoke vigorously on behalf of the necessity of pursuing academic studies into the history and geography of Manchuria and Korea.

When conditions calmed down following the Russo-Japanese War, the Japanese people began the economic management of southern Manchuria, and consequently the duty to protect and develop Korea fell upon our shoulders. I advocated at that time the urgency of our undertaking basic research into the regions of Manchuria and Korea from a scholarly angle. *I have two ideas in mind here: research from the perspective of the actual needs of the management of Manchuria and Korea; and from a purely scholarly point of view.* All the matters before us now must, needless to say, be built on a firm scholarly basis, and of course the management of Manchuria and Korea must as well. [Emphasis Itō's]

Gotō's response was as follows: "In order to make known Japan's distinctive mission in Asia and thus clarify the basis for the activities of Asian peoples in Asia, an investigation of historical customs is of great need to colonial policy." In January 1908, the Research Bureau for the Study of the Geography and History of Manchuria and Korea was established within the Tokyo branch office of the SMR. That day is very important in the history of the formation of Oriental historical studies in Japan. From the start academic scholars responded to this dream of a research institution that had been the brain-child of Gotō's taste for investigative research. It was a significant event both in the history of the founding of SMR research agencies and in the history of Japanese colonialism. This organ was regarded as a sort of favorite son of the SMR research facilities.

This date is etched into the history of Asian studies because it did not post marvelous achievements thereafter at the SMR. Let me touch first on the cause of this. I have already introduced Gotō's notion of "affecting a scholarly manner," his expectations deriving from it, and Shiratori's speech in response to it. The "cause" lay in the collision between the way the two men understood "reality" and "scholarship."

Shiratori's point, that he "advocated the urgency of our undertaking basic research into the regions of Manchuria and Korea from a scholarly angle," was in accord with Gotō's aspirations. By basic research he distinguished that undertaken from "a purely scholarly point of view" from "research from the actual needs" [of managing Manchuria and Korea]. However, Gotō firmly believed in the consistency between scholarship and practical affairs when he said: "Scholarship is only worthwhile when it is consistent with reality . . . and studying colonial civil and commercial activities will supply material for research." In accord with his belief, he expected the cooperation of the "scholarship" side in practical affairs and, by the same token, was prepared to have the "practical affairs" side be of service to scholarship. These two modes of thinking were tantamount to enemies in the same boat, for Gotō expected too much of Shiratori. The Research Bureau for the Study of the Geography and History of Manchuria and Korea took shape with the mutual misunderstanding of these two sides of the matter firmly in Gotō's mind. Taking advantage of what was referred to as Gotō Shimpei's "huge cloth wrapper," Professor Shiratori parasitically garnered research funds off the host of the SMR. This, I think, is the assessment one often gets of the Research Bureau for the Study of the Geography and History of Manchuria and Korea.

Establishment of the East Asian Economic Investigation Bureau and Foreign Advisers

Gotō's "huge cloth wrapper" was evident even in the formation of the East Asian Economic Investigation Bureau. He explained his object in setting it up: "Based on the collection and organization of a wide variety of materials concerned with the world's economy, particularly that of East Asia, we will gain a thorough knowledge of the economic position of Japan, Manchuria, and Mongolia." But you can equally see it as a necessary installation for Japanese imperialism in an era when the latter was just beginning. Global collection and analysis of information were thus absolutely essential. Because the scope of the work of the Research Section of the SMR was limited to China and Manchuria, the new body had to cover what spilled over from there.

Although essential, setting it up in Japan was quite a major undertaking at first. This "huge cloth wrapper" required an immense vision and a firm decisiveness, characteristics fitting Gotō Shimpei well. Nonetheless, since the first research organs were established to operate independently, very often inexperience afflicted their methods of collecting, organizing, and researching materials. Director Okamatsu Santarō, who was also the bureau chief, traveled about Europe and studied this matter until he found some guidance. He made a good number of appointments of Europeans and Americans with vast experience in these areas, and a succession of Westerners came to join the East Asian Economic Investigation Bureau. To provide a profile of these men, I should first mention Doctor Thiess, who was then a professor at the Danzig Senior Technical School. There is a brief episode concerning him that is worth recounting.

During his time in Taiwan, Gotō hit on the idea of the need for an overall research institute after having read an essay about such a venture in a German economics magazine. Afterward he apparently became absorbed in the idea. The author of the article was Thiess. When Gotō later became president of the SMR and undertook to create his heart's desire in a research organ, he was reminded of Thiess. And so, it was said, Thiess came to Japan, although one must take this story with a grain of salt.

Thiess accepted the invitation and came to Japan after having observed a variety of research installations in Berlin, Hamburg, Bremen, Paris, and Moscow. After taking up his post, he cooperated with Okamatsu to build the organization for a research facility based on the research department of the Parisian Crédit Lyonnais and seasoned with the strengths of various research institutes in Berlin. The project was nearly completed as his term of office to a close in 1911. He returned to Germany, although later during the Weimar period he became a minister in the Social-Democratic party. When I was temporarily at the East Asian Economic Investigation Bureau, he was extremely helpful in our efforts to get books from Germany. It was because of him that they used to say that to purchase books from Germany at that time it was cheapest to go through the East Asian Economic Investigation Bureau.

Following Thiess was Dr. Otto Wiedfeldt, who was then an imperially appointed counsellor to the German Ministry of Home Affairs. Making use of a rarely obtained temporary retirement, he made his way to Japan. According to Gotō Shimpei, he was

selected to be an imperial counsellor to the Home Ministry from a
rural district; and, as I heard from Mr. Matsuoka Kimpei who
worked with him, he was indeed a practical intellectual. In Germany he was apparently quite famous as a specialist in problems
of social insurance. After returning to his home country, he became a director on the board of the Krupp Company and ambassador to the United States. He was said to have been an extremely
brilliant man or a man able to cut such a figure. Thereafter Dr.
Behrendt, a teacher in the Mannheim Higher Commercial School,
worked for the East Asian Economic Investigation Bureau
through 1915. These three German specialists virtually laid the
foundation for this organization.

Next, let me introduce several foreigners who were hired to
work for the SMR. There was a German by the name of Baumfeld
who was an assistant at the East Asian Economic Investigation
Bureau. He came with Thiess to Japan and stayed for many years
after Thiess returned home. Through him the groundwork was
set for the organization of materials for this research facility. He
is still alive and well, I believe, in Japan. In addition, although not
in the East Asian Economic Investigation Bureau, a man by the
name of Musfeldt was employed as an adviser in the SMR Research Section when Ishikawa Tetsuo was section head. He had
been taken prisoner during the Tsingtao strife at the time of the
First World War. There was also a journalist by the name of
Robert Kinney, who was hired as a high-level consultant to Ma-
tuoka Yōsuke. He worked for the SMR in the capacity of a suppli-
er of publicity overseas and information on the foreign language
press. After the Manchurian Incident, it was suspected that he
was engaging in spying activities for the Americans and was
dismissed, but his son, Bishop Kinney, worked straight through
till the end of the war at the SMR.

The Natural Sciences Agency

Among the foreigners, a Czech by the name of Rudolph Jena was
employed for about five years at the Central Laboratory. He was
a glass-cutting technician, and through him the SMR learned his

trade, which has been bequeathed to the Asahi Glass Company to this day.

The Central Laboratory was the nexus of the Natural Sciences Agency's research institutes. The research facilities of the SMR were not limited to social and human science agencies—e.g., its Research Section, the East Asian Economic Investigation Bureau, and the Research Bureau for the Study of the Geography and History of Manchuria and Korea. As the sole colonial company in Manchuria, the SMR found it necessary to establish study organs for the natural resources that were to be expropriated, for the investigation and selection of resources, and for the industrialization and commercialization of the processes whereby these resources were extracted.

The Central Laboratory was first established for this purpose. Created in 1908 by the office of the Kwantung governor-general, rapid installation and expansion necessitated its control passing in May 1910 to the capital-rich SMR. The SMR invited Doctor of Engineering Takayama Jintarō, head of the Tokyo Industrial Laboratory, and entrusted him with planning for its expansion. Under his aegis it became an immense, comprehensive physical and chemical research institute, unprecedented in Japan at that time. Its structure entailed seven divisions: (1) analysis, (2) manufacture chemistry, (3) silk-thread manufacture and dyeing and weaving, (4) ceramics, (5) alcohol brewing, (6) health and sanitation chemistry, and (7) electrical chemistry. Each of these gave birth to advances in such areas as modern chemical means for soybean oil extraction, research into the diversification of soybean oil products, and coal liquefaction planning.

The establishment of the Geological Research Institute occurred at the same time, May 1910, that control over the Central Laboratory passed to the SMR. In actual fact it began earlier, at the same time that the SMR started business, under the name of the Geological Section of the Mining Department. Its first important task was an investigation concerning the opening of the Fu-shun coal mines. It was anticipated from early on that Fu-shun would provide a significant source of profit for the SMR, and a geological investigation was carried out to this end. As soon as the research was complete, a much broader study of the mineral wealth of all of Manchuria was implemented.

Once the Geological Research Institute came into being, Kido Chūtarō, son of Meiji statesman Kido Kōin, took over as its head. The great iron-ore deposits of the An-shan area were discovered during his tenure at the institute, and the An-shan Iron Works was built to extract this natural resource. The amount of iron ore in the ground at An-shan was enormous, but it was low-quality ore in that its iron content was low. Thus, tremendous effort went into its commercialization. During this process an original Japanese chemical technique—known in Japanese as *kangen baishō hō*—was developed with the cooperation of the technical staff of the Central Laboratory, and this made commercialization successful. Also, oil drilling enterprises from the waste oil shale of the Fu-shun coal mines as well as a coal liquefaction operation were made commercial by this method. The brilliance of the SMR's study institutions at the Natural Sciences Agency reverberated throughout the realm.

Agricultural Experiment Stations were set up at various sites in Manchuria, and they too supported one wing of the research organs of the SMR. The SMR was extremely enthusiastic about agricultural improvement from the very start. From 1908 on, specialists were often summoned from Japan, and they investigated the present state of farming and struggled to find ways to improve it. In addition, in 1913 an Agricultural Experiment Station was created in Kung-chu-ling. A branch station was set up in the city of Hsiung-yüeh and nurseries were built in Liao-yang, T'ieh-ling, and Ch'ang-ch'un. The following year they founded a trial manufacture site for alkali at Ta-shih-ch'iao, and the next an experimental manufacturing farm at Cheng-chia-ch'un; and at each site they built the facilities for agricultural improvement. It was the installation of the experiment station for agriculture and animal husbandry at Kung-chu-ling that passionately absorbed the youthful years of Mr. Komai Tokuzō, the subsequent governor-general of Manchukuo.

Among the experimentation stations set up throughout the region, those in the South [of Manchuria] were primarily devoted to experiments on rice culture and the cultivation of fruit trees. As a result the apple from the Kwantung Leased Territory became quite a menace on Japan's home market. In the North research was advanced into the improvement of soybean and animal husbandry products as well as into soybean fertilizer. Research and experimentation in the North were especially successful and led to a tremendous increase in soybean production. As a result the soybean began to be merchandised worldwide. This guaranteed an increase in railway and harbor revenues for the SMR, which took charge of the exporting of soybeans.

This story of the machinery of the SMR and the origins of its various research and study organs that I have presented as a kind of introduction has already grown too long. Established in this way, the SMR and its research institutes began activities in line with its objectives. When I entered the company in 1920, however, it lagged a bit behind the pace set by Gotō's original expectations. What compelled revisions in the implementation of the original plans was only natural, but I will spare you those details for now and move on to the story of my coming to the SMR Company.

2

I Enter the Company

My First Encounter with China

My Trip to China During High School

I became first interested in the Chinese people while on a trip with my high school friends to China; and I was further enlightened by the lectures on the Chinese revolution of Professor Yoshino Sakuzō at Tokyo University. I made many friends in school who later joined the Shinjinkai and became active in social movements. Whether that was the cause or the effect of my interest in China, it brought me to the research institutions of the SMR and enabled me to engage in the study of China. Thus, the initial point of contact between me and China and, hence, the SMR was my trip to Manchuria, Korea, and China during my last summer vacation of high school. This trip enormously stirred my interest in the Chinese people and made me feel that they were much more interesting than the Japanese.

At the beginning of July 1917, right in the middle of World War I, I began this forty-five day trip first to Tsingtao, then to Tsinan, Ch'ü-fu, T'ai-shan, Peking, Chang-chia-k'ou, Tientsin, Dairen, Harbin, and from there to Korea as one of over twenty members of the group organized by my high school. The previous year the high school had sent a group to the South Seas area, the newly occupied regions of the island of Saipan and the Truk Islands. Our group was the second such overseas trip. The aim of our voyage was to observe our newly occupied areas, and, by accepting offers of hospitality to stay at Japanese military installations along the way, we traveled extremely cheaply. In our case, this overseas trip cost each person seventy-five yen. Even considering how cheap prices were then, this was still very inexpensive. It also corroborates how well students were treated at that time. Among those in the group was a physicist by the name of Tsuji Jirō who later became chairman for public security of Tokyo municipality, a scholar of Chinese legal history named Takigawa Masajirō, and an overseas Chinese student named Han Shu-yeh.

Japan at that time was occupying Tsingtao, the former German military base in the Far East. Japan also controlled the Shantung Railway, which had been a German interest, and from that base, ignoring the protestations of the Peking government, exerted pressure on the whole of Shantung province. The imperialist countries were right in the middle of a life-and-death struggle on European battlefields, and there was no time to take the world of the Far East into consideration. Taking advantage of this situation, the newly arisen Japanese imperialism was enthusiastic about realizing its long-cherished desires with respect to the Chinese mainland.

Already in 1915 the Okuma Cabinet had thrust the Twenty-One Demands on China and fulfilled the majority of them, thereby enabling Japan to expand and strengthen its interests in Manchuria and Shantung. Furthermore, Japan fortified its influence in Chinese domestic politics by lending a hand to Yüan Shih-k'ai's imperial aspirations and to the establishment of the Tuan Ch'i-jui regime thereafter by offering huge loans. These activities on the part of the Japanese government gave rise to voices of criticism from Europe, let alone the resistance of the Chinese masses. The May Fourth Movement became the signal fire for the modern Chinese revolution and elicited the first birth pangs of the Chinese Communist Party, both of which, however, were inordinately weak at that time.

Our group began in Tsingtao, a city overflowing with the beauty of a modern European city. We proceeded through Tsinan, a

purely Chinese city with narrow streets in whose center, paved in
natural stone, stood the commercial houses in majestic architec-
ture next to each other, with people brushing shoulders in great
animation. We then went to Peking. We were put up at the
barracks of the Japanese detachment stationed there, and I remember that we were invited to a reception at the Japanese Club
by leading figures in the local Japanese community resident in
Peking.

We not only saw areas within Japan's sphere of influence, such
as Tsingtao, Peking, Tientsin, and Manchuria. We visited the
Confucian temple in Ch'ü-fu, Shantung; we climbed China's most
famous mountain, T'ai-shan; we strolled about the Great Wall and
the Ming Tombs; and we visited a purely Chinese social setting,
where there was not a single Japanese, when we entered Chang-
chia-k'ou, gateway to the North. We were surrounded in China
by rickshaw pullers who were speaking to us what seemed like
the jabbering of birds. Especially in Chang-chia-k'ou, when we
rode the railroad that was completely owned and operated by the
Chinese, we deeply felt how an inability to communicate brought
out in us a sense of disquiet and distrust. The only person in our
group at that time who could provide a means of communication
was Mr. Han Shu-yeh, the Chinese overseas student. Perhaps for
that reason, we encountered no real obstacles at all. We had been
informed in Japan, as was common knowledge then, that on the
railroad deep in the Chinese hinterland we would confront the
danger of "bandits," but we never met up with any. Instead, we
were profoundly impressed by the simple, hard-working, sincere
faces of the Chinese we saw.

The SMR in the Eyes of a Traveler

When our trip to North China was over, we headed toward
Dairen from Tientsin by ship. I remember being deeply moved by
my impressions of the group of coolies working at the Dairen
harbor and wharf, and as soon as I entered the SMR, I set my
mind on studying the Chinese laborers at the Fu-shun coal mines.

One could neither see nor hear a single thing that did not have some relation, directly or indirectly, with the SMR's activities in the lives of Japanese living along its rail lines beginning at Dairen. I was astonished to discover this. We spent several days sightseeing in Dairen, staying at a dormitory of the Dairen School of Engineering, which had been founded by the SMR. The factories we observed were of course managed by the SMR, as was the restaurant within the park where we escaped from our chaperones. Electricity, gas, water works—all had the SMR markings on them. In our youthful minds the SMR was merely a railway company, and we completely misunderstood its real character.

Heading north from Dairen, we separated from the SMR line at Ch'ang-ch'un. At the Kuan-ch'eng-tzu Station we transferred to the Chung-tung railway of Russian type with a 5'1" gauge and headed toward Harbin. I imagined northern Manchuria to be wild lands, but the scenery that drew near from the windows of the train revealed field after field of farms on the horizon. The area was sparsely populated, and there were very few forests. Where did these farmers come from to work the land? I had an eerie feeling about it all.

Mr. Han Shu-yeh

At the station at Shuang-ch'eng-pao, Mr. Han got off the train. All of us who understood not a word of Chinese owed him a great debt for taking care of the negotiations at the inn in Chang-chia-k'ou and with the rickshaw drivers. He had to spend the remainder of his summer vacation with his parents in Chilin, and so he left us. I remember certain things about Mr. Han. When he completed the preparatory course in language study at Japan's First High School, he transferred to a local high school and our contact thereafter died out. I later became a member of the SMR staff, and then the Manchurian Incident came along in 1931.

As that Incident developed, every single leading figure in the military administration of the three provinces that comprise Manchuria surrendered before the pressures of the Japanese Army. There was one hero among them who boldly hoisted high the banner of resistance against Japan. His name was Ma Chan-shan, and he had been the leader of an unnamed brigade in Chilin province. Evading one strategy after another of Kwantung staff officers Itagaki Seishirō, Doihara Kenji, and others who prided themselves on the ability to pacify the Chinese, Ma continued his resistance and for a short time was able to perk up the eyes and ears of the world. Eventually he shifted his position to Siberia and news of him died out, which disappointed those people opposed to the Japanese invasion of the mainland. Yet, after a while he reappeared in Sinkiang whence he came via the Soviet Union and surprised the world a second time. In this piece of news I stumbled upon, it was reported that the chief of staff of the Chinese patriotic army was a man by the name of Han Shu-yeh. It had been over a decade since he left us with briefcase in hand at the Shuang-ch'eng-pao station. This last piece of news of him came to me while I was head of the Research Section of the SMR.

Professor Yoshino Sakuzō on the Chinese Revolution

Having completed my summer vacation trip with the guidance of the Japanese Army and the SMR, at the end of high school in 1917 I entered the Law Faculty of Tokyo Imperial University in September. In those years the new term began in September after the end of summer vacation.

Awakened to a concern for China during this trip, I plunged first into the Faculty of Letters and attended Professor Shionoya On's lectures on *jibun*. *Jibun* was the term used in Japan at that time to refer to the contemporary Chinese language, principally newspaper usage mixed in with the oral language, in contrast to Japanese *Kambun*, which usually implied writings in the classical Chinese language. Since Chinese was written with characters, there were portions of it that we could understand by reading those same characters in Japanese, but *jibun* never provided genuine training in the Chinese language in any sense whatsoever. I learned Chinese from the first stages as a foreign language only when I later entered the SMR and was living in Peking. Professor Shionoya was, though, a very famous scholar of traditional Chinese matters. Although I was the same year as Mr. Kuraishi Takeshirō [who became a famous Sinologist], I had no connection with classical Chinese studies. My aim was to gain a broad and general knowledge of China, and then to pursue research into issues concerning Chinese coolies. Nonetheless, at the time I lacked the formal training in the Chinese language necessary as preparation to begin research on this topic.

In my second year at Tokyo University, I attended the lectures of Professor Yoshino Sakuzō on "The History of the Chinese Revolution." These lectures revised in a major way the view of China I had gained during my trip there. Professor Yoshino had a novel style of lecturing. His audience was not large, and I listened enthusiastically. It would be no exaggeration to say that I threw myself into school for those lectures alone.

As one of the many "educators" sent to Ch'ing China from Japan before the 1911 Revolution, Professor Yoshino had begun teaching at the North China College of Law and Government (Pei-yang fa-cheng hsüeh-t'ang) in Tientsin shortly after returning from study in the West. In addition he served as teacher to the family of the most powerful individual of the late Ch'ing, Yüan Shih-k'ai. He remained in China from 1906 through 1909 and devoted himself to learning about the country in a way different from earlier mainline China studies, which centered on the world of the Chinese classics. Thus, his lectures displayed remarkable insight into the problems confronting contemporary China. The observations gained from my high school trip there the previous year proved to be extremely superficial in thinking that China was hopelessly lost in confusion and collapse. Professor Yoshino taught in his lectures the meaning of the Chinese revolution through the thought of Sun Yat-sen as well as what the essence of this vague and nebulous China really was. For me this was the beginning of guidance toward a scientific knowledge of China.

The Shinjinkai and My Position

Taishō Democracy and the Shinjinkai

The full life of research that I enjoyed did not begin solely by virtue of a concern for China as I have described it. The fashion from the era when I received my education prior to my job with the SMR and the ideas that took shape within it exercised a great influence as well. And the contacts with friends I made during this period controlled to a certain extent my conduct after assuming the job. Let me speak just a little more about my life prior to entering the SMR Company.

Professor Yoshino, from whom I gained my first scientific knowledge of China, was known more as a leader in the Taishō democracy movement than as a scholar of China. And, more than as a university professor, he was famous as an advocate of "democracy" (or *minpon shugi*, as he called it), which he developed in popular magazines. That era was one in which even the word "democracy" was taboo. In the minds of bureaucrats and conservative militarists, democratic thought was heretical and would undermine the age. Adventurer groups based in the right-wing organizations Genyōsha and Kokuryūkai had occasion to confront Professor Yoshino. A group of university students who served as Yoshino's bodyguards when he appeared at the debating society took the opportunity to form the core of an organization that became known as the Shinjinkai (New Man Society). It was an early fruit of the Japanese student movement.

The following set of circumstances surrounded my joining the Shinjinkai. During summer vacation prior to the beginning of the semester that year, I was invited by several fellow students in the Law Faculty, Miwa Jusō, Kawanishi Taichirō, and Hayashi Kaname, to go and stay with them at Togakushi Mountain in Nagano prefecture. We had all been buddies together in the high school class that was required to take the special German course [as secondary education was organized in those days], and as such we were very close friends, a group of fighters for justice. In any case, that summer you could see cattle grazing in the overgrown grasslands and the southern Japan Alps in the scenery; around us lay Kurohime and Kōzuma Mountains. We passed the time in a serene world all its own.

Adopting an essentially neutral position in the world war, Japan at that time profited and enjoyed itself tremendously. A nouveau riche class appeared at all levels of the business world, singing eulogies to business conditions during the war. On the other hand, though, rice prices were on the rise. One *shō* [1.8 liters] of rice rose steadily from 14 or 15 *sen* to the 40 *sen* level. Despite this, the economic conglomerates, monopolizing rice imports from overseas, and the government did nothing at all, and domestic discontent rose as well. Internationally, the previous year had witnessed the collapse of czarist Russia and the spread of social discontent on a global scale. It was only natural, then, that doubts about tradition and concerns for social justice began to take root among the students. Furthermore, lectures at the university had no connection whatsoever with world conditions at the time.

Togakushi Mountain was known among a group of us as a place to study in preparation for the high-level civil official examinations, but that was not our objective. While we enjoyed living together, this was an era when a systematic social science literature had yet to appear. Groping in the dark, we would take at random for reading material translations of the Neo-Kantians, Kropotkin, Bertrand Russell, and the poetry of Walt Whitman in order to help clarify our search for intellectual liberation and for our discussions of issues of the day.

The war climate had led to a skyrocketing of commodity prices, and in July a printers' strike involving the workers in the print shops of the major newspaper companies brought about the inauguration of the era of Taishō "democracy." Also, in an effort to move away from soaring rice prices and domestic discontent toward foreign policy, the Japanese government directly in the face of public opposition sent a detachment of troops to Siberia. As the objective situation worsened, rice riots that began in August with housewives in a fishing village in Toyama prefecture spread throughout the country. Workers and students joined the movement, and then the police and the military were called out, as Japan moved just one step this side of martial law.

The situation at the time, from our student sense of righteousness, was unjust to an extent difficult to ignore. It made us harbor doubts about uncritically continuing our study of the university curriculum. In the two months we spent at Togakushi Mountain, we saw that our futures belonged not to civil service or to the directorship of a company, but to some other task in the genuine development of the Japanese people. Our careers had to be built on the creation of something. And so we arrived at this simple decision. At the end of the year when the opportunity to organize the Shinjinkai came up, our Togakushi Mountain group joined.

The Milieu in the Early Period

There was at this time in the Toyko suburb of Mejiro (3600 Taka-damura, to be exact) a home managed by Miyazaki Ryūsuke, the son of Miyazaki Tōten, who had participated in Sun Yat-sen's revolution and authored the *Sanjūsan nen no yume* (My Thirty-Three Years' Dream). There Huang Hsing, a leader of the 1911 Revolution, had once taken refuge. This home was offered as a meeting place for the Shinjinkai, and the organization set off on a course of vigorous activity.

Some of us lived communally at this house, and others commuted to and from it. Every day we studied, argued, and carried on discussions concerning human liberation. The participants included those in the leadership level such as third-year students Aka-matsu Katsumaro and Miyazaki Ryūsuke; second-year students, such as those of us in the Togakushi Mountain group as well as Hatano Kanae, Kaji Ryūichi, and Taira Teizō; first-year students such as Yamazaki Kazuo, Kadota Hiroshi, and Shimmei Masami-chi; and workers such as Kawai Yoshitora. In addition, some members of a group known as the Thursday Club, including Asō Hisashi, Tanahashi Kotora, Yamana Yoshitsuru, Katayama Tetsu, Takayama Gizō, Sano Manabu, and Okanoe Morimichi (whose pen name was Kuroda Reiji), joined us. Yamana and Asō were with the miners' union, Sano and Okanoe with the East Asian Economic Investigation Bureau of the SMR, and Ka-tayama was a lawyer at the time. Sakai Toshihiko and Hasegawa Nyozekan also came and lectured to us.

The general aims of the Shinjinkai were condensed into the following two items. (1) We would work for and promote the new spirit of human liberation throughout the culture of the world.

(2) We would support and engage in a just reform movement in contemporary Japan. We decided to publish a journal by the name of *Demokurashii* (Democracy). Its inaugural issue appeared in March of the following year, and its second number was banned. From the ninth issue the name was changed to *Senku—La Pioniro* (The Pioneer). Then, with the ninth issue of *Senku*, it was retitled *Dōhō* (Brethren); and the sixth issue of it, in turn, witnessed yet another name change to *Narōdo* (The People).

Inasmuch as many writers have already described the Shinjinkai, there is no need for me to belabor an introduction here. The fact that among the founding group were men such as Sano Manabu and Okanoe Morimichi, who both worked for one of the research groups of the SMR, provides a key to the link between the later research organs of the SMR and activists in the Japanese democratic and socialist movements. Following their lead, many of us took research positions with the SMR.

In 1918, the year after I entered university, World War I ended, and the next year (1919) Japan was troubled with how to bring the Siberian expedition—an unwarranted military adventure launched on the pretext of preparing for the end of the war—to a conclusion. That year the May Fourth Movement took place in China, but in Japan its significance was little understood by the larger public. In this regard Professor Yoshino was an exception. In an article entitled "The Explosion of New Thought Tides at Peking University" (published in the journal *Chūō kōron* in June 1919), he clearly explained the importance of "May Fourth" as a new democratic movement in China.

In April 1920, the year I graduated, we had the first postwar panic, but in July when commencement actually took place, the forces of prosperity still remained intact. There was no difficulty for a graduate of the Law Faculty of Tokyo Imperial University to find a job. Honored imperial university graduates still enjoyed a privileged position. The Shinjinkai group that graduated that year decided on their place of work on the basis of where they would retain comparative freedom of activity. Soon, though, many threw themselves into the labor movement. The one who seemed boldest among us was Miwa Jusō. He entered the law firm of Katayama Tetsu and Hoshijima Niro and wrestled with incidents related to labor disputes. Hayashi and Kawanishi took positions at private universities, and Kaji, Ishihama Tomoyuki, Hatano Kanae, and I took research positions for the SMR. (The following year Tanaka Kyūichi joined us.) Hatano and Ishihama soon returned to the university, however, and only Tanaka and myself remained with the SMR till the end; that is, until we were arrested late in the Second World War.

Recruiting Employees for the SMR

We got our jobs after seeing an SMR recruiting poster at the university, and we signed up to take a test. They called it a test, but it was a simple interview. We were not required to submit our school transcripts, nor was it a difficult written exam like they have nowadays. Also, our older colleague from the Shinjinkai, Sano Manabu, who was by this point with the East Asian Economic Investigation Bureau, provided us with all sorts of conveniences. But this proved not to be an influential connection. For Tokyo University graduates at that time, the SMR was not a particularly difficult place to get a job. Later in the Shōwa period conditions changed, and strict exams and severe interviews made it difficult for even the brightest university students to be accepted for employment.

Let me now say something about the SMR's recruitment of employees. In 1919 the SMR began formally to employ university graduates on its staff, particularly from Tokyo and Kyoto universities. This trend started when Professor Matsumoto Jōji of Tokyo University became a director. Until that point there may have been men among the graduates of Tokyo or Kyoto universities who joined the company on the basis of personal contacts, but not through a public recruitment. Staff recruited for executive positions, as the management system was referred to, were hired out of the commercial high schools, the East Asian Common Culture Academy, and the foreign-language high schools. Among the commercial high schools, Kōbe Commercial High conspicuously provided the largest number of staff, and occasionally Toyko

Commercial High (present-day Hitotsubashi University) was a
close second. Thus, when I arrived at the main offices of the SMR,
I remember that the majority of the executive staff were graduates of professional schools.

There was no particular rivalry between the employees who
had graduated from Tokyo University and those from Kyoto University. If any rivalry existed it was an attitude of the university
graduates toward the commercial school graduates. Only among
the SMR medical personnel did any significant clique consciousness develop; there were no Tokyo graduates at work there, but a
crowd of men from Keiō University, and a few Kyoto men mixed
in.

The Part-time Employment Policy of the SMR

Although they were not staff employees, let me mention the
employment of part-time workers or consultants that I touched
on earlier. The part-time system at the SMR was a kind of personnel system that distinctly illustrates one of the attributes of a
national company. There are all kinds of part-time work, and
there were various categories of it from the highest class at the
director level (there were also men formally known as advisers)
down to the ordinary staff level. Considering its manifold duties,
the SMR found it necessary to employ an extremely diversified
pool of talent. Without excessive fastidiousness to the staff system, the SMR was able to employ men with highly distinctive
skills, and much was made of the elasticity of its employment of
personnel. In addition, since there was no fixed staff system for
consulting work, this system was used a great deal to supplement
the permanent staff due to the expansion of responsibilities. It
also helped prevent bureaucratization, inasmuch as there was no
ossification of personnel.

There were many different kinds of part-time work. Some
men's work did not necessarily require full-time attendance on
the job, but ceased when they performed their duties. Some were
restricted in the short-term due to the specific needs of the mo-

ment. And some men's work required long-term attendance similar to that of ordinary staff members. Most enjoyed a tenure of from one to three years. There were men who joined in the capacity of a consultant to supplement the staff but eventually became permanent members of the staff. Most of them were regular employees with a three-year term.

The attitudes of certain party cabinets also had influence within the SMR, and top officials on occasion traded places. The ordinary staff employee was, of course, not influenced by such things, but there were cases of political consultants who quit their jobs to follow these top officials. Although some of these part-time employees who owed their posts to connections did serve for three years, the great majority usually served for a term of one year or less, often with a number of renewals.

Salaries were fixed, with no supplementary incomes. Some were on contract and others were simply given travel expenses to cover the completion of an objective. The amounts ranged broadly from the general employee line through to the high-level positions. Foreigners were usually hired as part-time consultants, and they were paid exceedingly well. I have already mentioned several of the Europeans, such as Thiess and Wiedfeldt, who worked for research organizations of the SMR, but let me now introduce several of the Chinese and Koreans who were hired in a part-time capacity.

When I joined the company there was a Chinese by the name of Huang Chung-hui in the Foreign Affairs Section. He worked for about two hours a day and returned home after jabbering some incoherent nonsense with the section head. At first I thought what he was hired to do was rather strange, but later I heard that he was an important figure who had been director of Chinese overseas students in America through an office at the Chinese Legation and had many friends in the Peking government. Thus, he had been hired as a kind of adviser in the tasks of the company's negotiations and in order to revise the drawn up forms of agreements with the Chinese side.

There were Chinese who worked as teachers of Chinese language and as interpreters on official tours of investigation. There certainly should also have been interpreters of Mongolian. Among the Koreans was a man named Yi Pom-jang, who was not a part-time employee but a regular member of the staff. Among those of Russian descent were a man who had been a White Russian general and others who served as diplomatic officials under the old system; their status was quite low, most of them working as translators.

Japanese military men on active service came by turns to the Railway Department as consultant officers to guide liaison in military transport. Later, consultants from the admiral level of the navy joined as well. They came for technical liaison on plans to produce gasoline for the aviation needs of the navy from the shale oil of the Fu-shun mines.

A staff officer from the Siberian expedition, Major General Takayanagi Yasutarō, was dismissed from the army and became a consultant to the SMR on publicity. He later became the president of the *Manchurian Daily News*. Although not at the rank of general, Kōmoto Daisaku, a schemer in the Manchurian Incident (the staff officer of the Kwantung Army who took responsibility for the murder of Chang Tso-lin, and later an SMR director), Amakasu Masahiko (said to be responsible for the Ōsugi Incident and influential in the state of Manchukuo, later chairman of the board of the Manchurian Film Company who shot himself when Japan was defeated at the end of the war), and others served in the capacity of consultants for a time under cover of the SMR. There were also military men commissioned for intelligence matters, but I would like to touch on these people later when I come to Tachibana Shiraki, who, though a civilian, joined the Intelligence Section.

Among the people of a "purely" scholarly bent, the SMR hired in a part-time capacity men whose knowledge was of an extraordinarily unique quality. These included Yagi Shōzaburō, who was famous as a pioneer in the field of Japanese archeology; Nakae Ushikichi, the scholar of ancient Chinese thought; Suzue Gen'ichi, a student of Chinese labor issues; Matsuzaki Tsuruo, who contributed to the immense collection of Chinese volumes in the SMR library and was known for his wide circle of friends among Chinese scholars; and Taoka Masaki, well known as an author of Chinese-style poems and the younger brother of Taoka Reiun.

A number of major figures from the world of journalism also worked for the SMR, including Zumoto Motosada, president of the *Japan Times*, and Sawara Tokusuke, president of *Seikyō jihō* (Sheng-ching Times) and the only Japanese to participate in the writing of the *Encyclopedia Sinica*. Hikasa Yoshitarō and Tachibana Shiraki might also be thought of as journalists.

During the Pacific War, known Japanese left-wing scholars were repeatedly hired as part-timers by the SMR. Ozaki Hotsumi, Hosokawa Karoku, Itō Ritsu, Itō Kōdō, Nishi Masao, and Horie Muraichi were all well-known names. The pioneer in this group was Kawakami Kiyoshi, who was famous during the early years of the Japanese socialist movement. In his later years, he took charge of lecturing on Japanese issues at Columbia University in his capacity as a consultant to the SMR in New York. I think that there were a fairly large number of right-wing individuals who emerged from the SMR, including Ōkawa Shūmei and Inoue Nisshō, but no other names come to mind. In hard numbers, though, the left-wingers far outnumbered those on the right. This was a peculiarity of the SMR.

The Research Organs at the Time I Joined the SMR

The Atmosphere at the East Asian Economic Investigation Bureau

From the very start we entered the company intent on working for a research institute. Kaji and Hatano, with whom I had joined the Shinjinkai, were sent to the East Asian Economic Investigation Bureau, while Ishihama and I were assigned to the Research Section at the main office. We did not, however, go to Manchuria immediately. We entered the company upon graduation in July and then spent a short period of apprenticeship working at the East Asian Economic Investigation Bureau.

At that time the bureau was housed in the Tokyo branch office of the SMR, along a corridor in a red brick building of the Mitsubishi Corporation outside the Babasaki Gate of the Imperial Palace. The bureau chief was Matsuoka Kimpei, a Tokyo University professor knowledgeable in economic policy. He, together with Nagao Sakurō, a director and head of the Materials Section, and Ōkawa Shūmei, head of the Research Section, formed its leadership structure. Our work began with learning what the collection of materials entailed. We learned the scientific methods of the day from one of the Germans I mentioned earlier, Baumfeldt. This involved the organization of foreign-language books and clippings from foreign-language newspapers as well as how to locate, organize, and preserve materials from Japanese monthly magazines and daily newspapers.

In Japanese companies after the First World War, a tendency gradually developed toward stressing research, and so research sections and research offices were being newly established. To form a nationwide federation of research agencies with the aim of establishing contacts between the various research institutions at this time, the East Asian Economic Investigation Bureau and the Research Department of the Bank of Japan, as models of these new research agencies, played managerial roles in working for its organization. Director Nagao was responsible for seeing this task through to completion, and observing his work from beginning to end proved to be very helpful to me in later years.

There is a famous story about the coexistence of both left- and right-wing groups within the East Asian Economic Investigation Bureau. Research Section head Ōkawa had been friendly with Director Nagao since their days together at a strike at the old Fifth High School, and it was on Nagao's recommendation that Ōkawa had initially entered the bureau. Ōkawa, together with Kasagi Yoshiaki and others, had gone ahead and organized the Kōchisha. The left wing was represented by Sano Manabu (who had been a leader in the Shinjinkai) and Okanoe Morimichi. Kasagi, Okanoe, and Taguchi Yasunobu all graduated from Tokyo University in 1919 and entered the company as a group. Riding the wave of Taishō democracy, Bureau Chief Matsuoka had lectured during those years on socialism from his rostrum at Tokyo

University. It was said that his lecture plan was actually prepared by Sano and Okanoe. These lectures, I believe, were the first introduction to Marxism offered at Tokyo University. Compared to the study of economics by Fukuda Tokuzō at Tokyo Commercial High School and Kawakami Hajime at Kyoto University, however, these were not terribly erudite; nor could they compare with the journalistic brilliance of Fukuda and Kawakami.

The activities of the Kōchisha were not that remarkable. After a short while, Kasagi quarrelled with Ōkawa and then moved to Manchuria. Sano Manabu, together with Asō, came in contact with the miners' union and participated in the labor movement of the miners, and this led to certain problems within the bureau. Under the pen name Kuroda Reiji, Okanoe continued to produce translations of books. After I was transferred to Dairen, Sano quit the SMR and took up a professorship at Waseda University; Okanoe joined the staff of the *Tōkyō nichinichi shimbun* (Tokyo Daily News, affiliated with the *Osaka mainichi shimbun*) and as an independent journalist became a correspondent in Berlin. Kuroda's reports on the conditions in Europe after World War I were outstanding for their excellence at the time.

It is not that the bureau was actually divided into left and right wings, for many staffers at the bureau were quite tame and neutral. For example, Mr. Sakura Shigeo, who was invited to join Mitsubishi's Economic Research Institute and became the central person in the equipping and developing of that institute, lived out his entire career as a "research man." After Ishihama and I went to Dairen and Hatano Kanae moved over to Dōshisha University, the liberals at the bureau were Kaji Ryūichi and Tanaka Kyūichi, who entered the SMR Company in 1921. Later, the liberal group of Matsukata Saburō, Mizuno Masanao, and Edayoshi Isamu joined the company through a special recruitment and became a lively force.

During this period, Bureau Chief Matsuoka Kimpei had already returned to the university, and Director Nagao had returned from Europe, gone to Dairen, and become absorbed in writing a doctoral thesis entitled "On the Colonial Railway as Seen from the Perspective of International Policy." In the bureau, I think someone who had been a petty official in the Imperial Household Department (I am told he was Itō Miyoji's secretary) was appointed bureau chief for reasons of personal favoritism, while Ōkawa Shūmei was director. Later, when Yamamoto Jōtarō was SMR president, it was reorganized into a foundation to give it a rational footing, and Ōkawa became chairman of the board. Until the time of the Manchurian Incident, a friendly coexistence was said to have characterized relations between the left and right wings at the SMR, but then the leisurely atmosphere completely dissolved as frightful world conditions would no longer allow such beneficence on the company's part.

Ōkawa Shūmei, the principal figure of the right wing, had close ties with the military, and as the bureau staff swelled coexistence with the Kaji group became increasingly difficult. As a result, in 1932 when I was head of the SMR's Research Section, the two factions confronted each other head on. Bureau Director Soejima Michimasa (grandson of Soejima Taneomi), who was a man of liberal bent, seems to have hastened the inevitable. The liberal group was crushingly defeated and the democratic base in the bureau was rooted out: Kaji was transferred to the *Asahi shimbun* office, Matsukata and Mizuno to the Dōmei tsūshin office (later known as the Kyōdō News Service), and Tanaka Kyūichi and the group beneath him were all removed to the main office in Dairen. After the establishment of the state of Manchukuo, the bureau again returned to be part of the structure of the SMR, and it continued until the very end in its research to serve the latest line faithfully and completely. I shall discuss it later, but my dismissal as head of the Research Section was not unrelated to this confrontation.

Knowledge about "Coolies"

If I might return to a story begun earlier, my life at the East Asian Economic Investigation Bureau was not long-lived. After about three months I moved to the Research Section at the SMR's main office in Dairen. My ambition at that time was to pursue research on the Chinese working class, and I hoped to do a study of the laborers at Fu-shun.

It was not that Chinese workers were limited to Fu-shun, but there were numerous coolies at the railway plant in the harbor of Dairen. The very first thing that caught the eye of a tourist to Manchuria were the faces of these coolies, half naked and covered in black grime, carrying with apparent ease seven or eight containers of soybean waste. I had been struck with this spectacle during my student trip several years earlier.

With a letter of introduction from Sano Manabu, I went to visit a Mr. Sugimura, the person responsible at the Fu-ch'ang Company (the only agency supplying laborers to handle cargo), and I observed the coolies' living quarters, the Pi-shan Dormitory. In Japan the fact that this company provided the coolies with living quarters was considered admirable as a public welfare installation, and it became a place of tourism, in fact a well-known one, for travelers to Manchuria. Its actual conditions were quite surprising though. I understood that the energy required for such heavy labor derived from the extreme poverty of foodstuffs at their disposal.

This alone was not surprising. Opium-smoking dens, though, were publicly built at a time when the Kwantung governor-general's office held a monopoly on the sale of opium. This system was aimed at preventing the spread of the poison, but a flourishing business in the drug went on in the workers' dormitories. I agonized in an effort to understand what was going on there. It seemed to me to be simply undisguised colonial control. On my inland trips in China in later years I learned in great detail about the spread of drugs through dealers of morphine who penetrated the hinterland beyond commercial port areas, taking advantage of their right of extraterritoriality. This deepened my initial impression. Several years after entering the company, when I was studying abroad, I heard a talk about the British opium policy in India given by an Indian student at the Student Movement Center in London. He described in great earnestness how this policy was causing the degeneration of Indian youth. At that time I was reminded of the sight of the Pi-shan Dormitory in Dairen.

Chinese laborers, not only as longshoremen, but also as wagon

drivers, factory workers, and coal miners, came pouring into
Manchuria. And peasants and laborers on the Chinese mainland
were an inexhaustible supply. Although they suffered severely
from the annual natural and human disasters and from the insa-
tiable exploitation of the imperialist Powers, these hundreds of
millions of people could not be worn down to exhaustion. History
has proven the impossibility of this. All of which is to say that
there would come a time when the great mass of Chinese coolies
would awaken. This experience was something I cannot forget,
and through it my study of the coolies formed the basis for my
knowledge of China.

The Atmosphere at the Research Section at the Main Office

So, I had gone to Manchuria intent on making a study of Chinese
coolies, though in fact I scarcely had enough time to do it because
of all the other work I was assigned. As to this other work, I was
provided with a staff to engage in the editing of what was considered the magnum opus of the Research Section of the SMR in
those early years: the *Man-Mō zenshō* (Comprehensive Collection on Manchuria and Mongolia).

This great task was first undertaken immediately upon appointment by Ishikawa Tetsuo, who joined the SMR shortly before we did. Ishikawa had taught German at the old Fourth High
School and had gone from there into the East Asian Economic
Investigation Bureau; in July 1919 he was appointed head of the
Research Section at the main office. He was a brilliant fellow who
was counted, together with Tsurumi Yūsuke and Maeda Tamon,
among the ten great disciples of Nitobe Inazō. The objective in
naming him head of the Research Section was to breathe new life
into its stagnating research activities. It seems to me that this
move was planned in the same manner as that of beginning to hire
university graduates like myself onto the staffs of the research
institutes from that very year.

The traditional atmosphere at the Research Section became
clear to me soon after I arrived. In the research machinery at the

main office in Dairen, one could not sense so much as a trace of the Research Section as one of the three original divisions from the founding era of the SMR. Organizationally, though, this element crept in by virtue of its being one section in the Executive Department on a par with the Liaison Section. It had scarcely developed at all compared to the other divisions—such as the railways, mining, and harbors, or schools, hospitals, and public utilities—which had grown a fair amount in the decades since their founding. Despite this lack of balance, we had about fifty members on our staff if you add the people at the Statistics Office.

The actual research staff there was a shabby array for the most part. The staff of the founding period had grown to maturity in their various areas of expertise although they were not exercising it. The practice of supplementing the staff with men particularly from the East Asian Common Culture Academy resulted in the spread of unmethodological topographical investigations for military needs. This bad effect had been brought about by the principle of using individual experts, which Mr. Kawamura Chūjirō, the first chief of the Research Section, had followed. When this linked up with a policy line stressing the investigation of natural resources, research activities were literally being carried out on foot. By following Kawamura's way of doing things, the level of the overall Research Section was not being enhanced, inasmuch as no research method could be established, even if superb experts did emerge. As a result, no research plans with any direction were forthcoming. This, it seems, was the root cause of its stagnancy.

I have already mentioned the Korean, Russian, and Chinese interpreters who were employed by the Research Section. When I came to the SMR, I thought it was a little strange. It seemed to me that there should be equal treatment between Japanese and other peoples, even though it was just a pretext, similar to the inclusion of a few Chinese among the stockholders. There were two or three Chinese: Yen Ch'uan-yüan, a graduate of Kyoto University; Lu Yüan-shan, from the School of Agronomy in Sendai; and Hsien Chen, a descendant of Prince Su of the Ch'ing dynasty and an elder brother of Kawashima Yoshiko, the adopted daughter of mainland adventurer Kawashima Naniwa and to whom much attention was later focused as the "Mata Hari of East Asia." I always thought of these three as one of the oddities of the Research Section of the SMR. But how should I have known? When the state of Manchukuo came into being, Mr. Yen became governor of Fengtien province, then Governor of Chilin province, and was installed as minister of civil affairs. Mr. Lu became head of the Education Ministry. Hsien Chen was transferred to be head of the Audit Department of Manchukuo. They all became major figures used by Japan. Consequently, they spent their rearing period in this research agency quietly.

The Man-Mō Zensho and Ishikawa Tetsuo

Mr. Ishikawa had two aims in planning the *Man-Mō zensho* (six volumes, with a volume of appendices). First was as an external demonstration. As he himself explained in the introduction to the first volume: "Since the World War the Powers have concentrated their interests to a remarkable extent on the Pacific and China. . . . This [set of volumes] introduces at home and abroad in a most precise manner an overall picture of the nature and culture of Manchuria and Mongolia which have become the focal point for the complexities of international relations." At the same time he also intended to "introduce at home and abroad" the name of the Research Section of the SMR. While achieving this aim on a large scale, he illuminated the obscure existence of the Research Section. One can sense this as Ishikawa's intention. Even more important than this, however, was the fact that by mobilizing the entire staff of the Research Section through this enterprise he hoped to give their subsequent activities some sort of comprehensiveness.

When Ishikawa left the East Asian Economic Investigation Bureau and arrived at his post in the Research Section, he soon decided to get rid of the principle of individual expertise there. First, using a method he had learned at the bureau, he transformed the modes of collection and organization of materials, not limiting this to individual book titles, but by using an itemized index of the contents including newspapers and journals. In this way he was trying to break down the separate, specialized sects among the researchers first through reference materials. He established the preconditions for conducting comprehensive research. To this end, he drew up a budget for a considerable amount.

Until this point we had been freely run in a laissez-faire manner, our research tasks having no meaningful planning whatsoever. Ishikawa decided to institute the practice of annual plans. The work of the members of the research staff was strictly apportioned in each case, while at the same time it became possible to follow a preestablished plan and bring about exchanges for common research work. Ishikawa adopted this approach in order to effect an integration and orderliness in our overall research work. Without these latter two qualities, no amount of time would have made possible the organization of research work that accorded with the present demands both of company business and of colonial management. These demands necessitated an overhauling of the research activities based on the earlier principle of individual expertise.

Ishikawa's description of the research activities makes one think of Gotō Shimpei's policy of "affecting a scholarly manner." "In handling all cultural and economic business, the question to be settled first of all has to be an exacting and unified knowledge of a wide variety of facts for the appropriate localities. In other words, entering from the door of research and study, we must advance to the inner sanctuary of actual management." This constituted a revival of a consciousness from the founding period of the research agencies. Also, he pushed one step further the reform of the system supporting the research activities by establishing liaison meetings for economic research.

Ishikawa's project, which aimed at the mobilization of the entire staff for the *Man-Mō zensho*, for cooperative research in practice, and at an organizational reform for mutual exchange among the research staff, began in late 1920 to fill the five of us newly employed freshmen who entered the Research Section with vigor. With this immense task on our hands, work proceeded on the *Man-Mō zensho* from 1921 through 1922. His aim, however, was not fully realized. This point becomes clear as one reads through the seven volumes that appeared. Although there was abundant "collective knowledge" there, it lacked for theory and system.

There was a great deal of disorder as well in the pace at which the editorial staff worked. The writing battalion was conscripted from the ranks of the East Asian Common Culture Academy, the group that had investigated old customs, and the recent university graduates who had entered the SMR, but this tripod was not well balanced. In particular, the discord between my group of university graduates recently having joined the company, Ishihama Tomoyuki, Okumura Shinji, who later became an executive director of the Manchurian Heavy Industry Company, Ltd., and Satō Teijirō, on the one hand, and the people associated with the East Asian Common Culture Academy, on the other, was severe. Inasmuch as the new learning of the social sciences now existed, our group impetuously advocated the need for a theory and a system in the editing of the *Man-Mō zensho*. The researchers from the East Asian Common Culture Academy did not understand this. What's more, they disposed of the matter by laughing at us. All of this is meant to say that we newcomers from the universities had no knowledge whatsoever about actual conditions in Manchuria. We remained stubborn, however, fighting recklessly against them.

When I think back on it, it seems to me now that they did not know what to do with us, which makes me feel rather ashamed. Our influence was not especially strong, and as such it was not reflected in the *Man-Mō zensho*. Despite our calls for theory and system in this work, when the time came to write it, they had no choice but to rely on the old materials. The significance of calling for theory and system, though, was in its own way part of the history of the Research Section, and eventually this trend was realized.

If I might raise one distinctive trait that characterized the entire *Man-Mō zensho*, it would be the fact that in it Manchuria was described as the territory of China. This was not, however, an attainment that the text consciously sought out. In fact the formality involved validated it as an object for invasion. The attitude concerned in this description, though, was not something to be found at the time of Gotō Shimpei and at the time when the Manchurian Incident was near. In Gotō's day there was no conception of differentiating China and Manchuria, and as the era of the Manchurian Incident neared, the trend to consider the two as separate grew consciously. I find the fact that this was also the very period in which the *Man-Mō zensho* was compiled very intriguing.

Volume 2, Military Affairs

The section of the *Man-Mō zensho* that I was put in charge of was that dealing with military matters in volume 2. When Satō Teijirō, who was in charge of the chapter on law, first broached the subject with me, I was actually rather perplexed because I had just arrived and completely lacked any hard knowledge of the situation. Well, with the knowledge of a first-year student in Manchuria, I accepted the charge and set out directly on a firsthand inspection tour.

From the SMR rail line I made a connection in Harbin with the Chinese Eastern Railway as I departed on my first trip. Three years had passed since the 1917 voyage of my student days, and the appearance of the rail lines had changed as well. With the inroads made by Japanese merchants who had accompanied the troops dispatched to Siberia, the development along the rail line had been phenomenal. A Japanese hotel fostered by the SMR now stood in Harbin, and I stayed there. I enjoyed the exotic flavor of Harbin's houses of religious worship, bazaars, and cabarets, all relics from the days of the czars.

Harbin was a scene of thriving activity. But, with the breakdown of the discussions on American-Japanese cooperation in sending troops and joint control over the region, the return of Japanese troops stationed along the Chinese Eastern Railway pressed near at hand. Unable to stem the tide of domestic public opinion, the military authorities decided to go along with it. When

I arrived there, Harbin was the bustling epicenter of this very issue. I plunged right into this busy center by going to the headquarters of the Japanese Army stationed in northern Manchuria, located at the heart of the city. When I asked if they had any materials on military relations between Manchuria and Mongolia, I was given the military's investigative report. This document was the result of a detailed study of the circumstances of the Chinese military in the Three Northeastern Provinces (Manchuria). So I took a copy of this report prepared by specialists and returned home.

The report alone was not going to do the job, so when I arrived back at the office in Dairen I did a search of the Research Materials Division of the Research Section and of the Dairen Library. Was I ever surprised! I had imagined that a fair amount of material existed concerning military matters, but I never expected so much. Virtually all of the documents from the early period concerning Manchuria had been prepared by the military itself. But these all seemed to be of a sort cataloguing military requirements. Notable among them were Koiso Kuniaki's "Memorandum on an Investigation of Manchuria and Mongolia" and Endō Moritoshi's "Investigation of the Cities of Manchuria." In addition there was a document stating that in 1872 Saigo Takamori had written a piece entitled "A Chronicle of Manchuria" (Manshū kiroku); I looked for the original text but it was not forthcoming. Well, I was again made to recognize that enlightened documents concerning Manchuria, not limited to military affairs, had all been prepared or collected by the military. With this as my point of departure, I began to write on military affairs in Manchuria.

The Chinese armed forces in Manchuria at that time were like a dumping ground for vagabonds or, essentially, men who were out of work. "Good metal is not to be used for nails, and good men are not to be used as soldiers," as the Chinese saying goes. Soldiers were considered in a class of men beneath coolies, formed in the same cauldron as bandits. A good example would be Chang Tso-lin, who rose from the ranks of bandits. From a robber-hero used by Russian troops in guerrilla warfare at the time of the Russo-Japanese War, he grew to establish a regime of his own in the Three Northeastern Provinces.

In the founding period of the SMR, the Chinese central government appointed Hsü Shih-ch'ang to be governor-general of the Three Northeastern Provinces and T'ang Shao-i to be the viceroy. They were resident in Fengtien, and it was there that Gotō Shimpei had once engaged them in various negotiations. After the 1911 Revolution, however, the control of the central government was ineffective and all real power passed to the hands of warlord Chang. Well over 100,000 troops were under his control, and the land he personally held grew to an area the size of the island of Kyūshū. His hegemony blanketed the North as a warlord leader who managed all manner of enterprises including warehousing and banking and who controlled the market price of specialty products and the value of the paper currency he issued.

Warlord Chang owed his wealth and power first and foremost to the rapid speed at which the newly opened lands in Manchuria had developed. I have stressed on the Japanese side that this phenomenon was based upon the backing of the Japanese military and the economic development caused by the SMR rail lines, and these factors cannot be ignored. In particular, the stability of Chang Tso-lin's regime vis-à-vis the inconstant situation of warlords rising and falling was greatly aided by the Japanese. As a result high-level, active commissioned Japanese officers responsible for communications with the Japanese military joined him as advisers. These overseers cum coordinating officials carried with them profound implications.

The other military force at work in Manchuria, the Japanese military structure, relied on the Portsmouth and Sino-Japanese Manchurian Relief Treaties. The railway garrison was divided into six battalions along the rail lines, with a headquarters set up at Kung-chu-ling. Later, a Kwantung Army headquarters came into existence in the Kwantung Leased Territory. Police power for the protection of resident Japanese in Manchuria was exercised by the Police Affairs Bureau of the Kwantung Governor-General's Office and by the consular police in places where Japanese administrative powers did not extend.

The scope of the Japanese garrisons was limited to the Kwantung Leased Territory and areas attached to the rail lines, but it is well known that under the pretext of protecting the resident populace, these Japanese garrisons were often used to cause international troubles, such as the incidents at Hun-ch'un, Hsin-min-ch'un, and Cheng-chia-ch'un. The Japanese Army, which had had complete control over Manchuria during the years it had spent in Siberia, decided to withdraw in 1920, but in its own way it continued to exercise influence thereafter in the region. We should also take special note of the fact that it had a powerful spying organization in such major cities as Fengtien, Harbin, Chilin, and Chichihar, among others.

Adding a postscript on the ratio of Chinese civil to military expenditures in Manchuria and Mongolia, I put together the section on military affairs for volume 2 of the *Man-Mō zensho*. I am disappointed now at how little I really knew of Manchuria and that I was unable to prepare my account with an additional analysis of the strata that comprised the military.

Expansion of the Research Facilities

I remained in Dairen for about one year. Shortly after I finished my portion of the *Man-Mō zensho*, I was sent on to Peking. In 1921 the SMR established a research agency in Peking, and I was appointed to a position in it. At our facilities in Peking the tentacles of SMR research now ate their way from the remote Northwest directly into China proper. Then, in 1923, the Research Section planned a massive structural reform and expansion. Since I was in Peking away from the main office in Dairen, I cannot describe the inside story of this change in much detail, but let me for a moment describe my life in Peking.

Section head Ishikawa Tetsuo was the man who sent me to Peking, but of course this was not merely his doing. You might say it was the hope of the SMR and hence Japanese imperialism to anticipate renewed advances into China after World War I. They especially hoped to attain essential intelligence concerning the unfolding of China's complex political situation, and to that end the Peking research organization came into being. For Japan, it was essential that not only China but Soviet Russia to the North also be studied. With the collapse of czarism, Japan now frustrated at the dispatching of its troops to Siberia, stood face to face with Russia in Manchuria. This situation was met with the installation of a research section at the Harbin office at the time of the reform and expansion of the research structure in April 1923.

The SMR's studies of Soviet Russia were famous for the scale and tremendous expense with which they were undertaken. The full picture, though, was as if wrapped in a veil and thus hidden from sight. Well known is the fact that in its early years the Harbin Research Section was the center for a collection of a massive quantity of documents. Shortly after the facilities were set up, its first task was the publication of the *Rōnō Rokoku kenkyū sōsho* (Research Series on Workers' and Peasants' Russia) in six volumes and the *Roshia keizai sōsho* (Series on the Russian Economy) in eight volumes. Miyazaki Masayoshi and Shimano Saburō were the central figures in the work of these compilations. They had been trained by the SMR years before as scholars of Russia, and naturally they were concerned with the North from the inception of the SMR.

I will speak later about Miyazaki in connection with his cooperation with the Kwantung Army, but let me just touch on his background. Upon graduating from the Russo-Japanese Society's school in Harbin, he soon went to work for the SMR and entered the company before I did. Sent by the SMR to study in Moscow, he witnessed the Russian Revolution first-hand. After returning to Manchuria, he became the SMR's first "Soviet hand," and as such he became a valuable asset to the Japanese military and civil authorities in Manchuria later.

Mr. Shimano was of a different sort. He was a man of scholarly disposition who had spent many years with the East Asian Economic Investigation Bureau in Tokyo. Under the auspices of the bureau, a massive *Ro-Wa jiten* (Russian-Japanese Dictionary) was published by the Dōjinsha in 1928, and this work was the crystallization of over ten years of Shimano's research. Later he moved to Dairen and engaged in the early research on the Soviet Union. The role he played for the SMR, though, was considerably different in nature from that of Miyazaki.

The structural expansion of April 1923 did not merely entail the founding of an institute for the study of the Soviet Union. Until that point the duties of the Research Section had been confined to general research centering on the study of colonizing enterprises. In addition, matters concerned with rail lines, transportation, and general intelligence became the responsibility of the Research Section. As our tasks expanded, the weight of the Research Section within the SMR became increasingly heavier.

To expand and diversify the work of the SMR, a need was seen to unify the lines of intelligence in the various areas and concentrate them at the center; and the arena controlled by the Research Section was seen as that place. The measures taken involved the organization of necessary intelligence for management, a systematization intimately linked to basic research. This, it would seem, was the result of a return on the part of the leadership of the SMR to the early, founding spirit of the research agencies in which research and management plans had been inseparable. Perhaps this might best be regarded as the period in which Gotō Shimpei's will had come to fruition.

Gotō's hope was in part betrayed at the time of the founding of the research division, and there had been an era when the only work done was inferior even to research on military needs for the army. This poor record lay in the lack of general rules in research methodology and the principle of expertise. It was also due to the lack of social science methods. The efforts of section head Ishikawa Tetsuo compensated for this deficiency, but the comprehensive research methods that Ishikawa sought simply did not take root. Strictly speaking, this task was never fully accomplished.

In any case, though, the efforts continued. From that year the Research Section began a study of conditions of the soybean crop. We became engrossed in studies of the circulation structure of agricultural products, such as soybeans, soybean oil, and soybean waste, and research on Chinese labor relations. These studies were indispensable in response to the international merchandising of the soybean and the increased opportunity to employ Chinese laborers. We could not carry out these studies using our past static understanding. We had to reorient our methods to dynamic research. The methods of economics were introduced at this point. Researchers who worked according to the old framework lost all influence as a result of these changes. Young men who had graduated from university departments of economics and law willy nilly took the lead. The April 1923 reform and expansion of the research structure were bolstered by these internal changes and indeed furthered this trend. Ishikawa Tetsuo was at this time transferred elsewhere, and the reform might be seen as the final fruit of his continuous efforts ever since the *Man-Mō zensho* project. In a word, then, my going to Peking was one action in this larger reformation of the research structure.

3

My Years in Peking— Japan in China

Peking Friends and Acquaintances

Japanese Society in Peking

I believe that the SMR established its office in Peking in 1919–1920. I was called by section head Ishikawa in the early summer of 1921 and told that I was being appointed the first resident official in Peking of the Research Section. The announcement came as quite a surprise to me, inasmuch as I still was not very comfortable with the Chinese language. I felt I could not accept the position immediately. But I was drawn to the wonders of Peking, which I remembered from my former visit, and eventually consented. I returned to Tokyo and then left to take up my post in Peking in October 1921, as I remember it.

As insignificant as the Research Section of the SMR may have been at that time, this was the first extension of its research tentacles into China proper. The SMR had indeed already established organs within China proper. As a beachhead for maritime transport, they had set up a Shanghai office and appointed as its head Mr. Sakuragi Shun'ichi from the Tōyō Kisen Lines. Furthermore, they had made contact with railway transport interests in Peking and established a Peking office for negotiating business with the central government there. Only the Research Section had no facilities in Peking as yet.

The project Ishikawa gave me concerned China's fiscal administration. Because the central government in Peking at that time had not had a moment of peace since the 1911 Revolution, it was always falling into financial trouble and was incapable of satisfactorily repaying its foreign loans. Warlords throughout the land set their sights on control over the central government, while the imperialist powers were absorbed by competition over establishing spheres of influence. My job was to complete a study of this state of affairs.

My knowledge of things financial was limited to a few hours of lectures at Tokyo University from Professor Ōuchi Hyōe after he had finished his years as an official in the Ministry of Finance. To be quite frank, I knew nothing. How did I carry out my assignment over the next four years? This becomes the main theme of my discussion from this point.

Once I had arrived in Peking, I settled down at the company living quarters of the SMR's Peking office at No. 2 Ch'un-shu Lane in the eastern part of the city. The building had been purchased by the SMR from Ting Shih-yüan, a high official in the Old Communications Clique who later became minister to Japan from Manchukuo. According to international law, foreigners were not allowed to own property within the city limits of Peking, but in fact it was possible despite the illegality.

Of all the cities of the world, Peking together with Istanbul are considered unique as tourist attractions. The fall scenery in particular proves endlessly fascinating to the traveler. Groups of white doves in an endless azure sky fly about in the dry air, echoing the sounds of the flutes attached to their feet. Beneath them the red leaves of creeping plants coil themselves around the pale, dark walls of the gardens. Countless numbers of rickshaws come and go, as the major means of transportation in Peking, along the wide avenues that seem ill matched with the rows of low stores dating back to the Ch'ing dynasty. Foreigners in a few automobiles race through the yellowish dust storm of the rickshaws to enjoy a drive through this capital of forests.

Peking was not a commercial treaty port. In one corner within the city walls the Legation District (known in Chinese as the

Chiao-min-hsiang) had been built, and as a consequence of the Boxer Treaty foreigners had the right to reside in this quarter. Within this area each nation placed its diplomatic office, troop garrison (there were forces present from the American marines as well as from Japan, France, and Italy), consular police, a foreign post office, and banks. These institutions, however, were only accommodated in this particular section of the city. An overflowing number of foreigners did live illegally amidst the 900,000 citizens of Peking. The majority of Japanese residents, who numbered about 3,000 at that time, had homes spread out in this way. Among them were the offices of the resident officials from the Japanese Railway and Finance Ministries, as well as the offices of staff members for such companies as Mitsui, Mitsubishi, Ōkura, Tō-A kōgyō, and Taihei. Aside from the military officials attached to the legation, there were such military establishments as the Aoki Residence, the Banzai Residence, and others named or unnamed. The SMR was mixed in among all of these.

The homes of Japanese advisers who worked for various organs of the Chinese government—such as the army, the communications office, the telephone bureau, the banks, and the botanical gardens—were referred to as "residences." Japanese newspaper offices—the *Asahi*, *Mainichi*, *Jiji*, *Fukunichi* (now, *Nishi Nihon shimbun*), and *Kokusai tsūshin* (forerunner of Kyōdō News Service)—each had correspondents in Peking. Their buildings were referred to as "press offices." Japanese working for the offices of the Chinese customs and the Chinese salt administration (internationally run establishments), those intellectual types teaching in Chinese universities or high schools or studying in China, or the daily supply shops with Japanese partners, together with Japanese doctors and Japanese adventurers, all formed the resident Japanese population of Peking.

Japanese society in Peking took shape around the Japanese Club created by influential men residing in the area: legation officers, army garrison officials, and employees of the Yokohama Specie Bank. While outwardly saying that Chinese and Japanese shared the "same written language" and were of the "same race," these Japanese still enjoyed the same extraterritoriality as the Europeans in China as well as a leisurely style of life far above the Chinese people whom they looked down on.

I still knew nothing of it at the time I arrived two years after the May Fourth Incident, but in July of this year (1921) the Chinese Communist Party (CCP) was being founded. China's capital, Peking, appeared calm and tranquil at a glance but was in fact on the eve of great change with disturbances brewing. The sight of Japanese society there enjoying a leisurely, completely nonchalant existence struck me, a recent arrival, as very disquieting. I had expected the dawn of student and labor movements for a new China, and I had thought I would see an extension in China of the atmosphere and my experiences with the Shinjinkai. Thus, I had prepared myself to cope with such a view of life in Peking.

I think I was most sensitive to social movements, and I tried to make contacts with members of the press because I thought they would be most sensitive to social movements. In addition to Japanese correspondents, there were men working for the English-language *North-China Standard* and the Japanese-run, Chinese-language *Shun-t'ien shih-pao*, and I questioned them all about the May Fourth Incident and the student movement after it. They all answered me that the students had been merely the tools of political cliques agitated by politicians, that the May Fourth demonstrations had been led by Lin Ch'ang-min of the Progressive Party, and that they had been used in his in-fighting with the Communications Clique.

It seemed to me that these reporters were excessively concerned with reporting on the struggles over the largely fictitious central government and the fighting over regional bases between the feudal warlords. By the same token, they seemed completely oblivious to or unconcerned with what was occurring beneath this ostensible confusion and what that might mean for the future of China. Since our newspapers were not free of such views, it was only natural that ordinary Japanese people as well retained the notion that nothing had proceeded so much as a single step from the old view of China as the crumbling "Chinese empire." I could hardly set to work based on this kind of general knowledge of China, gleaned from Japanese society there. Having come to this judgment, I ceased getting too involved with Japanese in Peking. I diligently studied Chinese and decided to begin my work by reading the Chinese press.

Mr. Nakae Ushikichi

When I say that I was not going to get too deeply involved with Japanese society in Peking, that did not mean I avoided all Japanese living there. I imagine the reason that in the five years I lived in Peking I was unable to make friends with Japanese with whom I felt comfortable engaging in serious conversation was this nagging sense of discomfort with respect to the Japanese community. All of the friends I made there were people who lived consciously separate from the Japanese community. Although few in number, these remarkable friends made my years in Peking among the best of my entire career. I think I should say a few words about two of these friends first—Nakae Ushikichi and Suzue Gen'ichi.

Nakae took up residence in Peking shortly after graduating from Tokyo University in the early Taishō period. He initially came to China together with Ariga Nagao, a professor of law who had been recommended by the Japanese government as a legal adviser to Yüan Shih-k'ai, and Nakae later settled there. Ariga took him along because his mother, the widow of Nakae Chōmin [the famous activist of the popular rights movement in Japan], had asked him to, for it seems that Nakae himself had no particular interest in China. He had shown no inclination whatsoever to pursue a bureaucratic career or to enter a company upon graduation. Passing his time in Peking listlessly, he found himself unable to melt into Japanese society there and had no one to talk with. He spent his days in what he himself called the life of an "indolent villain" at a geisha house known as the Chōshuntei.

This behavior did not continue for long, however, for he soon turned over a new leaf, spurred by reading a work by the German legal scholar Georg Jellinek. Eventually he absorbed himself in studies of ancient Chinese political thought. At the time I came to know Nakae in 1923, he was already reputedly an obstinate and fiercely independent, eccentric scholar. One day he abruptly came to visit me, without anyone's introduction, and began the conversation with his own history of "indolent villainy." He went on to discuss his research, and this really surprised me. It seemed that he had no one in Peking with whom he could engage in a scholarly discussion and was extremely lonely. We became close friends thereafter, and he offered me guidance on many points in the years that followed.

Nakae lived along Eastern Kuan-yin-ssu Lane (near the present-day public square in front of the new station in Peking). The home was given to him by Ts'ao Ju-lin. Ts'ao was repaying Nakae's mother a favor, for when he had been a student at Waseda University he had stayed with the Nakae family. At the time of the May Fourth Incident, Ts'ao Ju-lin was regarded as first on the list of traitorous officials, and he became famous for having his home attacked by student demonstrators. Nakae was at that moment visiting with friends, and upon hearing the news he rushed over to Ts'ao's home and saved Ts'ao from the assault of a club-wielding group of students. The incident was reported in the Japanese newspapers at that time. Nakae's mental attitude at that moment may be summed up in his single expression that he did "what he ought to have done as a human being." While Ts'ao faced this critical juncture, Nakae was concerned that he warn Ts'ao and not take the wrong course of action. Ts'ao remained thankful for the rest of his life.

Nakae's initial living and research expenses came out of Prince Saionji's pocket. Saionji had been a close friend of Nakae's father since their days together as students in France and at the *Tōyō jiyū shimbun*. As a result, Nakae dedicated his first essay, "Shina kodai seiji shisō shi" (A History of Ancient Chinese Political Thought), to Saionji and Ts'ao. Around 1924, however, shortly after I had gotten to know Nakae and become sufficiently close that we spoke about conditions of our private lives, Saionji's available resources had dwindled, and he sent word to have the SMR look after Nakae. I ended up going on the errand of carrying Prince Saionji's name card, on which this instruction had been written, to SMR President Sengoku Mitsugu. The conditions Nakae gave the SMR are interesting: "The money I receive is for research expenses. If there are any demands for counterservice on my part as 'consultant,' then I refuse it. However, when my research is complete, I will send you a copy of it."

I negotiated these conditions with the main office. At that time the head of the General Affairs Department of the main office was Mr. Ishimoto Kenji. He had known Nakae since they had been in the same year in kindergarten (the Yamada Kindergarten in the Suidobata area of Koishikawa, Tokyo). Thus, the arrangements went without a hitch, and we paid him a monthly salary of 300 yen—quite high for that time—over a three-year period. This three-year contract was renewed throughout Nakae's career. Nakae's case typifies the work arrangements of SMR consultants, as I described them earlier.

Sano Manabu

Around the time that I got to know Nakae, I learned that Sano Manabu, a leader of the Japan Communist Party, had paid a visit at Nakae's home in the year prior to my settling in Peking. Having decided to make a secret trip to the Soviet Union via Peking, he stopped at Nakae's residence on both legs of the journey. Sano and Nakae both were graduates of the Seventh High School in Kagoshima, but it was not through alumni connections that this meeting was arranged. Sano rather had an introduction from Shimizu Yasuzō, who was then known as the Saint of Peking.

Sano first went to visit Shimizu, who had contributed an article from China to the Japanese journal *Warera* on the Chinese literary revolution. Perhaps for fear of some bad aftereffects, this saint entrusted Sano to Nakae, who was seen as an oddball and had no contact with Japanese society in Peking. Shimizu was a graduate of Oberlin College in America, and whenever Nakae referred to him, he called him by the nickname "Oberlin." At this time Shimizu was managing a school to educate poor Chinese girls in Peking and had thus gained himself the title of "Saint." He returned to Japan after the war and opened the "Oberlin"

School in Kanagawa prefecture.

Sano visited Nakae's home one other time, and on both occasions he laid out for Nakae the arguments in Marx's *Capital*. This was the point from which in later years Nakae would become an avid reader of *Capital*. Nakae disclosed his opinion of Sano only after the latter's ideological conversion years later. He said that this leader of Communists in Japan seemed only to have read the first volume of *Capital*, and that perhaps he would have been better off to have died in prison without relinquishing his belief in communism. Nonetheless, Nakae was truly helpful to Sano. When Sano escaped from Japan the next time and visited Nakae, Nakae had his wife show Sano the sights of Peking; and when Sano left for Shanghai, Nakae had his Chinese cook accompany and wait on him prior to arrival there. In any case, Nakae's home in Peking became a Mecca thereafter for visiting left-wing Japanese following in Sano's footsteps.

My Meeting with Katayama Sen

On a blistering hot day in Peking in June 1925, Nakae's servant came to my home and asked me to come with him. When I reached his house on Eastern Kuan-yin-ssu Lane, wondering the whole way why I was wanted at all, Nakae spoke to me in an exceptionally serious tone: "An extremely rare person has appeared, and I would like to introduce him to you. But, there's a condition. You must refrain from raising the topic of 'revolution.'" He then led me off to a remote room. Upon our arrival I saw a small-framed, white-haired man seated cross-legged in a narrow Japanese-style room. "This is Mr. Katayama Sen." I remember being startled, but what conversation ensued I no longer clearly remember. Following Nakae's condition, we did not mention the Soviet Union or Japan, but mainly discussed the labor and student movements in China.

At the time of the centenary of the birth of Katayama Sen, the journal *Zen'ei* put out a special issue. The editors quoted from his "Chūgoku ryokō zakkan" (Impressions of a Trip to China), and these lines reflect well the atmosphere of our discussion:

The Chinese labor movement is overdue, but its leaders who are intellectuals are all men of principle. They are all thorough. . . . The movement in China is more reliable than that of Japan, and in their solidarity also the Chinese laborers are much stronger than the Japanese. The power of the Chinese revolution will advance with a tremendous force like the unblockable flow of the Yangtze River. These were my candid feelings upon coming to China.

After our meeting Katayama proceeded to Shanghai and then returned again to Peking. I met him at Nakae's home again, and this time he showed us some neckties he had bought in Shanghai as souvenirs for friends. The discussion was enlivened by the question, "Don't you want to return to Japan?" I remember that he confided that he really did want to see his daughter Yasuko.

I think Katayama's main task during his visit to China was to investigate the May Thirtieth Incident. This was an event of international proportions, not even ignored by the Japanese social movement. Known as one of the leaders in the famous strike at the Nippon Musical Instrument Company in Hamamatsu, Mitamura Shirō visited Nakae's home through Sano's contact, and I met him through Nakae. When I showed him a copy of a translation of Marie Stopes's *Married Love*, he said he would be happy to give it to Yamamoto Senji, and he brought it back with him to Japan. Yamamoto did later quote from the book, so it seems to have been useful.

From the radical student organization Gakuren came Kyoto University student Ishida Eiichirō to China to make contact with students at Peking University. He came directly to my place with a letter of introduction from Professor Hatano Kanae of Dōshisha University. In the May Thirtieth (1925) period, numerous other refugees and revolutionaries came and visited me. I accommodated them as best I could, and where it was impossible for me I sent them on to my friend Suzue Gen'ichi.

We were able to carry on such relatively free exchanges with these left-wing figures because we belonged to an imperialist country that enjoyed extraterritoriality. Peking offered this odd variety of freedom to the lives of the Japanese there. The consular police at the Japanese Legation in Peking had a responsibility to oversee the comings and goings of left-wing figures. Also the Ministry of Home Affairs had a public censorial office, and it had dispatched Tatsuta Kiyotatsu to Peking and stationed him there. Although I am sure he kept a watchful eye on all these activities, he did it without ostentation. The atmosphere in Peking was unfit for becoming immersed in ridiculous matters. There were no incidences in which he directly brought harm to anyone.

Later, however, there was a severe roundup and arrest of Gakuren people in Japan. Ishida's trip to Peking was revealed, and my name appeared widely in the Japanese press. Inquiries apparently went as far as the main office of the SMR, but I was then on a trip overseas. Seeing the newspaper clippings sent by my family during my stay in beautiful Paris, I could not help smiling wryly, but the matter ended there.

Mr. Suzue Gen'ichi

I came to know Suzue Gen'ichi shortly after I met Nakae Ushikichi. At that time he was living in the rundown residence of an old Manchu bannerman in the northern part of the city where no other Japanese lived. He went by the name of Wang Shu-chih or Wang Tzu-yen. With his friend, the impoverished artist Ch'i Pai-shih, they painted, played the four-stringed hu-kung (a Chinese musical instrument), and helped each other out in those chaotic times in Peking. In April of the year after I arrived in Peking, I attended an exhibition of contemporary Chinese paintings at the Japanese Club, and from then forward I remained attentive to the name and the art of Mr. Ch'i Pai-shih. Over the next few years, Suzue and I became close friends. I remember being rather surprised to hear him mention the name of Ch'i Pai-shih and to hear that he was his music partner.

Suzue informed me about the actual state of the Chinese labor movement, and one by one he introduced me to Peking University students Huang Jih-k'uei, Hsieh Lien-ch'ing, and Ch'eng Heng. From them I got hold of publications then illegal, such as the journal *Cheng-chih sheng-huo* (Political Life) and *Hsiang-tao* (The Leader), an organ of the Chinese Communist Party (CCP) published in Hangchow. Needless to say, obtaining these basic documents was a great boon to my research. Suzue's devotion to the Chinese revolution expressed itself in remarkable ways, and from his experiences were born several superb works: *Shina kakumei no kaikyū tairitsu* (Class Conflict in the Chinese Revolution), *Son Bun den* (Biography of Sun Yat-sen), and *Chūgoku musan kaikyū undō shi* (History of the Chinese Proletarian Movement).

Suzue was actively involved in the Chinese revolutionary movement. Around the time of the May Thirtieth Incident, he went to observe a strike of textile workers in Tsingtao, and when he returned he informed me of his conversations with the Chinese laborers he met there. When surrounded by a crowd of workers, a middle-aged man who looked like a coolie cornered him and showered him with a series of rapid-fire questions: "They say that in Japan universal suffrage is going to be enforced, but does the emperor allow it? Do the aristocrats consent to this? I saw in the Japanese newspapers and magazines that have come to China that supporters of the Second International and those of the Third International have split apart, but I don't know which one is correct. I've read both sides' writings. I was convinced by the first argument I came across but I can't come to a conclusion."

At this time Suzue made his first friend among the Chinese laborers, Su Chao-cheng, and thereafter he made many more acquaintances in the Chinese revolutionary movement. It is remarkable that this man till the very end never forged an abiding relationship with Japanese society in Peking. Only one person, Nakae Ushikichi, made him his "sole friend among those [Japanese] resident in Peking," and they shared an intimate friendship. Nakae encouraged him to devote his career to studying the Chinese revolution, and he helped Suzue to read through *Capital*. My acquaintance with Suzue helped my research immeasurably. Perhaps I should now touch on the history of the Chinese liberation struggle that we witnessed, pondered, and discussed together.

In the History of China's Struggle for Liberation (1)

My Impressions of Li Ta-chao

In addition to officials of the Peking government, we had contacts in the Peking offices of the SMR with so-called pro-Japanese Chinese from nongovernmental walks of life. But it was impossible to make friends through such people. Before assuming my post in Peking, I had made a trip to Tokyo and there received letters of introduction to two Chinese residents of Peking from friends in Tokyo. One of them was Peking University professor Ch'en Ch'i-hsiu, who was later to become well known as an economist. I first met him at a gathering of Chinese and Japanese members of the Gakushikai [the association of graduates from the imperial universities in Japan], but no friendship developed out of our acquaintance.

The other one was the first Chinese friend I made in Peking— Li Ta-chao. I paid a visit to the Peking University Library with a name card from a Tokyo friend who had several years earlier met with Li through a letter of introduction from Professor Yoshino Sakuzō. This was shortly after I arrived in Peking, and Li Ta-chao was then head librarian at the university. When I opened the door and entered his office in the library, he held out his hand to me. His first words were: "Is Professor Yoshino in good health? I was a student of his in Tientsin." Li was one of the principal leaders of the spectacular New Culture Movement, which had created such a sensation in China. As an eminent author of articles for the journal *Hsin ch'ing-nien* (New Youth), as professor as well as head librarian at Peking University, and as a leader of the youth movement and the student movement, Li Ta-chao was already well known at the time of our meeting. He had also been one of the students during Professor Yoshino's tenure (1906–1909) at Tientsin's School of Law and Government.

Li had a quiet manner and spoke slowly. I felt none of the sharp impressions one often has of a university professor as I had imagined prior to meeting him. At first glance he struck me as a mild-mannered village school teacher. Later I visited him many times at his modest home along Shih-fu-ma Avenue outside Ch'ien-men (the front gate of the old city of Peking), though this first impression never left me. Through my friendship with Professor Li Ta-chao, my research found a direction, and in due time I will describe just what that was.

Of course, at the time of our first meeting, I did not know that he had been the leader of a study group on Marxism, nor that he had met in Peking in 1920 the East Asian representative of the Comintern, Grigori Voitinsky, nor that he had planned the founding in Shanghai of the CCP. These are facts everyone now knows, but in July 1921 I was not concerned with the convening of the First Congress of the CCP. Later he was always active in the North, rallying students "to go to the people" or "to go among the troops," as he held positions of responsibility in the party organization. I came to realize this gradually the more we met.

Observations of the First Hong Kong Strike

Around the time that I began working in Peking, the Kuomintang government in the South, which stood in opposition to the Peking government, began to effect a series of administrative reforms. In particular, my attention was drawn to Sun Yat-sen's eldest son, who become the mayor of Canton, and his implementation of city planning. This aroused my interest in investigating the South. Also, soon after the year began, a tremendous strike of seamen erupted in Hong Kong, and news of it intermittently was reported in the North. This only spurred my desire further to carry out a first-hand investigation.

The solidarity of the strike that had begun in January was extraordinarily strong. Despite repeated suppressions by the government office in Hong Kong, the strike was not easily disbanded. I knew that for England this movement had become a severe blow that extended to debates in its own Parliament. It seemed to me that one was witnessing here the first modern strike of Chinese workers as well as the sprouts of an anti-British nationalistic movement. Oh, how I wanted to go just to take a look! But, I had only been in Peking three months, and my Chinese still was not very good. I gave up when it looked as though my wish would not be granted. But, the SMR was quite a magnanimous institution. As a result of the negotiations of my co-worker Ōya Nobuhiko, for some reason I was readily given permission to go to Hong Kong and Canton.

Full of high spirits I headed south, as I recall, in the springtime, March, when prospects for the resolution of the great strike that had gone on for fifty days were in sight. I followed Ōya, who left before me, and all alone boarded the Chin-p'u rail line. The train went via Nanking (at that time, there was a ferry between P'u-k'ou and Nanking) to Shanghai. From Shanghai's north station, I heaved a heavy sigh of relief when, relying on the one expression in the Shanghai dialect taught me by Ōya, "Yang-ching-pang" [the name of the old creek running by the International Settlement, and hence implying that area in Shanghai], I made my way by rickshaw along a bumpy road to the SMR offices on the Whampoa Bund. It also made me quite happy that I had the self-confidence to negotiate this trip all alone. Here I met for the first time Mr. Sakuragi Shun'ichi, the early head of the office, and Consul-General Funatsu Shin'ichirō (he would later become very important in Sino-Japanese relations in a nonofficial capacity for Japan). Since there were no Japanese ships out of Shanghai, I boarded a Chinese vessel for Hong Kong and from there went by ferry into Kwangtung.

When I arrived the great strike had already ended in a victory for the Chinese people. All the same I decided to take a room in the hotel on the fifth floor of the Hsien-shih Department Store, which overlooked the shore of the Pearl River, and from there I made a study of the remains of the battle. Still, I did not know any Chinese people, so I took a leisurely walk around the Japanese quarter and was able only to ask local Japanese about their impressions. The Consulate staff had maintained contacts with a fair number of important members of the Kuomintang (KMT), including such men as Liao Chung-k'ai, and they introduced me to the mayor of Canton, Sun K'o.

The Japanese Consulate, the resident military offices of the

Japanese Army and Navy, the Bank of Taiwan, the Mitsui Bank, and the Nisshin Kisen Lines had all taken up positions in the Shameen concession area among the virtual forest of foreign offices there. The meeting place for the Japanese was at a restaurant on the other side of the Pearl River. I mixed with Japanese residents there and went around asking them about such issues as the influence of the South, the future of the KMT, and their impressions of the strike.

When you are in the cradle of Sun Yat-sen's revolution, the base of Southern influence, the local environment controls your understanding of things. Unlike the Japanese in Peking, the local evaluation of the KMT and the might of the South was right on the mark. Most people had only scorn for the view that the odds-on favorite in China's future political developments would be resolved by the struggles of the Northern warlords. Yet, on the question of a perspective on China's future, I felt there was no major difference with the people in Peking.

Japanese intelligence on the Hong Kong strike, based on information gained on the spot, reported that the leaders were Hsieh Ying-po and T'an P'ing-shan. In fact, however, it was the organizational leadership of the secretariat of the Chinese Labor Union, which was created just after the founding of the Chinese Communist Party. The actual leader of the Seamen's Union was a Cantonese sailor by the name of Su Chao-cheng. I learned of this when I made his acquaintance through Suzue Gen'ichi. The information in the hands of the Japanese accorded with the general contours at the time, even in the details.

The Third Anniversary of the May Fourth Incident

Shortly after I returned from Canton, fighting broke out in Peking between the Fengtien and the Chihli warlord cliques, which became known as the first Fengtien-Chihli War. Right in the midst of it came the third anniversary of the May Fourth Incident.

With the German camera I had just bought in my hands, I went over to the public square in front of the Gate of Heavenly Peace (T'ien-an-men). I was the only Japanese standing there amid a crowd of students. I cannot remember who the speakers on the platform were. When the gathering was over, I walked along with the demonstration of young men and women students into the center of town. It was a quiet demonstration, and I recall being slightly disappointed that it failed to live up to my expectations. A special correspondent for the *Asahi* carried out his journalistic responsibilities by using one of the amateur snapshots I took. The Japanese had hardly any interest in the student movement. I myself came to the hasty conclusion from the atmosphere of this mild meeting that the Chinese revolution had a long way to go.

The Kailan Coal Mine Strike

Suddenly, however, in September a strike broke out in the Kailan coal mines. It was a great surprise to me, completely unexpected. Having observed the situation in Kwangtung and having witnessed the development of the Chinese labor movement there, I had come to the judgment that several years would be necessary before these trends would spread to the North. People generally anticipated that workers in the North would enjoy a late marriage with the labor movement. Even if they were instigated to riot, it was said at the time, they would quickly be put down.

First of all, I went to visit Li Ta-chao at the Peking University Library. There I was quite embarrassed by the naïveté of my judgment. Li spoke to me in his usual soft tone. Workers on the Peking-Hankow Railway centering around the Ch'ang-hsin-tien Railway Factory and laborers at the factory workers' association at T'ang-shan on the Peking-Fengtien line (the site of the Kailan mines) had both participated in the May Fourth Movement of 1919. In the spring of 1921 an organized labor movement began at the Kailan mines. At present, Li continued, along the Peking-Hankow Railway, a Ch'ang-hsin-tien factory workers' school had been founded and sixteen workers' clubs were being formed. Also, a workers' preparatory committee for a general organization of labor unions would soon be meeting in Cheng-chou.

Li's story was not carried in any of the newspapers at the time, but it made me reflect on just what I had seen and been living through in my one year in China. I realized the ignorance of the Japanese residents in China, but I was in fact not much different from them. Although I was there on the spot making observations, it made me realize how hard it was for a foreigner to comprehend the real situation.

When I had pulled myself together and acquired some knowledge from Li Ta-chao, I decided to venture to the T'ang-shan area of the Kailan mines, where there was not a single Japanese except for one or two morphine smugglers. T'ang-shan was a prominent industrial city in the North in which were located the Kailan mines with five mine locations around it, the depot for cars on the Peking-Hankow Railway, the Ch'i-shan Cement Factory, the T'ang-shan Textile Mill, and a branch of Chiao-t'ung University.

As I got off the train in front of the station, the T'ang-shan Theater straight ahead looked like the strike headquarters, and workers who looked to me like coolies were busily coming and going there. Along the road, students from Chiao-t'ung University were soliciting for a strike fund. Huge slogans, such as "Down with Imperialism" and "We Demand Economic Freedom," hung in the open area in front of the station. Also hanging was an enormous placard with the amounts collected in the campaign from the union branches, including overseas Chinese in the South. There was a tremendous hustle-bustle of activity.

I did not go over to the headquarters but headed directly to the residential quarter of the workers. I went through the central city of T'ang-shan and walked for two or three kilometers toward a distant heap of coal sludge, along a rural road through a bleak field in which the sorghum crop that fall had already been harvested. There I came upon a lonely workers' waiting area where large lifting machinery was parked. I hoped to hear the living voices of laborers from the Lin-hsi and Ma-chia pit sites here. A handful of workers, indistinguishable from the peasants who happened to be there, responded to my questions in hushed tones in the rush-mat cottage where we spoke.

"We're treated worse than the donkeys that carry the coal.

One donkey costs sixty *yüan* and we only get five or six *yüan* a day in wages. If one of us gets killed in a mine disaster, twenty *yüan* is sent to the family as condolence money. The English are more concerned with an injury to their donkeys than they are with the casualties we may suffer."

As is well known, the Kailan coal mines were a joint capital venture between England and Belgium, although management rights were held solely by the British. Thus, disputes with them were fought as a part of the anti-imperialist movement. When I visited there, the struggle was still at a very early stage, opposition between capital and labor. After I left the area, however, Great Britain called up Indian troops from Shanghai to protect their interests, and the antagonism became much fiercer. At the same time, the Tientsin police force, which was backed up by the Fengtien warlords, began a military repression causing several dozen deaths and injuries among the workers and eventually suppressing the strike altogether.

Although defeated, the social influence of the strike was immense. More than anything, the strike brought solidarity to the semilaborers of rural origins in the North. Also, it concentrated itself against imperialist enterprises. These two points forbode an uneasy future for foreigners resident in Peking. As I mentioned earlier, the SMR employed numerous Chinese laborers at the port of Dairen, in the Fu-shun mines, and on railroad construction. It was only natural, then, that at our main headquarters in Dairen wariness was on the rise.

The Great Peking-Hankow Railway Strike

The Chinese laborers also learned many things from the Kailan strike. In particular, the lesson of this defeat taught them to be critically aware of the immaturity of the cohesion of workers of peasant origins and their as yet insufficient capacity to fight against the military forces surrounding them. More than anything, it was firmly recognized that, unlike the Hong Kong strike in the South where the Canton government provided a stronghold, in the North they had to fight without such a stronghold for support. And, that represented not only a difference of conditions but also a weakness of the workers' movement in the North. This fact was bitterly felt in the great Peking-Hankow Railway strike of February 1923, the following year.

The Peking-Hankow line was at that time under the control of Wu P'ei-fu, the strong man in the Chihli warlord clique. Wu had spoken of protecting workers so he could take advantage of them in his confrontation with the Fengtien clique. Li Ta-chao used this protection and, through political negotiations with Wu, created a union of railway laborers. As the union neared the stage of formal organization, though, Wu P'ei-fu resolved to crush it with military force. The General Labor Union reacted with a strike along that entire rail line, and finally the curtain fell on the great Peking-Hankow Railway strike. On 7 February 1923 when Wu P'ei-fu issued the order with armed coercion along the entire rail line to board the train, the conflict met its climax. The workers rejected his order. Over ten strikers, including the Chiang-an branch secretary of the union, Lin Hsiang-ch'ien, were tied to telephone poles and slaughtered one after another.

Several years ago when I was visiting the People's Republic of China, I stayed for awhile in Cheng-chou. On the street during our planned tour, I found a building on which was written "February Seventh Memorial Museum." I had the car come to a stop and when I entered the building, numerous scenes from that time were portrayed in paintings. The figure of Lin Hsiang-ch'ien, bound to a telephone pole, conspicuously caught one's eye. A group of men there seemed extraordinarily moved by this gruesome picture. At that time, our guide introduced us to an old man by the name of Chiang Hai-shih, the superintendent of the museum. In response to my questions, Mr. Chiang said he was a worker who had survived the events of 1923. Thinking back on that time is still very moving to me.

Martial law was eventually imposed along the entire Peking-Hankow rail line, and a naval landing party from the foreign powers anchored off Hankow came ashore. A state of war was developing. By this point, the strength of the General Labor Union and the Alliance of Workers' Corps was spent, and they issued a pathetic order for patience and a return to work. The workers had been defeated once again. Seizing the advantage, Wu P'ei-fu went about destroying their organizations in various places. The movement that had risen nationwide since the Hong Kong seamen's strike was forced into inactivity in the tempest of reaction. Li Ta-chao took refuge in the Soviet Union for a time.

Well, let me momentarily interrupt this discussion of the liberation movement in China to that point and return to the story of my own research on China at the Peking Institute, which had progressed in the meantime.

The Peking Institute

I Begin Research

Life in Peking from late 1921 through the middle of 1926 proved decisive to my life's work. As I mentioned earlier, the Research Section of the SMR gave me the mission of studying China's financial administration and stationed me in Peking. For myself, however, I decided to comply with this task by seeing Chinese problems globally and without necessarily following the SMR's guidelines too strictly. The overlap between the theme given me by the company and my own research was not that great. There are people who are fastidious about differentiating the various areas of knowledge, but at that time insofar as China studies were concerned nothing of this sort existed. This was an era in which everyone strove for a way to capture the vibrancy of Chinese politics and economics. I did my research amidst this trend with the intention of studying China's real financial administration.

I understood the problems of foreign loans and the Chinese government's finances as one phenomenon of the imperialist encroachment on China. A string of devolutionary phenomena in Chinese society, such as the fighting of warlord cliques and the political strife among corrupt bureaucrats, originated in the competition among the imperialists to offer China loans. At one pole of this phenomenon of decay was warlord fighting, and at the other were the student and labor movements. These movements were born and bred in the process of this social devolution, but at the same time brought this process to its end. My study was concerned with what place these social movements would occupy in the China of tomorrow.

The origin of this concern of mine was the fact that I had been able to gain the invaluable experience of witnessing firsthand the early climax of the history of the Chinese struggle for liberation. If the SMR found fault with my attitude and my activities, it is interesting that they never interfered.

Inauguration of the Pekin Mantetsu geppō

For over two years I visited various places from my base in Peking, and I amassed a fair amount of personal experience. Now I felt inclined to put this all together and publish it. The Research Section of the SMR had, as its published organ, a research report as well as a monthly journal by the name of *Chōsa jihō* (Research Review), which was later renamed *Mantetsu chōsa geppō* (SMR Research Monthly). Practically everything that the *Chōsa jihō* carried in its pages, however, had to do with affairs in Manchuria. Since my reports from Peking were indirectly concerned with Company business, they carried little weight with the SMR. Also, the main theme that I earnestly pursued had a tinge of the intellectual about it, so it would not necessarily be reported in full.

In 1924 we planned to inaugurate the journal *Pekin Mantetsu geppō* (SMR Monthly of Peking), because we needed to have our own publication in Peking. This new journal would list the research essays on its frontispiece, and in addition to these articles it would include explanations of contemporary political and economic events as well as introduce newly published books and materials in Chinese and foreign languages. We decided to divide it into these three parts for editorial purposes. If some major social event were to occur, we would organize a special issue of the journal. Although in name a monthly, it did not necessarily come out every month; about ten issues were published each year.

The articles that I wrote for this journal concerned the devel-

opment of capitalism in China: a history of the imperialist encroachment on China, the national revolution, the revolutionary
political parties, the student movement, the strikes in the textile
mills, and Chinese guilds and modern labor unions. Among the
shorter pieces I wrote on China concerned the issue of poverty in
Peking, a study of the Peking population census, a study of rickshaw pullers in Peking, a history of the development of newspapers in Peking, and a study of Jesuit missionaries in China.

I was in charge of editorial work on the journal through 1926
when I went overseas. After I left, Miyamoto Michiharu replaced
me in Peking and continued publishing *Pekin Mantetsu geppō*. It
continued as such through 1929. When I returned from overseas
study in 1929, I was stationed in Nanking. In conjunction with
this period when the center of politics moved to the Nanking
government of Chiang Kai-shek, the SMR organ also moved to
the South. At that time the research institute of the Peking office
moved to the Shanghai office. Miyamoto became head of research
in the Shanghai office and carried on the editorial work on the
journal in Shanghai. At that point it was no longer *Pekin Mantetsu geppō*, but had changed its name to *Mantetsu Shina gesshi*
(SMR China Monthly).

I now have neither *Pekin Mantetsu geppō* nor *Mantetsu Shina
gesshi* in my possession. If I could now see all the issues of these
journals, I think I could add some vividness to these memories,
but unfortunately I have no way to locate where in Japan they
exist. Perhaps they no longer exist as a body within Japan. I have
heard that the only full set is in the collection of the Library of
Congress in the United States. From 1924 through August 1926 I
was in charge of editorial work, and we recorded material in detail
on the spot from the infancy of the great revolution, centering on
the early Chinese labor movement and the May Thirtieth Incident. In the subsequent period, Miyamoto worked enthusiastically in my absence and made the journal a rich chronicle of the
times.

Although only two volumes now remain in the Waseda University Library, one of them is the special issue on the May Thirtieth
Incident. It explains and analyzes in detail conditions in various

places around Shanghai at the time of the May Thirtieth Incident. Numerous manifestos were issued at that time, and the journal ran many of them, including that of a group of Peking University professors.

While I was overseas the journal was once seriously endangered, in April 1927, when both sides in the great revolution were in retreat. Prior to Chiang Kai-shek's coup d'e'tat in Shanghai, General Chang Tso-lin carried out a raid on the Soviet embassy in Peking and captured Li Ta-chao and other members of the Chinese Communist Party. Of course, he did this with the understanding of the ministers of the imperialist powers. An SMR consultant on intelligence matters, Noda Ranzō, played a part in all this. When they captured Li Ta-chao and investigated the books and materials in his possession, they said that there was an entire set of the *Pekin Mantetsu geppō* there. How did they get there? Who brought them there? These were really puzzles for us. Inquiries came through Japanese officials to the head of the Peking office of the SMR. In actuality, Suzue Gen'ichi brought them to Li. The head of the office, Mr. Ushijima Yoshirō, answered them frankly that it was not a secret publication, but a research organ of the company and engaged in exchanges of materials with the Chinese. So, the story came to a close.

The Peking Institute

The editorial and publication work for *Pekin Mantetsu geppō* was assuredly not something any one individual could do. For that reason we hired Mr. Mitani Tōru as a special assistant, and on my own I decided to name our center the Peking Institute. Fortunately, the head of the SMR office in Peking, Ushijima Yoshirō, was an intelligent man; he agreed to my request and guaranteed us a room in the SMR offices. Although the Peking office was at that time referred to as an "office," the staff only included about five members. There was the office head, the business manager, myself (resident staff in charge of research), and an additional Chinese employee. To allocate an entire room for my "Peking Institute" in such cramped quarters and to allow me to hire a special assistant within the budget of the Peking office was assuredly a decisive action on the part of Mr. Ushijima.

I became acquainted with Nakae Ushikichi just before the institute came into being, and he was delighted with my plans. He encouraged me to furnish the newly founded institute with a complete set of the *Ku-chin t'u-shu chi-ch'eng*, the famous compilation of the Chinese classics. The next year (1925) friends of mine with whom I had worked at the main SMR office in Dairen transferred to Peking, and I dragged them onto the institute staff where I had them assist in our editorial work. Eventually Mitani was also hired onto our permanent staff and our organization was complete. We put together a budget and it was approved by the SMR's board of directors.

From 1925 the SMR paved the way for a system of study in Peking, according to which about ten staff members would come each year to study language or contemporary Chinese affairs. The SMR itself was aware to an unusual extent of the upheavals in China on the verge of the period of the "great revolution." I think that this was one part of the activities of the company, as it was wholeheartedly determined to study conditions in China in order to prepare itself for these events. As for myself, inasmuch as these budding research staffers had come to Peking and were now close at hand, I was happy to have them cooperate in the publication of *Pekin Mantetsu geppō*. When their period of study came to an end, they returned to the home office, but among them were some promising scholars who I tried to get to stay on the staff of the institute. While I was away from Peking, the institute filled up in this way and matured into an array of four research staff and two assistants. Nonetheless, at this stage of things the institute itself had yet to be formally approved as an institution. Only the *Pekin Mantetsu geppō* had attained the position of an official published organ of the SMR research facilities.

The institute still had not attained "institutional" security. This did not mean that the SMR lacked any enthusiasm concerning China studies. The *Pekin Mantetsu geppō*, which I had started up on my own, had received official approval. Similarly, the activities of the "institute" were fully accommodated in both personnel and budget matters. These facts illustrate the concerns of the main office. In 1926 I had occasion to request a special budget for the purpose of purchasing a collection of essential materials. I expected that my monetary request might be cut a bit, but it was approved without a word of complaint. I took this money and went over to the storeroom of the French Bookstore, which had opened a shop in the Peking Hotel. I discovered there classics of Sinology, and I remember buying them on the spot. Among these volumes were the works of Henri Cordier, a collection of the letters of Jesuit missionaries, the writings of Richtofen and of Yule. The main office raised no complaint about the purchase of these historical materials because somehow they understood the needs of the institute.

Furthermore, since I was about to leave Peking, I was worried about the future of the institute. My requests were approved: they accepted my selection of Miyamoto Michiharu, a remarkable researcher at the Research Section of the main office, as my replacement, and Suzue Gen'ichi's appointment as a consultant was also approved. In this way the subsequent life of the institute was secured.

Exchanges Through the Institute

The institute belonged to the SMR and in principle was not for public use, but in fact using it became comparatively easy, and as a result we had occasion to engage in cooperative ventures with Chinese. Mr. T'ao Meng-ho, the assistant head of the Chinese Academy of Sciences who recently passed away, was a professor at Peking University at this time. One day he dropped in unexpectedly at the institute to ask my advice on a matter concerning research into social conditions. He said he had been reading the *Pekin Mantetsu geppō* and praised it highly. He and his students wanted to put together a study of the living conditions of workers, and he had come to inquire what sorts of materials existed. I and all the staff at the institute were more than happy to show him a wide variety of material, and we gave him four or five volumes as specimens. From our cooperation there evolved under T'ao's direction the earliest Chinese *Lao-tung nien-chien* (Laborers' Year-book).

If I might say one more thing about the *Pekin Mantetsu geppō*, it apparently was even more useful in stimulating China studies in Tokyo than within the SMR. Virtually all the articles introducing events in China that were carried in the newspapers and magazines of the time traced the superficial, frothy phenomena of warlord fighting and the Peking bureaucratic realm. They offered not a clue about the true state of affairs in China or in what direction China was likely to go in the future. In a word, they became the stereotyped reports of Japanese "China hands." Our journal as a result played an enlightening role and was very well received in certain quarters back home as well.

The fresh style of our journal was appreciated among academic scholars in China and gained us a certain esteem, and it was for this reason that T'ao Meng-ho had paid me a visit. From this connection T'ao and I later became close friends, and through him I became acquainted with professors at Peking University. I was invited to dine with such scholars as Kao I-han, Hu Shih, and Ku Chieh-kang. I received materials from them and I asked them questions.

Mr. Hu Shih

When I came to know Hu Shih, he had already attained a world-wide reputation as the representative of the group of scholars who were known as "Young China." His name was even known among Japanese society in China. The Japanese, however, thought that the "Young China" group was identical with the anti-Japanese activists. Thus, it seemed as though none of the Japanese had approached Hu Shih, the leader of "Young China."

When I got to know him, Mr. Hu had written a piece entitled "Problems and Isms" for the journal *Nu-li* (Endeavor) in which he had called for "government by good men." He had already carried on a vitriolic debate with Li Ta-chao on the issue of problems and isms.

He also pointed out for me errors in an essay on the liberation movement that I had written for the Japanese journal *Kaizō* (Reconstruction). In this article I never mentioned the role played in the May Fourth Movement by Li Ta-chao and the young people in the Marxism Study Group led by him. Hu Shih said that any writing on the May Fourth Movement that failed to mention the role played by Li and the young Marxist group would never portray it accurately. All of which is to say that, myself included, among Japanese generally at that time there were numerous lacunae in our understanding of the dawning of China.

A Meal with Lu Hsün

I met Lu Hsün, too. Actually, I had been inattentive enough to dine with one Chou Shu-jen, without recognizing him to be Lu Hsün. Tendencies in taste are frightful indeed. At the time I was trying to investigate such radical-minded Chinese, and I was unaware that the person with whom I was enjoying a meal was Mr. Lu Hsün.

The venerable Uchiyama Kanzō, who passed away two or three years ago, once asked me: "So, you met Lu Hsün, eh?" I tried to remember such a meeting, but I could not. "It's in his diary, you know," Uchiyama carefully added. I was a bit confused, went home, and quickly checked Lu Hsün's diary. I diligently read through the pages covering the time when I was in Peking, 1921–1926, and there it was in the entry for 17 September 1925: "The 17th, clear. . . . In the evening I visited Chi Shih [Hsü Shou-ch'ang], but he was out so I couldn't see him. I went to the Ishida Restaurant at the invitation of Mr. Minehata Yoshimitsu. Seated there were Itō Takeo, Tatsuta Kiyotatsu, Shigemitsu Mamoru, Chu Tsao-wu, and Chi Shih."

Eventually I remembered. I had met a man by the name of Chou Shu-jen who was at that time an official in the Ministry of Education. Had the old Mr. Uchiyama not brought my attention to this fact, I probably would never have been aware that that Chou Shu-jen was in fact Lu Hsün himself.

Needless to say I have not the slightest memory of what we spoke of at that meeting. We had been invited to the dinner by

Minehata Yoshimitsu, a consultant for the SMR. He had been invited as an instructor to China at the end of the Ch'ing era, in a way similar to Professor Yoshino's experience, and had made many Chinese friends. At this time in 1925 he was both an SMR consultant and an adviser to a jointly managed company in Chilin, and from time to time he came to Peking from Chilin. He introduced his friends in China to Japanese people. It was part of his job. He must have been very close to Lu Hsün, for his name appears a good many times in Lu's diary. Tatsuta, who had eaten with us, had been sent to Peking and stationed there by the Home Office; he was in charge of the suppression of leftist thought. Shigemitsu Mamoru was at that time still a second-rank secretary in the Japanese Legation.

In the History of China's Struggle for Liberation (2)

The May Thirtieth Incident

After the suppression of the great Peking-Hankow Railway strike, Wu P'ei-fu of the Chihli Clique reigned supreme in the North and squashed radical movements wherever they arose. The labor movement headed toward a period of inactivity. I have already touched on this story, and I won't continue at length. At the time of the second Fengtien-Chihli War in October 1924, one force within the Chihli Clique, led by the Christian General Feng Yü-hsiang, boldly and suddenly carried out a coup d'état in Peking. This became the starting point for the loosening of the reactionary warlord structure in the North. Abolishing the reactionary policies enacted by Wu, Feng opened up freedoms of speech, assembly, and organization. The order for the arrest of Li Ta-chao and others was rescinded at this time. No one then realized that Li Ta-chao had been influential in Feng's coup d'état. Li and Feng had been in contact for many years, ever since Li in his youth had planned the Luan-chou Uprising of 1911.

Calling his forces the National Revolutionary Army, Feng Yü-hsiang greeted Sun Yat-sen in Peking. The United Front policy had already been enacted at the Second Congress of the Chinese Communist Party, Li Ta-chao had met with Sun in Shanghai, and the negotiations had been a success. In January 1924 the Kuomintang underwent reorganization. A detailed discussion of all the political upheavals at this time is unnecessary. In any case, a major turning point ensued shortly after Sun Yat-sen's death in Peking in March 1925. Supporting and propelling the momentum at this time, labor unions were formed and reorganized in many places from late 1924 through 1925, just at the time that Feng lifted the ban on the labor movement. And the wave of strikes came seething to the surface. Strikes at the Japanese textile mills in Tsingtao and at the cotton mills in Shanghai were the sparks that set off the May Thirtieth Incident.

I was sorting out the developing situation in the labor movement that had reached this climax for an article entitled "The Background of the Chinese Liberation Movement of 1925," which was published in *Shakai shisō* (Social Thought). This journal served as the organ of the Shakai shisō sha (Social Thought Society), an association of many of us who had been together earlier in the Shinjinkai. Members of the Shinjinkai who were still in school had already in the time of Koreeda Kyōji outgrown Taishō democracy and plunged into practical activities; these people were quite apart from the group of us who had graduated together. The Shakai shisō sha was built by graduate members who were not involved in social activism. Since I was one of them at this time, I published my essay in *Shakai shisō*.

In China the May Thirtieth Incident is accorded the status of the start of the era of the "great revolution." It is on a par with such events as the Boxer Rebellion and the 1911 Revolution insofar as they captured the outside world's attention. Perhaps it was for this reason that my article was taken much notice of in Japan. Subsequently, people who came to China from Japan with the aim of engaging me in democratic interchanges thronged my library along Ch'un-shu Lane. Ishida Eiichirō of the Gakuren, which I have already mentioned, and Mitamura Shirō of the Council of Japanese Labor Unions both paid me visits at this time. In addition, such different and varied men as Taguchi Unzō, on his way back from Russia, Ch'uan Li-yü of the Manchurian cultural movement, Pak Sok-yun of the Korean student movement, and Raja Mahendra Pratap of the Indian independence movement all came to my home.

Raja Mahendra Pratap

Among these men, my extraordinary impressions of Raja Mahendra Pratap are difficult to forget. The storms of May Thirtieth had not yet subsided and tumultuous days passed one after the next. I have forgotten the name of the person who introduced us, but I received a phone call out of the blue that said he was waiting at the Peking Hotel and wanted to meet me. I raced over.

I had imagined a dare-devil, patriotic type from a fierce independence movement, but when he introduced himself in the lobby, I found him merely an advocate of the "religion of love" and an exemplary individual. He had a certain softness about him as he explained that he had been deported from Japan. He described for me in detail the story of the repression of the Indian independence movement by British government officials. I explained by comparison the present situation in the Chinese anti-imperialist movement. His aim was to forge contacts with the anti-imperialist and anti-British movements in China, and he wanted me to help him if I could. Several times during his stay either I visited him or he visited me.

Apparently he met with leaders on the Chinese side in Peking on several occasions, although there seems to have been some ideological differences between them. He often complained to me of his dissatisfaction. He finally felt he could not get to the truth of things in Peking; he said he wanted to go to Shanghai and asked if I could help him with the preparations so that the British authorities would not be informed. I put him in the hands of Hidaka Matsushirō, who ran the administrative committee of the Tientsin foreign settlement and was an in-law of mine. Then I sent him off on a Chinese ship bound for Shanghai. He found the situation there the same, though, and ultimately left China very despondent.

My Observations of the Kuo Sung-ling Affair

It was not at all easy to bring the agitated atmosphere of May Thirtieth under control. It continued to meander along. In the spring of that year, 1925, on my way back from a trip to Dairen, by chance I happened to witness the Manchurian assault of the army of Kuo Sung-ling at Shan-hai Pass.

Kuo Sung-ling had many reasons for rising in revolt against Marshall Chang Tso-lin, but one should also take into account the nationwide revolutionary trend of events from Feng Yü-hsiang's coup d'état continuing into the May Thirtieth Movement. The movement's influence extended into the Fengtien faction, a typical warlord army, and the Commander Kuo Sung-ling of the advance guard took the crack troops of the Fengtien Army with him to the Chinese side of the pass and made a compromise on his own with Feng Yü-hsiang. After issuing an anti-Chang manifesto, he tried to attack Chang's Manchurian base. The train car I was riding in met up with Kuo's advancing army and was not permitted to go beyond the city of Ch'in-huang-tao.

I had no choice but to remain in Ch'in-huang-tao, and I decided to wait at the Japanese inn there until traffic was reopened. This inn was often turned into a place where negotiations were conducted between Kuo Sung-ling, whose troops were invading Manchuria, on the one hand, and Chang Tso-lin's son, Chang Hsüeh-liang, later known as the Young Marshall, who had come to pacify Kuo's attack, with Army Major Giga Seiya (an adviser to Chang Tso-lin) assisting him, on the other. I observed the course of events from beginning to end.

Despite the intermediary role played by Japan in these parleys, Kuo remained firm and the negotiations broke down. Kuo's troops attacked Chin-chou and Ying-k'ou and then advanced as far as Hsin-min-ch'un in the suburbs of Fengtien. I heard later that Chang Tso-lin's personal property had been transported to the SMR office in Fengtien, so that for a time Chang had lost all hope and was prepared to retire from public life.

However, the Japanese side, that is, the Kwantung Army which supported Chang's Manchurian kingdom, issued a statement that it would under no circumstances allow a crossing of the SMR rail line. Kuo Sung-ling's political advisers, Lin Ch'ang-min and Yin Ju-keng, both of whom had spent periods of time as students in Japan, responded to this announcement by trying to gain the understanding of the Japanese government. Kuo issued a statement to the effect that he respected Japanese interests even in Manchuria, and he further engaged in a variety of maneuvers to influence the governmental authorities. On the Japanese side, one group of the army and one group among the mainland adventurers (Komai Tokuzō [who would later become one of the most important Japanese officials in the puppet state of Manchukuo] among them) were said to be planning to support Kuo. Finally, though, the situation was completely reversed when Japan carried through its support for Chang Tso-lin and with military force prevented Kuo's troops from entering Fengtien.

As Kuo's troops hesitated about cutting across the SMR line and attacking Fengtien, the army of Heilungkiang warlord Wu Chün-sheng, whose military operations were guided by his Japanese adviser, Major Hayashi Daihachi, came up from behind him and attacked his rear. Kuo's army was routed. The whole matter was brought to a close by the end of the year when Kuo Sung-ling and Lin Ch'ang-min were murdered, and Yin Ju-keng took refuge in the Japanese consulate. In the final analysis, they had merely succeeded in throwing Chang's kingdom and the Japanese government into a temporary state of confusion. The following year at the central park in Peking, the Chinese Students Association had a gathering together with workers and conducted a solemn anti-Japanese meeting in memory of Kuo Sung-ling.

The Second Hong Kong General Strike

Following this memorial an anti-British, anti-Wu P'ei-fu mass meeting was held in Peking amidst the fierce opposition between Feng Yü-hsiang's National Revolutionary Army and a diplomatic delegation of the imperialists. Wu's Chihli Army had been crushed by Feng's coup d'état, and Wu now sought a comeback with his base in the Yangtze delta where British interests were concentrated. As the movement in Peking flared up further, the National Assembly on 18 March 1926 announced that the number of dead had swelled to 47 and the injured to 164. In the South a second general strike in Hong Kong, which began following the May Thirtieth Incident, gradually demonstrated immense proportions to the world. I wanted to take a look at it with my own eyes, so in March I planned a second trip to the South.

In the hope that this would prove a highly fruitful trip, I made a fair number of preparations before leaving. Making use of my friends in Peking to the utmost, I secured letters of introduction to important government functionaries in the South. First of all, through Suzue Gen'ichi's introduction I received a letter from Kan Shu-te, head secretary of the party department of the Kuomintang in the North, to Lin Tsu-han, head of the agricultural department in the Kwangtung government, and Yang Pao-an, secretary to Chiang Kai-shek. He also enabled me to get a letter from Peking University student Hsieh Lien-ch'ing to the All-China Student Alliance in Shanghai. Suzue himself wrote me a letter of introduction to Su Chao-cheng, chairman of the Hong Kong strike committee.

I recall arriving in Hong Kong in the middle of March. Already ten months into a general strike since the May Thirtieth Incident of the previous year, Hong Kong had fallen into a state of paralysis like an asphyxiated corpse. Contact with the mainland by either land or sea was severely blockaded. The only way to get to Canton was by boat through Portuguese-controlled Macao.

It was four years since I had seen the streets of Canton, and they bustled with activity beyond my expectations. The reorganization of the streets had made advances; the distinctive red-light district had disappeared; and practically every street was covered with modern pavement. The names of the party, governmental, and union organs were scribbled in white on green backgrounds of every building and street corner, and from the rooftops flew the Nationalist Chinese flag. The walls were painted in green, and they were filled with the slogans "Down with the Warlords" and "Down with Imperialism." I wrote a piece for *Shakai shisō* as a record of my observations of the conditions in

Canton, and I described it as the "green capital." The most glorious episode in the history of the Kuomintang regime was experienced here in this city of green.

The freedoms of speech and publication were protected in the extreme, and translations of anti-imperialist works that could not be had in Japan rose like mountains in the bookstores. I wrapped in newspaper Chinese translations of the *Communist Manifesto* and sent them to my friends in Tokyo.

Impressions of Su Chao-cheng

I took up lodgings at a small Japanese inn in Sha-chi [Shakee], where at the time of the May Thirtieth Incident, I heard, numerous sacrifices had been suffered in the confrontations with the British troops from Shameen. I first went out to pay a visit on Su Chao-cheng, chairman of the executive committee of the Hong Kong strike committee and vice-chairman of the General Labor Union. The committee was in the famous Eastern Garden, protected by worker pickets. Su Chao-cheng had the gentle look of a man thirty-five or thirty-six years of age, and he began the conversation by asking me for news of Suzue Gen'ichi. He had gotten to know Suzue in Tsingtao at the time of the May Thirtieth Incident. Since I had often heard Suzue speak about Su, I felt as though this was not our first meeting as he proceeded to fill me in, with complete self-confidence, on the situation in the Hong Kong strike.

At that time 200,000 laborers who had returned from Hong Kong to Canton were being accommodated. One group among them served as pickets and formed an armed workers' brigade. Another group served as a contruction brigade and did work on public roads and general urban construction. The 80,000 men out of work lived on a patriotic fund contributed by overseas Chinese. Since they were in high spirits and their money was abundant, the strike would not be broken even if it went on for any number of years into the future. As he spoke politely, Su's look of trust made me believe that what he said was not idle chatter.

The Young Mr. Liu Shao-ch'i

The following day Su Chao-cheng invited me to dinner, and he introduced me there to the leaders of the General Labor Union. I believe that Li Sen, the chairman, and about ten other members of the executive committee were present. Liu Shao-ch'i was among them. The reason I'm able to remember Liu's name and have forgotten the faces and names of the others is that among the people seated there it was he, a lad presumably in his twenties, who was most gracious toward me.

When the desultory conversation after dinner was over and I was about to return, he gave me the official journals of the various labor associations and very simply invited me to come to a meeting of the executive board of the General Labor Union the following day. I could not pass up this rare opportunity, so on the appointed day I strolled from my lodgings over to the General Labor Union. On the way, Mr. Liu Shao-ch'i walked up to meet me. He said he was lucky to have caught me en route to say that the meeting had had to be cancelled due to circumstances. So, he apologized but asked me to leave. That seemed pointless to me, but without questioning him too closely on it, I took a snapshot of Liu on the street and returned to my room. It was 20 March 1926.

When I read the newspaper the following morning, I understood why Mr. Liu had backed out. Chiang Kai-shek had pulled off his coup d'état. On that very day, Chiang had seized the battleship *Chung-shan*, arrested the military and party representatives who were from the Communist Party, disarmed the Hong Kong pickets, and raided the headquarters of the Soviet advisory delegation and the Soviet consulate.

What had actually happened only became clear three days later. Li Chih-lung, the deputy head of the naval bureau within the military department, received a falsified order from Chiang Kai-shek as part of a right-wing plot. Without understanding the situation well, he had the battleship *Chung-shan* prepared for war and gave it sailing orders to proceed offshore the Whampoa Military Academy. At the same time Chiang Kai-shek received the false information that the Communists, at the head of a force of military and labor troops, were plotting to incorporate the Nationalist government into the Soviet government. He reacted with lightning speed.

Because of this incident Chiang's secretary Yang Pao-an informed me over the telephone that the chances for my promised meeting with Chiang looked considerably dimmer. It in fact did wipe out my opportunity ever to meet with Chiang in person.

The circumstances behind the incident were not deeply investigated, but clearly Chiang Kai-shek had availed himself of this opportunity. The matter was resolved as a misunderstanding between the Kuomintang and the Communists, and responsibility was placed on the shoulders of the leader of the KMT's left wing, Wang Ching-wei. Using the chance this incident provided, a party reorganization plan was issued on Chiang's initiative, and the KMT-CCP cooperation moved to a new stage, well known in the history of the revolution.

I returned from my trip to Kwangtung and wrote an essay evaluating the incident; it was entitled "The Kuomintang and the Chinese Communist Party." In it I examined Chiang's conversion to rightist ideas, which were publicized for a time after the incident. I offered the judgment that in view of the present situation in which relations with the Soviet Union continued as before, Chiang's right-wing views could not be trusted. Due to my lack of adequate knowledge, though, this conclusion was found to be entirely incorrect.

A Meeting with Lin Tsu-han

For these reasons I never met Chiang Kai-shek, but Kan Shu-te's introduction did enable me to meet Lin Tsu-han as promised. Since the previous year Lin had been serving as the head of the Kuomintang's agriculture department, and he led the farmers' cooperative movement in Kwangtung province. The building housing the party department of the KMT where I made contact with him was enormous, though the room allotted him as head of the agriculture department on the second floor was covered with a musty rush-mat rug. In the corner of the room sat a Chinese man with an appearance of magnanimity, a gentleman past forty with a head of hair streaked with gray: Lin Po-ch'ü (Tsu-han).

He had attended a senior normal school in Tokyo, so he spoke to me softly in Japanese. What I can now remember is a man, with sparkling eyes, telling me that the phenomenon of wandering vagrants turning to banditry was not confined to Manchuria for there were quite a few of them in Kwangtung province. He then moved on to emphasize strenuously the importance of the peasant movement in the Chinese revolution, pointing out the present situation of peasant associations which had already begun to be organized, and he spoke enthusiastically about various aspects of the revolution. He had the most beautiful and piercing eyes. When I was about to leave, he gave me several issues of their journal, *Nung-min yüeh-k'an* (Farmers' Monthly); then we shook hands firmly and parted. Several years ago on my second trip to China I saw him for the last time when he presided over a conference in support of the South Korean people's struggle. It was a profound sadness for me when he passed away in 1961, one of the Chinese Communist Party's "five old men."

Headquarters of the All-China Student Association

After the *Chung-shan* battleship incident in Kwangtung, the flourishing center of the revolution, power concentrated under Chiang Kai-shek. He himself took on all the important positions of head of the military department of the KMT, chairman of the government's military committee, head of the standing committee of the government, and principal of the central military-political school. Furthermore, in July he assumed supreme command of the Northern Expeditionary Army. When I left Kwangtung, preparations for the Northern Expedition had already made steady progress. They had put together a network of nine army battalions in which the army in the lead organized numbered battalions from the military school troops.

My aim in coming from bustling Kwangtung to Shanghai was to visit the headquarters of the student association, which seemed more like the general headquarters of the antifeudal and antimilitarist struggle of that time. During the upsurge of May Thirtieth, Shanghai was for a time called the Mecca of the world revolution. But the Shanghai I saw one year later was one of comparatively quiet streets. The center of the revolution had already moved to Kwangtung.

Since this was my third visit to Shanghai since 1922, I dispensed with general observations of the city and went straight to investigate the building housing the student association. I have forgotten whether it was located in the general concession area or in the French concession, but the headquarters was not a particularly secret building. I do in fact remember a placard reading "Student Association" that hung in public.

When I showed them the letter of introduction that I had carried from Peking from Hsieh Lien-ch'ing, the Peking University student, I was permitted to go upstairs to a room resembling a conference chamber and consult innocently with a group of students from the headquarters. I no longer remember what our subject was that day, but they gave me a complete set of back issues of their journal, *Cheng-chih sheng-huo* (Political Life). I gathered that anything I might want to know was written therein.

The glorious history of the student movement in China from the May Fourth Movement on is well known. Within it, the All-China Student Association played an immense role, relying on its nationwide structure, as the central organization of a widespread national movement. However, the "class nature" of the student movement, as elsewhere in China at the time, led to increasingly fierce struggles, and accordingly the signs of rupture appeared. At the same time, the leadership of the radical movement in China moved toward the working class.

In my opinion the transition point for the changeover was in the period of the May Thirtieth Incident. In Kwangtung I had heard criticism of the leadership powers of student intellectuals, and the defeat of the general strike planned for March of that year by the student association illustrated the conclusion of this process.

In March the student association persuaded the Shanghai Merchants' Association in their plan for a nationwide general strike along a common front against warlordism. When the comprador capitalists vacillated, though, the plan ended in failure because of the opposition of workers along the Shanghai-Nanking railway line. Later that year no major movement could be held on the anniversary of the May Thirtieth Incident. In June, though, the workers showed a phenomenal rise in strength. The student movement itself split into those who accepted the Communist Party's leadership and those who did not. In the midst of all this, the wave of a large-scale general strike came surging forward initially from a strike in a Japanese-owned textile mill in Shanghai.

I Leave Peking

I returned to Peking from my trips to Kwangtung and Shanghai with a very profound personal sense that a great wave in the Chinese revolution was close at hand. Over the next year or two there would unfold in China the most lustrous spectacle. Believing this firmly, I intended to expand and replenish the institute.

It was just at this time that the Japanese government, having attained a compromise with Chang Tso-lin over the pending issue of the four railways in Manchuria and Mongolia, embarked on negotiations to compel the Chinese central government to sign a contract for a loan. The SMR office in Peking took over the guiding hand in these negotiations, and all of a sudden the importance of our office's job rose tremendously. While I was traveling, Takenaka Masakazu, who had been the head of the Administrative Bureau of the SMR (later a director), took over as the new head of the office, superior to Mr. Ushijima who had served in that capacity until then. Also, the office moved from Ch'un-shu Lane to a new business office, purchased (and then remodeled) from an old Chinese restaurant on a corner that faced out onto Eastern Ch'ang-an Street.

Taking advantage of this expansion, I secured for the institute a corner of the new business office and increased my research staff as well as the quantity of materials. At this time I requested a special budget from the main office and bought from the French bookstore the classics of foreign diplomacy. I was really in great spirits. Then, one day toward the end of May, I was suddenly informed by Mr. Takenaka that the board of directors had decided that I was to go on a two-year period of study to Europe and the United States. I was stunned, for I had never expected that my turn for study in Europe and America would come so soon.

The SMR overseas study system was divided into three categories of two-year, one-year, and half-year programs, based on applications after five or six years of work in the company. I had just finished five years the previous year, and I was told to apply in writing to the personnel department concerning my reasons for wanting to study abroad. I wrote for my "reasons" the pretext: "to study the policies toward China of the nations of the West and their Sinological research and study institutions." Overseas study was guaranteed in the future when one became a company executive, and given the results of my work since entering the company, my selection was truly unexpected. Also, the approval had been granted so rapidly that I vaguely wondered if there was something fishy going on. This was, as it were, an "order to leave my present position."

To leave the scene of action at this moment, the opportunity of a lifetime for a China scholar, was unthinkable. My first thoughts were of what had been the purpose of four and one-half years of diligent research in Peking. Yet, overseas study in Europe and the United States was not without its own attractions. When the opportunity presented itself, I tried to bargain for an extension with Director Ōkura Kimmochi who came to Peking for a liaison meeting between Chinese railways and the SMR line. I told him the decision for overseas travel was a blessing but just now I did not want to leave China. Director Ōkura's answer was one line: "Such self-indulgence is impermissible."

I didn't know what to do, so I went to seek the advice of Nakae Ushikichi. "How can you be so narrow-minded?" Nakae said to me. "China's problems aren't going to be solved in a year or two. They're international problems of long duration. You can't understand China's problems by only looking at China. This is a great chance for you to get a global perspective."

"And you, Nakae," I retorted, "you study ancient Chinese history and, instead of keeping a watch on movements in world history, you don't take a single step outside of the city of Peking, do you?" Nakae laughed out loud and then whispered something I didn't understand at the time: "Soon enough it's going to be time to get out of Peking, you know."

My mind was made up to accept the period of overseas study. As I think back on it now, I don't fully understand why I decided to choose that course of action.

The Death of Li Ta-chao

I accepted the overseas study in Europe and America and left Peking in the late summer, August, as the Northern Expeditionary Army subdued Hunan, Kiangsi, and Hupeh and with the force of raging billows continued its assault on the North. I returned to Tokyo, again a passenger on the *Taiyō-maru*, and then headed for America in December of that year. My life as an overseas student lasted for over two years, from then until the spring of 1929, but I will foreshorten my discussion of that period here. There is only one thing I would like to mention by way of concluding discussion of my years in Peking.

One of my aims in going overseas was "to study the Sinological research and study institutions of Europe and the United States." When I arrived in America, I decided to attend Professor Williams's seminar on China at the University of California, and for a time I rented a room in Berkeley. Berkeley's local newspaper concentrated on local society and scarcely carried any general or international news stories. However, since this was an era in which the world's attention was focused on China, reports (albeit simple ones) about developments in the Northern Expedition were carried in the newspaper that I read at home. I lived impatiently, inferring from the short telegram news items the situation in the Chinese revolution.

In a corner of this newspaper one morning early in April 1927, I read a telegram to the effect that Chang Tso-lin had laid siege to the Soviet embassy in Peking and captured Li Ta-chao and some twenty or more members of his party. Then, just after Chiang Kai-shek's coup in Shanghai was reported, there was a simple telegraphic message, like a line in book, saying that Li Ta-chao and his followers had been hanged without a trial. I have never been able to forget the unbelievable shock I suffered that morning. Memories returned to me from the time of the *Chung-shan* battleship incident of the previous year, mixed in with feelings of irritation for not being in China, as I realized this setback to the "great revolution."

4

The Study of China and the Invasion of China

Modern China Studies at the SMR

A Study of Contemporary Chinese Society

Following his coup d'état in Shanghai, Chiang Kai-shek established a government in Nan-ch'ang in opposition to the regime in Wuhan, and a campaign of terror to suppress leftists, primarily the Chinese Communists, raged. None of the students in Professor Williams' seminar at Berkeley understood what had precipitated this sudden change of circumstances. An ex-missionary, Williams was a China scholar best known for his book *China Today*, although at this time he did not seem to have much knowledge of the liberation movement in China. Prior to the "great revolution," studies of the Chinese revolution in the United States had progressed little.

The members of the seminar asked me, having just arrived from East Asia, for an explanation. I began the story, in my terrible English, with a history of the collusion between imperialism and warlord power, and I discussed the history of the opposition between the left and right wings of the Kuomintang. Although I revealed no new information, the direction in which the revolution was developing was clear, and the members of the seminar, including the professor, all seemed quite impressed. At this time I just happened to receive from Japan my first publication, *Gendai Shina shakai kenkyū* (A Study of Contemporary Chinese Society), and I presented a copy of it to Professor Williams. Since it was written in Japanese, I was dubious about its utility to him, but between my "class report" and now this piece of written work the class began to look at me in quite a different light.

A Study of Contemporary Chinese Society was a collection of my articles that had been published during my years in Peking in the *Pekin Mantetsu geppō*, *Shakai shisō*, and *Kaizō*. These essays were compiled from the perspective of the historical relationship between the development of Chinese capitalism and the imperialist invasion. I had delivered the manuscript to Mr. Kaji Ryūichi, and at the time I left Japan, it was to be published as the second volume in the *Shakai shisō sōsho* (Series on Social Thought). In late April 1927, when I had settled down in Berkeley, it arrived in book form.

For reasons of editorial convenience, certain sections from the manuscript I had handed in, such as "A History of the Development of the Newspaper Industry in China," "The Peking Census and Social Research," and "The Problems of Poverty in Peking," were cut. Also, since I hadn't copyread the text, there were numerous incorrect or missing characters, so I was not especially gladdened by the appearance of my maiden work. However, this book did serve as a summation of my research life in Peking. I learned that in book reviews by Yanaihara Tadao and Yamakawa Kikue, written in Japan at the time, my book was said to be a scientific interpretation among studies concerning China. Later, I read in a collection of materials on the CCP held at the East Asian Institute of Columbia University a bibliographical note that said my book was an objective evaluation. Ozaki Hotsumi later urged me to revise it for republication, but since I was still unsatisfied with it, it was never reissued. Perhaps it may have been important as a book that made use of the social sciences and appeared relatively early in Japan among studies of contemporary China.

Contemporary China Studies Prior to the "Great Revolution"

As I have pointed out, my study of China was directly motivated by the trends in China from the May Fourth Movement through the May Thirtieth Movement and derived from events I had witnessed with my own eyes. Under the influence of the "great revolution," studies focusing on Chinese society began to draw attention, a little after the period in which I had begun my work. It was only around 1927 that Americans finally started to work in this area, as the situation in Professor Williams's seminar would indicate. In China as well, editorial work on a *Lao-tung nien-chien* (Laborers' Yearbook) was stimulated by my work. Amano Motonosuke and Kaji Ryūichi pointed out to me that Li Ta's *Chung-kuo ch'an-yeh ko-ming shih* (A History of the Chinese Industrial Revolution), which was written rather early on, merely rearranged some of the material on the history of the development of capitalism from my book. Similarly, I heard directly from Hosokawa Karoku that his *Shina kakumei to sekai no asu* (The Chinese Communist Party and the World Tomorrow), written when he was working at the Ōhara Institute, owed a great deal to my book.

In Europe, men such as Karl A. Wittfogel had begun research in this area fairly early. His *Das erwachende Chinas: ein Abriss der Geschichte und der gegenwärtigen Probleme Chinas* appeared in 1926, and his edited volume of the writings of Sun Yatsen, *Aufzeichnungen eines chinesischen Revolutionärs*, was published in 1927; and Wilhelm Wagner's *Die chinesische Landwirtschaft* came out in 1926. My book was on a par with these works in terms of early attention to the issues at hand.

China studies undertaken as analyses of social structure deepened only after the "great revolution," or actually after its collapse. The work of Wittfogel, Wagner, and Georgii I. Safarov in the Soviet Union were its cornerstone. My book did not go as far as theirs. It was fatal to be writing before the advances of the Northern Expedition and to be separated from the scene of action, because the main focus of China studies centered on the problems of counterrevolution that emerged with the unfolding of the Northern Expedition and aimed at an elucidation of Chinese society.

As for studies of the "great revolution," before leaving Japan I had written an essay entitled "Shina musan kaikyū seitō" (The Chinese Proletarian Party) for the book *Kakkoku musan kaikyū seitō shi* (A History of Proletarian Parties in Various Countries), volume one in the Series on Social Thought. Together with Hosokawa Karoku's work, mentioned above, these were the first essays to introduce the Chinese Communist Party to Japan.

Let me say a few words about what might be called the basis that sustained my research in Peking. Inasmuch as my first book was published as a volume in the Series on Social Thought, it was linked [through the publishers] to the democratic movement in Japan. I have already mentioned several articles I submitted for publication on the Chinese labor movement to *Shakai shisō*, the journal a few of us from the Shinjinkai had founded. The position on the Chinese revolution taken by Professor Yoshino Sakuzō, the man who had originally drawn me to the subject, examined the Chinese democratic movement from the standpoint of Taishō democracy. Although my study of the Chinese social movement was different in nature from Professor Yoshino's, both were carried out through a linkage with the democratic movement in Japan. As a member of the Research Section of the SMR, my study was protected. However, aiming at making China's contemporary reality understandable to the Japanese population at large, I paid close attention to the world of journalism and to the organization of my writing.

Four Lineages among Early Japanese Studies of China

After my period of overseas study, what accomplishments could the SMR show for itself concerning postrevolutionary Chinese politics and economy? In the spring of 1929, I returned to Dairen and got ahold of them, but before I touch on these let me first look at early Japanese studies of China that predate our efforts. There were a number of different lineages in this field, which I think can generally be categorized into four schools: (1) historical studies; (2) geographical studies; (3) literary studies; and (4) politics, or Sino-Japanese relations in the international relations surrounding China.

By historical studies I mean the field of "Sinology," both the Tokyo school and the Kyoto school of Sinology. The Tokyo school refers to the work of men engaged in East Asian historical studies, under the tutelage of Shiratori Kurakichi, based at Tokyo Imperial University. Although this school took form in imitation of European Sinology, it distinguished itself in research on Manchuria and Mongolia. By contrast, the Kyoto school of Sinology originated in ancient classical studies, and having gone beyond classical understanding developed to encyclopedic proportions. The achievements of such men as Naitō Konan, Kano Kōkichi, and Ojima Sukema, who began their careers with training in textual critical research, emerged from this school.

Geographical studies began with information from local gazetteers for the General Staff Headquarters of the army and can be divided into three parts. From the early Meiji period, the General Staff Headquarters poured its research energies into, particularly, gazetteers from North China. The military itself diligently translated documents concerning the travels in China of European missionaries. When I was writing the section on military affairs for volume 2 of the *Man-Mō zensho*, I mainly used materials published by them. I have already noted that the Research Section of the SMR was heavily influenced by them.

While military research focused on Manchuria, Mongolia, and North China, concerns for trade and commerce spurred research on Central and South China. Results could be cited from the earlier period due to the propelling force of Arao Sei's Nis-Shin bōeki kenkyūjo (Institute on Sino-Japanese Commercial Research) and Tō-A dōbun shoin (East Asian Common Culture Academy). The East Asian Common Culture Academy's *Shina shōbetsu zenshi* (Complete Compendia of China by Provinces) and *Shina keizai zensho* (Compendium on the Chinese Economy) were well known. In addition the research reports made by Shiraiwa Ryūhei's Nisshin Kisen Lines, businessmen in the textile industry, and trading companies in the Mitsui conglomerate as well as materials from the Trade Bureau of the Ministry of Foreign Affairs can all be counted among China studies of this sort. Ranking third among these geographical studies were the academic achievements of the journal of the Geographical Society of Tokyo. The work of the Ōtani exploration party [to Northwest China], spurred by the teams led earlier by Paul Pelliot and A. Le Coq, fell into this category.

As a layman, I find the third grouping, literature, difficult to discuss. Aside from the translation already completed in Kumamoto City during the late Meiji period of the [famous Chinese novel] *Hung-lou meng* (Dream of the Red Chamber), we can generally divide this group into two subcategories: traditional Chinese-style poetry and classical Chinese prose, and tasteful, modern "Chinese literature." Contemporary literature was left completely unstudied in this early period.

The fourth group of political essays or journalistic views on China would include, among others, Ozaki Yukio's *Shina bunkatsu ron* (On the Partition of China), Tarui Tōkichi's completely opposite work *Daitō gappō ron* (On the Confederation of the Great East), and the editorial essays of Yamaji Aizan, Miyazaki Tōten, Naitō Konan, and Kita Ikki. Japanese expansionist concerns in Asia, from the debate over the invasion of Korea on, were expressed conspicuously and vividly in this category of works. Jumping into the Shōwa era, men like Hatano Ken'ichi, Kanda Masao, and Tachibana Shiraki were all part of a grouping of China studies by newspapermen such as Hosokawa Karoku and Ozaki Hotsumi. Writings on contemporary China were tied up with other disciplines, such as political science or law, and gave rise to a variety of writings, such as Imai Yoshiyuki's *Shina kokusaihō ron* (On International Law in China), Takayanagi Ken'ichirō's *Shina zeikan ron* (On the Customs Duty in China), and Yoshino Sakuzō's *Shina kakumei shōshi* (A Short History of the Chinese Revolution) and *Shina kakumei ron* (On the Chinese Revolution). Professor Yoshino's works were based on his personal experiences when he had been invited to China.

SMR Studies after the Pekin Mantetsu Geppō

China studies centering on the *Pekin Mantetsu geppō* began in the 1920s with the foregoing as background. It played the significant role of trailblazer in studies of Chinese society that used social science. I have already mentioned how, when I had arrived in China, general knowledge of China, which is to say journalistic knowledge, was cut off from contemporary realities. Our task had been to shed this skin, and the role of enlightener that the *Pekin Mantetsu geppō* played in Japanese studies of China was the product of our efforts. As a result, around the time I left Peking, I was on several occasions approached by the Japanese journalistic world to contribute manuscripts on China.

From the essential position of the SMR's research institutions, however, this enlightening function was really secondary or derivative. Our main task remained the collection and scientific summation of information linked to the actualities of Japan's management of Manchuria. What was strange was that the SMR was not all that scientific. Responsibility for conveying information to the general public was what journalists generally undertook to do. However, they did not fulfill their task in a consistent manner, for even into the first decade of the Shōwa era (1925–1934), a situation persisted that was deplorable to one journalist, Ozaki Hotsumi, who covered China superbly. To explain the situation in China, I felt in my work that it was necessary to point out the larger framework, that lack of which prevented Japanese journalists from understanding that Chinese society was in the midst of development and, specifically, from understanding the essence of the Chinese revolution. They had felt compelled to adhere to the notion that, as an invading nation, Japan was more progressive than China. From this position they could not understand or approve of the radical changes transpiring in Chinese society.

Groundbreaking efforts in this direction emerged from two exceptional points. One was Japanese journalism, which is to say the recognition expressed therein of a position that rejected Japanese imperialism, and this meant studies of China by Japanese revolutionaries. The recognition in this case arose simultaneously from a sense of solidarity with the Chinese revolutionary movement. This role was played in Japan, I believe, by the Proletarian Scientific Institute, formed in 1929, and its study group on Chinese issues. At that time, I had no contact with it at all.

The other impulse came from studies carried out by our research institutes at the SMR as well as by arms of the Japanese government and military from a fully imperialist position. One simply could not use the concoction created earlier by Japanese journalism skillfully to pressure or repress the Chinese popular movement. Without approaching the realities of the movement one could not hammer out an effective countermeasure. Of course, it was futile for studies undertaken from this perspective to grasp comprehensively the necessity of the Chinese revolution. However, studies were undertaken from this limited field of vision, and a certain factual understanding could be reached through a process of trial and error, insofar as such studies were linked directly to the aggressive activities of imperialism. These were the conditions surrounding China studies at our research facilities at the SMR, which put us in an extraordinary position.

Let me mention two or three academic projects I was involved with at the SMR. As I have already mentioned, Miyamoto Michiharu took over the *Pekin Mantetsu geppō* after I left to study overseas. I returned in 1929. During my absence the state of affairs in China had undergone rapid change, as seen in the shift of the political center after the Northern Expedition from Peking to Shanghai and Nanking. In conjunction with these changed circumstances, we moved the journal to our Shanghai office and changed its name to *Mantetsu Shina gesshi*. As a notice in the new journal, I wrote a piece entitled: "Toward a Scientific Synthesis of China Studies." In it I offered a general overview of European studies of China and argued that Japanese studies had not gone beyond the methods and approaches of economics and textual scholarship. I concluded that the new scientific approach could not elucidate matters unless it was based in Marxism. Noting that since Marx's views on China had arisen from the writings of missionaries in China, I called for a wide variety of responses to them. In addition, I planned to trace America's China policy systematically, but the journal ceased publication after only two or three issues. I basically completed this plan, albeit roughly, under the entry "Imperialism in China" for the *Shakai kagaku jiten* (Dictionary of the Social Sciences).

We gave the editorial tasks of the *Mantetsu Shina gesshi* its special character by inaugurating a joint Sino-Japanese research approach, and we gained the cooperation of Ch'en Han-sheng and Hsiung Te-shan. Hsiung died a young man, but Ch'en is still alive and active in the Peking academic world, and he published a number of pieces in the *Mantetsu Shina gesshi*. From that period Marxist analysis of Chinese society began to appear in the studies by Chinese themselves. The same was true in Japan, as the influence exerted by translations of the work of Liudvig I. Mad'iar and Wittfogel was immense.

As for materials concerning revolutionary matters, I first got my hands on a copy of *Hsiang-tao* (Guide) from a a group of scholars at Peking University through the intermediacy of Suzue Gen'ichi. This actually substantiated the existence of the CCP. It was a secret publication at the time and was first published in Soochow and, later, I believe, in Kwangtung. It was sent to me through the mail because it was a secret publication. *Hsin ch'ing-nien* had been discontinued temporarily, but I remember that it reappeared around this time.

The SMR issued all sorts of materials, such as *Shanhai o chū-shin to suru Shina no rōdō undō* (The Chinese Labor Movement, Centering in Shanghai, published 1928), as documents "concerning the great revolution." In 1929 Suzue Gen'ichi, on a short-term consultancy from the SMR, completed his *Shina musan kaikyū undō shi* (A History of the Proletarian Movement in China, published as an internal document without editing). Later, his *Shina kakumei ni okeru kaikyū tairitsu* (Class Conflict in the Chinese Revolution) was published by the Taihōkaku Press.

Tachibana Shiraki, who wrote a variety of unusual stories and articles in the years 1922–1923 for the Japanese-language newspaper *Kei-Shin nichinichi shimbun* (Peking-Tientsin Daily

News), moved to Dairen, and it was in this period that he began publishing the journal *Shina kenkyū* (China Studies) in which he inserted his well-known essays on Chinese guilds and on Taoism. Tachibana's essays and critical works were collected by a group of younger staff members of the Research Section, such as Ōgami Suehiro, and they were published during and after the war in three volumes by the Nihon hyōronsha: *Shina shisō kenkyū* (Studies in Chinese Thought), *Shina shakai kenkyū* (Studies in Chinese Society), and *Shina kakumei shi ron* (On the History of the Chinese Revolution). From about 1927 Tachibana became a consultant to the SMR on the staff of the Information Section, but I shall come back and touch on this later.

The first SMR collection of documents concerning the Chinese Communists was compiled by Ōtsuka Reizō, entitled *Chūkyō bunken shiryō* (Documents and Materials on the Chinese Communists, in two volumes), under the guidance of Tachibana Shiraki. It was published to complement a collection first put together as Institute of Pacific Relations (IPR) materials. Among the Chinese Communist documents were special dispatches compiled by Himori Torao. Although I think this fellow's level of understanding of Marxist thought and, thus, the information he provided had strengths and weaknesses, he did diligently put together this collection of leaflets and pamphlets which at that time could not ordinarily be obtained. I believe it has been rather widely used.

Let me go back momentarily to the period when I had returned to China. Nakae Ushikichi had become an SMR consultant and continued his own distinctive research. His studies were entirely different in kind from what we even today refer to as Sinology. In methodology his work had the unique quality of combining an extremely broad area of the social sciences with German philosophy, including Marx, which Sinology until then had lacked. From 1924 on he produced articles from time to time, the first being "Shina kodai seiji shisō shi" (A History of Ancient Chinese Political Thought), and they were assembled and published after the war by the Iwanami Publishing Company under the title *Chūgoku kodai seiji shisō* (Ancient Chinese Political Thought).

SMR Investigations of Rural Chinese Villages

In any event, just as research that approached the trends in modern China got underway, we were confronted with the Manchurian Incident of 18 September 1931. After it had occurred, analyses of the structure of rural villages in Manchuria became exceedingly popular. Two motives for this development can be cited. First, with the upsurge in the "great revolution," debate on the "Asiatic mode of production" became widespread in European studies of China, and a great deal of interest coagulated around the structure of Chinese villages. In this instance Japanese scholarly concern was aroused by an international debate. The second cause was the popularity of a method which by investigating the structure of agriculture gave one a basic position for the analysis of society generally, as might be seen, for example, in the *Nihon shihonshugi hattatsu shi kōza* (Symposium on the History of the Development of Capitalism in Japan).

Riding the crest of this vogue for methodology, we carried out rural village investigations in Manchuria on a massive scale. To investigate regions that had been newly incorporated under Japanese dominion, to obtain policy materials, and to understand accurately these newly seized objects for exploitation: these were the objectives. The SMR sent a group of village investigators led by Amano Motonosuke to the Interim Industrial Research Bureau, an organ created by the government of Manchukuo. It engaged in research with a staff of forty or fifty men. The real leader here was Shiomi Tomonosuke, who after the war was a bureau chief in the Japanese Ministry of Agriculture and Forestry and finally quit as vice-minister there, and he received the cooperation of men such as Suzuki Tatsuo.

The result of this research was five or six volumes in folio, comprising an enormous amount of material. But it was only raw materials, and no summary of it was ultimately forthcoming. The SMR issued it as a development in Marxist theory in the *Manshū keizai nempō* (The Manchurian Annual Economic Report). While taking many suggestions for their research methods from the investigations of Soviet economists, such as Iashinov and Mad'iar, the report was not well compiled, as compared to its models by Soviet economists. The group that carried out the investigations continued their analyses of villages in the pages of *Manshū hyōron*, run by Tachibana Shiraki. It was these investigators who kept the *Manshū keizai nempō* in print and whose writings in it raised the spirits of the SMR researchers by criticizing the Kwantung Army and the political administration of Manchukuo.

After the village investigations in Manchuria, a group centering around myself carried out field research in thirteen counties in eastern Hopeh (North China) just before the beginning of the Sino-Japanese War. These materials later came into the hands of Yamada Seitarō, who developed a theoretical system for Chinese villages.

When the war with China began and military force was put to use deep in the Chinese hinterland, investigations of Chinese villages were carried out on a large scale and in a detailed fashion. A study of customs in North China villages and an investigation of commercial practices in Central China were prepared by the Research Committee on Chinese Customs under the leadership of Dr. Suehiro Izutarō in the field. The materials resulting from the former of these two were published by Iwanami after the war and received the Asahi Prize. I shall discuss in detail later the projects with which I was directly involved in Shanghai, but they included research on Chinese commercial products, a study of industry in the Wusih area, and research on native shipping in Central China; also, among the joint topics of research at the Research Department were a study of the resistance capacity of the Chungking regime and a study of inflation, and these were primarily conducted from the Shanghai center.

Such investigations were carried out in a colonial China and during the waves of an aggressive war. How should they be treated as a scholarly inheritance today? There are still materials of value to scholarship here. It was at the height of the Sino-Japanese War that the Publication Committee for Materials on East Asia was founded, and it published the famous written works of Richtofen and Shirokogorov. The Ministry of Foreign Affairs invested several hundred million yen of the money from the Boxer Indemnity and created the Tōyō bunka kenkyūjo (Institute of East Asian Culture) in Tokyo, the Jimbun toshokan (Humanities Library) in Peking, and the Shizen kagaku kenkyūjo (Institute of Natural Sciences) in Shanghai; several hundred yen were given monthly to researchers, with the aim of training young scholars, and with this amount they were to study for a one- or two-year period. The model for all this came from the example of the United States, which had used its Boxer funds to build Tsinghua University and invite Chinese students to study in the United States. This American tradition is related in spirit to its offering of study funds to developing nations today, and I think it is a tradition worthy of consideration.

The Research Section and Intelligence Agencies

Ties with Military Intelligence Agencies

Research staffers traditionally looked down their noses at the intelligence activities directed solely at contemporary trends. I knew nothing of this before I entered the SMR, but before I traveled overseas I don't think there were close relations between the government and the military, on the one hand, and the Research Section, on the other. However, during the period between my study and my return to Dairen, the bond between the Research Section and the military became extremely close among a certain group of people. This was one of the troubling changes that had transpired while I was away.

In the tumult following the Northern Expedition of the National Revolutionary Army, Japan attempted an act of imperialist intervention by sending troops to Shantung. This occurred in the midst of a period when the Nanking regime was enjoying a brief moment of stability and in the few years of so-called Shidehara diplomacy prior to the Manchurian Incident. The military laid down its arms for a time, and Sino-Japanese relations had a short respite when friendship prevailed. Shidehara diplomacy, though, with the inexplicable suicide of one of its advocates, Minister

Saburi, moved toward an unclear future. The circumstances surrounding this complex and eerie future involved, I believe, a number of people in the military and in the research institutes of the SMR.

Following the Siberian Expedition, the Special Services Unit (or secret police) was created as an organization within the military, and it gained considerable notoriety on the mainland in later years. At that time a Special Services officer was sent from General Staff Headquarters to forge a liaison between the tactical leadership of the White Russian military forces and the Japanese Army, and he saw to the initial formation of a Special Services Unit, at that time in Harbin, as an organ to supervise them. Following the withdrawal of Japanese troops after the Siberian Expedition, this organ continued in place primarily to collect political and military intelligence on the Soviets. From that time, a dangerous atmosphere emerged in relations with China; whenever trouble erupted and the military stepped in, the agency that carried out special intelligence and strategic activities was the Special Services Unit.

Not formal organs of the military but of a slightly different nature were the so-called Residences. The Aoki Residence and the Banzai Residence are well known, for they were the organs that engaged in various diplomatic parleys with the Chinese military, in part planning strategies as well as collecting information. Although it was the legation that formally handled diplomatic negotiations with the Chinese government in Peking, the main actors in the Peking government were warlords, and accordingly these organs (the "Residences") undertook such tasks as handling preparatory negotiations before the Japanese Ministry of Foreign Affairs would make an appearance, seizing intelligence for that purpose, and maneuvering with leading Chinese military people. In matters such as military pacts, the legation simply stepped aside altogether. Thus, we had this dual or two-tiered diplomacy.

In addition to its role in liaison and negotiations between the Manchurian railways and the domestic Chinese ones, the Peking office of the SMR was involved in a variety of activities. After its formation, the SMR set up offices in Chilin, Fengtien, and Chichi-har to handle negotiations directly with the officials of the provincial governments on the Chinese side. In 1917 an office was established in Harbin, and its primary function lay in negotiations with officials of the Chinese Eastern Railway.

At first the Special Services Unit and the research facilities of the SMR had no direct connections. The first links between them formed at the branch offices of the SMR around Manchuria. There was an inseparable relationship between the capacity to transport and intelligence activities. From there they traded all sorts of political and economic information, and gradually the relationship grew closer and closer. As the political demands on the military's intelligence activities multiplied, the intimacy of the bond with the Research Section of the SMR grew increasingly necessary. And, from exchanges of simple information, they eventually moved to a relationship of mutual assistance and sharing.

The close ties between the Research Section and the military date from the period when Sada Kōjirō was section head, before the Manchurian Incident, at the beginning of the Shōwa era, I believe. Mr. Sada graduated from the Gakushūin (College of Peers), entered the Mitsui Company, and then came to the SMR. He was an extraordinarily eccentric man. He was, for instance, author of an essay suggesting the institution of a national lottery, and in that he was indeed a pioneer. His enthusiasm was such that he delivered a speech to everyone he met, and everyone who had the opportunity to meet him in person would inevitably hear such a speech.

On the military's side, information necessary to their activities included more than just military matters. The complex movements in Chinese politics at this time necessitated the military's getting their hands on information from the political and economic arenas as well. These were areas beyond the control of military men. In such cases, leaving rice cakes to the rice cakes dealer, as we say, they wanted information at that time in the hands of the research organs. You might say that section head Sada responded to the changes in this situation. The crux of the cooperative bond between the military and the SMR was in railway transport, and the other areas emerged auxiliary to this and gave the relationship between the research organs of the SMR and the military its nature. In any case, around the time of the Manchurian Incident, this cooperative bond began to strengthen.

The Establishment of an Information Section

The collection of information for research on SMR projects, which was the original function of the Research Section, and the collection of political intelligence, which the military needed, were, however, slightly different in nature. Those people who lived in the tradition of Gotō Shimpei or were reared as researchers with an academic tint under the influence of Ishikawa Tetsuo wanted limitations placed on cooperation with the military. There was, in other words, opposition within to serving the military. Although cooperative relations did emerge in spite of this, there were points at which we did not get along well with each other.

Thus, an Information Section was created, under company management separate from the Research Section and actively engaged in cooperation with the military. This occurred in April 1927, shortly after I left to study overseas. The first head of this section was Ishimoto Kenji. Son of Ishimoto Shinroku, who had been minister of war, Mr. Ishimoto later became one of the executive directors of the SMR. Under his auspices the new Information Section was created, consisting mainly of consultants in intelligence matters. This group included a wide variety of men engaged in the gathering of information, such as China adventurer types, journalist types, and intelligence hands from military backgrounds. Among them were Tachibana Shiraki, who was off wandering around China with his Japanese-language newspapers, and Noda Ranzō, the expert on Soviet intelligence. They passed critical judgment on the information received from various offices.

The Information Section soon changed its name to the Research Materials Section and later to the East Asia Section. I came to know these people when I moved from Nanking to the main office in Dairen and was attached to their section.

Mr. Tachibana Shiraki

My attention was first drawn to the name Tachibana Bokuan (the pen name of Tachibana Shiraki) shortly after arriving in Peking when I became aware of his social commentary with an extremely modern consciousness in the pages of the *Kei-Shin nichinichi shimbun*, the newspaper he published in Tientsin. No one among the Japanese then resident in the Peking-Tientsin area was writing such social commentary. To this day I still remember that it was through his articles that I first learned of the existence of Chinese guilds and gangs. We later met when I moved to the main SMR office. I first imagined that, being a veteran journalist, he had had to leave the world of journalism and come to the SMR for sustenance, but I found that, judging by his attitude at the company, he was not about to sell his honor as a journalist for a salary. The first opinion I heard from him involved the problem of the An-shan Iron Works as one link in a move toward heavy industry on the part of Japanese capitalism. This later turned out to be an accurate approach, and in 1929, when I had just returned after several years abroad, I remembered that these words reminded me of just how important Manchuria was.

When one thinks of the intellectual and scientific pedigree of the Research Department of the SMR, the scholarly debt owed to Tachibana Shiraki, both directly and indirectly, is enormous. In August 1931, just before the Manchurian Incident, Koyama Sadatomo began to publish in Dairen a weekly journal of political and economic criticism by the name of *Manshū hyōron* (Manchurian Critique), under the editorship of Tachibana. It continued publication for nearly fifteen years till April 1945, the year World War II ended, altogether reaching 675 issues. Even Kwantung Army staff officers Katakura Tadashi and Imada Shintarō, both disciples of Ishiwara Kanji, contributed essays to the journal. The main contributors, though, were young staff researchers from the research agencies of the SMR, and through this journal Tachibana exercised a tremendous influence on the members of the research staff.

Active debates on such issues as the Kyōwakai (Concordia Society) and [the slogan of] "Kingly Rule" unfolded in the pages of this journal, although it became principally concerned with debates over the nature of Manchurian agriculture; and young Marxists like Ōgami Suehiro distinguished themselves on this issue. In the process of the creation of a empire in Manchuria, from the Manchurian Incident forward, the *Manshū hyōron* took a critical stance toward the politics and policies of the military, for the actual state of Manchukuo, from Tachibana's point of view, turned out to be very different from what he had initially expected it to be. He treated problems like Japanese emigration with the most acute critical acumen. In the last days of the Pacific War, when the Tōjō government's thought suppression was focused directly on the Research Department of the SMR, this group of commentators were first and foremost made an object of attack because of their critical stance.

While Tachibana and Koyama typified a kind of idealism in Manchuria at that time, dopesters of the class of Noda Ranzō were of a different sort. I have already noted the part Noda played in the 1927 raid on the Soviet Embassy by Chang Tso-lin and the seizure of Li Ta-chao. We worked together for a time when I, having returned to Dairen from Peking, was attached to the Information Section, by now renamed the Research Materials Section. Noda used to jabber triumphantly about the arrest of Li Ta-chao and emphasize to me what a debt I owed him because when they were checking through confiscated documents my *Pekin Mantetsu geppō* appeared, and as editor I would have been in trouble with the military police. Since I had been overseas at the time, he intimated, I had not been arrested.

Tachibana, Noda, and others affiliated with the Information Section found the bond with the Kwantung Army in matters concerning the exchange of collected intelligence growing closer, and this foreshadowed the specific role played by these men in the commotion of the Manchurian Incident and the creation of Manchukuo. The links between the Research Section staff and the

120 STUDY OF CHINA, INVASION OF CHINA

Kwantung Army also arose on various other fronts, such as the relationship between Soviet hand Miyazaki Masayoshi and Ishiwara Kanji, but the great majority of the researchers found cooperative work with the military repulsive, particularly before the Manchurian Incident. Even after it an antimilitary air remained. There were those who took a different attitude, and I hasten to point out this fact. Intelligence gathering activities, as I have noted, did simultaneously form a hidden side of the strength of Chinese studies at the SMR.

5

The Manchurian Incident and the Reorganization of the South Manchurian Railway Company

The SMR Is Outwitted

The Manchurian Incident and the Heads of the SMR

Although Tanaka Giichi's report to the throne, the so-called Tanaka Memorandum, was in fact spurious, it certainly expressed popular Japanese designs on Manchuria and China. Prime Minister Tanaka himself often spoke of "an active policy in Manchuria and Mongolia," and during the period of the Tanaka Cabinet, a hard atmosphere prevailed with respect to China. In June 1928 a joint plot of a group of adventurers and a Kwantung Army staff officer, Kōmoto Daisaku, succeeded in killing Chang Tso-lin in an explosion. This incident and the hard-line policy taken by the Tanaka Cabinet toward China were not unrelated. Tanaka was vigorously pursued in the Diet by the opposition fighter Nagai Ryūtarō, and he ultimately took responsibility for the incident before resigning. Shortly thereafter Tanaka died suddenly, and this caused the affair from developing further on the Japanese side. Such was not, however, the case on the Chinese side. Pro-Japanese elements in the Manchurian regime of Chang Tso-lin's successor, the Young Marshall Chang Hsüeh-liang, were immediately removed, and following an earlier plan a line of encirclement around the SMR was put into effect.

The SMR now found itself in the most difficult position since its founding. The root of these troubled circumstances was the world depression of the 1930s, for the Japanese economy was exposed to instability and fluctuations, and the SMR could not remain unaffected by all this. Revenues from the SMR rail lines dropped dramatically. In over twenty years that I was with the company, this was the only period in which regular staff salary increases ceased and various allowances were decreased. Accordingly, Japanese businesses conditions and Japanese living conditions in Manchuria became quite severe. It was a time when rural privation back home was even worse.

If some sort of remedy were not found, such an atmosphere would continue to prevail. The crisis in Manchuria and Mongolia, primarily in the military, was sounded loudly. Japanese living in Manchuria and Mongolia were becoming agitated, and a tendency sympathetic to this emerged within the SMR as well. It was in this situation that the Manchurian Incident exploded.

Now, when the SMR rail line was bombed, however, and the military activities of the Kwantung Army pushed forward, the SMR itself was still surprised. There is an immense gulf between the sense that "it has to happen" and the actual act of trying to do it. Even after the Incident occurred, we did not immediately all fall in line. Of course, one segment of the staff of the SMR, within the research organs as well, worked actively with the military, but that was only one segment. As a whole we were not at first cooperative.

At the time of the Manchurian Incident, the heads of the SMR Company were President Uchida Kōsai (from the Ministry of Foreign Affairs), Vice-President Eguchi Teijō (from the Mitsubishi conglomerate), and Director Kimura Eiichi (originally Asian affairs bureau chief in the Ministry of Foreign Affairs). In their negotiations with Chang Hsüeh-liang, they followed the Shidehara foreign policy line of trying to protect Japanese interests. Thus, the Ministry of Foreign Affairs and the financial world did not immediately collaborate with the military at the time of the Manchurian Incident. The SMR was of the same inclination.

Mr. Kimura followed the course of those gifted men under Shidehara in the Ministry of Foreign Affairs. To negotiate with Chang Hsüeh-liang about the railway, he entered the company as a director. Creating a "negotiations department" in the SMR, he steadfastly sought a conclusion to the railway talks. Before the eruption of the Incident, just before I was made head of the General Affairs Section, for a short time I held responsibility for the Research Materials Section. When the Incident occurred and the military became increasingly active, this man, Mr. Kimura Eiichi, was completely ignored.

Even though the leaders of the SMR did not collaborate with the military, they of course could not stand in total opposition either, and for the time being they chose a wait-and-see policy. Yet, the attitude of Vice-President Eguchi was crystal clear. He among the group of leaders of the SMR had the capitalist's disposition. When the Manchurian Incident occurred, and just after it the Shanghai Incident of January 1932, he claimed: "This is Napoleon's Moscow. It will end in dismal failure." And he resigned. President Uchida, until this point a follower of the Shidehara line, saw what had transpired and made a 100 percent conversion. He worked to convey the wishes of the military to the home government and to secure its understanding. Later he was recommended by the military and became foreign minister.

The Kwantung Army may have controlled Uchida, but it could not shake up the SMR. Furthermore, without securing the cooperation of the SMR, the Kwantung Army would find it extremely difficult to rely on the Manchurian economy as well as to engage in military activities. Mr. Uchida was followed by the scholarly Count Hayashi Hirotarō, one of the leading members of the Kenkyūkai group in the House of Peers. The skillful technician Hatta Yoshiaki, from the Railway Ministry, became vice-president. Director Kimura left the SMR during this reshuffling.

In response to these new circumstances, Vice-President Hatta gradually hammered out a structure cooperative to the Kwantung Army. Even before this, people associated with research were organizing a cooperative structure early in 1932. I will touch on this later. The leadership of the SMR submitted in this reshuffling. Although the leaders recanted at the time, this did not at once became the stance of the entire staff of the SMR.

The Issue of the SMR's Reorganization

A wide variety of attitudes existed among the SMR staff members from the Manchurian Incident until the founding of the state of Manchukuo. The groups that formed around the Manchurian Youth League and the Yūhōkai (Majestic Peak Association), both of which I shall introduce later, took the lead in cooperation, though their beliefs were not uniform. The general staff members, particularly those in the research area (from the directors on down) were critical at first and made no moves whatsoever. It was in this situation in the middle of 1933 that the SMR reorganization incident occurred.

To explain this incident, I have to touch on the Kwantung Army as well as the policies for dealing with the SMR and for the administration of Manchuria adopted by the Secretariat for Manchurian Affairs of the Department of the Army (Japanese Ministry of the Army), which supported the Kwantung Army. When Manchukuo came into existence in March 1932, it was primarily the Kwantung Army and the Secretariat for Manchurian Affairs that established the basic plan for subsequent policy in Manchuria. The central task before them was what to do with the SMR. At the time of the Manchurian Incident, the SMR was not simply a railway company. It was a huge concern spanning the entire territory of Manchukuo. When it was founded, the SMR was a corporate body standing on three legs of on-site work (railways, mines, and harbors) and running the local administration of the associated regions. Diligently over the subsequent twenty-five years, it directly managed, in addition to these three enterprises, the An-shan Iron Works and assumed among its tasks the operation of a huge number of affiliated enterprises. The following is a list of its enterprises with more than a million yen in capital (figures in parentheses represent millions of yen in capital):

South Manchurian Sugar Company (10)
Manchurian Spinning Mill (5)
Manchurian-Mongolian Woolen Goods Company (3)
Ch'ang-kuang Glass Company (3)
Manchurian Dock Company (2)
Manchurian Mineral Medicine Company (1)
East Asian Industrial Company (20)
Joint Chinese-Japanese-Russian Timber Company (6)
Manchurian-Korean Timber Company (3)
Dairen Steamship Company (10)
Korean Railway Company (54.5)
East Asian Engineering Enterprises (5)
Fu-shun Coal Company (3)
Dairen Maritime Fire Insurance Company (2)
Ch'ang-ch'un Trading Trust Company (2)
K'ai-yüan Trading Trust Company (2)
T'ang-kang-tzu Hot Springs (2)
Ying-k'ou Hydroelectric Company (2)
Fu-ch'ang Industrial Company (1.8)

After the Manchurian Incident the number of affiliated enterprises increased, reaching the figure of about eighty companies in
1938. In this way the SMR held firm control over the entire
economy of Manchuria in all of its departments. This situation
was not so desirable for the Kwantung Army, whose intention,
after the Manchurian Incident and the establishment of Manchukuo, was to encourage the rapid influx of domestic capital from
Japan and to turn Manchuria into a base for heavy industry.

By breaking down this huge conglomerate the military intended to open the doors of Manchuria widely as free investment sites
for domestic capital. Thus, the SMR was to be turned into solely a
railway company. Various related enterprises, be they directly
managed by or affiliates of the SMR, were to be severed completely from the company.

Behind the emergence of this new conception of things was an
opposition to the overdiversification and inefficiency of the enterprises subsumed by the SMR and to the fact that the military
could not necessarily control the entire machinery of the SMR by
controlling its highest executives alone, nor could its power of

control extend to domestic monopoly capital. An antimonopoly view was also present in the Kwantung Army, and the notion of rejecting the monopoly on enterprises in Manchuria held by the SMR ran through the military. For a time they had accepted only middle-size and small companies from Japan, following the spirit of ethnic harmony, to manage Manchuria. The military now sounded this position in a loud voice, and it left a trail that influenced the dissolution of the SMR conglomerate.

Ayukawa Yoshisuke of the Nissan Corporation took advantage of this view in the military. He inspired the military with the idea that, with funds raised through the sale of all his stocks held in Japan, he would engage in economic construction in Manchuria, suggesting as well the possibility of taking development loans from the United States for similar use. It is impossible to estimate to what extent Ayukawa had financial backing in the United States or his self-confidence and foresight so far as attracting capital was concerned. The notion, though, of investing foreign capital in the economic contruction of Manchuria delighted the military, opposed as it was to a Japanese monopoly.

From late 1932 through early 1933, news of all this appeared in various forms in the press. Neither the leaders of the SMR nor Japanese public opinion expressed any particular criticism of it. A kind of unease as well as a discontent with the Kwantung Army's unilateral actions were hotly discussed among the staff members of the SMR. This feeling led to an atmosphere among the staff that the employees' association—the overall body for all staff members—might have the power to deal effectively with the Kwantung Army. After the Manchurian Incident, employees on the scene were compelled to cooperate with the military's activities (including military operations against anti-Japanese guerrillas) whether they approved of them or not. Thus, an antipathy to the military emerged among the staff members, as they felt indignant at the Kwantung Army's ruthless "reorganization" in which they had been forced to cooperate despite the fact that they were in no way civilian employees of the military. Although the employees' association had originally enjoyed a rather low status among the staff, after the Incident the level of trust in the directors fell off and a sense that our own employees' association was a dependable body began to run deep. It was then April 1933, time for a reelection in the association, and I was elected executive director.

From the late Taishō period, there was a trend afoot within the SMR to form an employees' association. As background to this, there had been a movement toward requiring that the directors of the SMR be appointed from within the staff. Until then the directors had changed with every change in government back home, and the various SMR presidents and directors, who came from the political parties, exploited the company and violated its rules, which adversely affected staff morale. Also, during periods of inactivity when personnel reductions were carried out and regular salary increases were forestalled, a severe shifting of the burden fell upon the lower level of workers, and another element among the staff members wanted the treatment of these employees bettered. In these circumstances the employees' association was formed. Earlier some of the lower-level employees had taken part in the affair known as the Manchurian Communist Party Incident among workers at the railroad yards in Sha-ho-k'ou and along the Ying-k'ou branch line.

I believe the employees' association was formed in 1927. Since I was overseas at that time, I did not know of its founding. In the summer of 1926, just before I left to study abroad, I submitted an essay to *Dokushokai zasshi* (Magazine of the Readers' Association), which was prepared among the staff members, and by chance that article happened to call for the need for staff solidarity.

When I returned from abroad, the employees' association that had come into existence comprised the entire staff membership (including high-level employees); delegates selected at the work places organized a council from which was established a board of directors and an executive committee; and the chairman of the board of directors served as the representative of the employees' association. The chairman had departments for the performance of his duties, and some men of either section head status or chief clerk status from the delegates were selected to be head of these departments.

For delegate selection when the issue of the reorganization of the SMR was at its height, there were only one or two other section heads in addition to myself, and I had to serve as chairman of the board. We had to assign the post of department head to men of chief clerk level or below. From the perspective of office organization, this inordinately weak employees' organization stood up to the SMR reorganization.

Since my position in the company at that time was an easy one of counselor, I had lots of time to wrestle with this task. From the time I took up the post, I was attentive to strengthening our organization in preparation for the problems anticipated in the "reorganization." As I mentioned earlier, though, the leaders of the SMR Company, while opposed to control by the military, did not openly resist the Kwantung Army. Yet, the tendency in the employees' association did not especially run counter to the feelings of the SMR leaders. Preparations were made for fighting with the Kwantung Army. My opponent at the time I was selected chairman of the board of directors, chief clerk Hōjō Hidekazu, organized separately a group of young staff members into the Association of Young SMR Comrades, and he and I worked to breathe vitality into the employees' association.

I think it was in the early summer of 1933. Lieutenant Colonel Numata Takezō, who had come on a mission to the Kwantung Army from the Secretariat for Manchurian Affairs, was interviewed in An-tung by an anxious reporter named Maeda of the *Manshū nippō* (Manchurian Daily News). There the plan for the reorganization of the SMR was openly disclosed, and the employees' association rose up at this signal. In the opening lines of our manifesto at the time, we set forth the laudable phrase: "The SMR is an inheritance bequeathed by the Meiji Emperor, and it will permit no arbitrary violations." We had wise men among us who knew that this was the only way to resist the military effectively.

The organizational structure of the employees' association, including the staff at the far reaches of the railroads and at the Fu-shun site, was in excellent running order. However, since department heads in the office organization did not necessarily agree, I had to use individual persuasion. The most obdurate person was the railway department head who was responsible for military transport. The company leaders, though, completely assumed the attitude of bystanders (as Director Sogō Shinji once cynically put it). Eventually I reached accord, and unity throughout the entire staff was fortified. The eyes of the military police and the regular civilian police focused on the employees' association and myself, and persons who considered themselves activists in the Manchurian Youth League came all the way from Ch'ang-ch'un to my home to criticize me on matters concerning the employees' association.

The major newspapers in Manchuria reported on the activities of our association in great detail. I remember in particular that Mr. Wake, a reporter for the *Manshū nippō*, and Hatanaka Masaharu, a special correspondent for the *Asahi shimbun*, both faithfully supported the position of the association. It was advantageous to our organization that the journalistic world was generally antimilitary.

Our next move took place on the occasion of the general meeting of SMR stockholders in Tokyo. We decided to send representatives of the employees' association to attend that meeting, and we authorized them to speak on behalf of all stocks held by staff members. This all transpired in an atmosphere in which to defy the Kwantung Army's desires was an unthinkable absurdity given the conditions of the time. Thus, it was the perfect theme for journalists in Tokyo. The SMR board of directors could no longer remain outside the fray, and through the head of the General Affairs Department they interfered to say that we had gone too far. We rejected this, and our representative left Dairen with loud cheers on the very same boat as the SMR directors.

At the same time, there emerged the view that the employees' association itself had to come up with a reorganization plan that responded to the circumstances of the time, because our conduct of resisting the military simply for the sake of resistance was considered unworthy of a national policy corporation. We agreed then on the following points: to exchange a segment of the department and section heads in the office organization, to establish a committee of responsible executive staff officials, to make the affiliated enterprises (including the An-shan Iron Works) and the Commercial Affairs Department independent, and to return the SMR to the form it had possessed in its founding years as primarily a railway and coal mining company. This plan was not so enormously different from the wishes of the company's board of directors. At our final committee meeting we decided on a plan but chose not to announce it; the next day, however, the *Manshū nichinichi shimbun* scooped the story. Both the public and the military were dumbstruck by our plan.

At that point the Kwantung Army had no choice but to give in. When the employees' association requested a meeting with the Kwantung Army to convey the intentions of the staff, they consented to see us, and the entire board of directors of the employees' association traveled to Ch'ang-ch'un. Separate meetings with Chief of Staff Koiso Kuniaki and Assistant Chief of Staff Okamura Yasuji were conducted in the presence of their staffs. We "appealed" that the reorganization ignored the SMR employees' devoted spirit as trailblazers in Manchuria and was disadvantageous and irrational as far as future development was concerned. This meeting occurred on the very day in Tokyo that the stockholders meeting convened, and as a result this was the high point reached by the employees' association in the Japanese journalistic accounts.

Several days later General Hishikari Takashi, commanding officer of the Kwantung Army, in his capacity as governor-general of the Kwantung Leased Territory, headed south to Port Arthur and invited the board of the employees' association for talks. There was quite a scene, upon hearing this news, as men from the various newspapers chased after us, riding a string of cars along the road from Dairen to Port Arthur. Our association was now fully resplendent under the attentive eyes of the world.

The reorganization issue proceeded according to the plan of the employees' association (and in accordance with the wishes of the SMR) in principle and was resolved by concessions made by the Kwantung Army. The reason the Kwantung Army retreated a step was attributed to the fact that Ayukawa's proposal did not attain his initial aim and the hopes for financial cooperation with the United States were dwindling; as a result, the capital procurement with which he had inspired the military could not be realized to the extent he had anticipated. Furthermore, as this situation emerged, the military turned to the notion that they had to welcome capital investment by Japanese financial conglomerates for the development of Manchuria. Neither Mitsui nor Mitsubishi had any intention of being placed under the control of Ayukawa. Only Sumitomo, with its ties to the navy, invested in the machinery industry in An-shan.

The major result of this "reorganization incident" was the increased voice of the employees' association vis-à-vis the heads of the company. The pending issue until then, the desire of the staff (mainly the blue-collar and clerical workers) for the dissolution of the clerical work system and for a single blue-collar system (later, it became a single white-collar system), was completely accepted. After this incident, the SMR directors got along well in talks with the Kwantung Army, so it had been worth it to them.

Another Anti-Kwantung Army Incident

Because Japanese influence and interest spread throughout Manchuria as a result of the Manchurian Incident, a simplification of the administrative structure there was concocted. There were international problems involving legal procedures, and things did not advance smoothly, but the essential and urgent issue was that of a uniform military and police structure; that is, placing the civil Police Administration Bureau of the Kwantung Leased Territory under the auspices of the commander of the military police, in the name of centralizing the local security structure in Manchuria. Since the military commander assumed the tasks of the Kwantung governor-general, these police structures would be nominally unified, but in actual practice the civil police would not necessarily fall under the control of the military.

This issue was debated for some time, and the civil officials at the Police Administration Bureau, seeing how the SMR employees had risen up to wrest concessions from the military, tried to attain the same. Police officials in the bureau first issued a mass resignation. This was late in 1933. They were dissatisfied with their being reorganized under the control of the military police of the Kwantung Army. The military police and the Police Administration Bureau had a long history of mutual opposition, so this impasse was not going to be easily resolved. However, a strike of policemen was out of the question. Since these civil officials, like the SMR, carried no weapons (the decisive factor), they were quickly crushed. The result was that later in the cases of public security, we were arrested not by the police but by the military police.

It was pathetic that a group of counselors in the Manchukuo government—the Yūhōkai Clique—should have taken advantage of this opportunity created by the military police and (as I will discuss later) eliminated the Conscience Clique led by Kasagi Yoshiaki.

Manchukuo and the SMR

Let me just say a few words about what seemed to be the basic cause of the reorganization incident. The intense hope contained in Japanese imperialism ever since the Russo-Japanese War was in part realized with the creation of Manchukuo. Why, then, did this sort of trouble between the Kwantung Army, Manchukuo, and the SMR crop up? Although the role of the SMR Company as a monopolistic colonizer was in principle realized, this role at the same time represented the SMR's last stand of resistance in which Gotō Shimpei's early colonial policy of "military preparedness in civil garb" was defeated: they had to rely on direct military force. Manchuria practically became a Japanese possession, even though disguised as Manchukuo.

This was something, I believe, that the employees' association had not as yet considered. That is, the SMR as the vanguard of Japanese imperialism was the organization that planned the monopoly over Manchuria. Its objective was attained even when things went wrong and military force was used. Thus, the function of the SMR as an organ of national policy was already finished. The aim of reorganization, then, was to return the SMR to its origins as a railway company. This may have seemed perfectly obvious, but the employees of the SMR were extremely skeptical of the military's leadership in political and economic matters and proud of the fact that without our cooperation the military could do nothing. Thus, when the military attempted to move ahead, ignoring the employees of the SMR, they encountered our resistance.

The Fantasy of a State in Manchuria: The Ideology of Ethnic Harmony

"Ethnic Harmony"

From the Chinese perspective, the Three Northeastern Provinces, that is Manchuria, were regarded as an area beyond the perimeter; and the Ch'ing dynastic house, considering it the area in which its ancestors had arisen, long forbad Han Chinese from migrating there by sealing off the region. Having subdued Siberia, Czarist Russia seized the region in Manchuria north of the Amur River and east of the Ussuri and then began laying the ties of the Chinese Eastern Railway, striving hard to bring Manchuria within the Russian sphere of influence. After using the area as a battlefield in the Russo-Japanese War, Japanese interests, under the name of the SMR Company, first solidified in southern Manchuria and later began extending their way into northern Manchuria. For its own part, China drew up basic demands for the formation of a Manchurian granary kingdom with the massive numbers of the domestic Chinese population migrating there after the 1911 Revolution.

As Japanese imperialism intensified its opposition to the Chang family, "Kings of Manchuria," it brought the annihilation of this "grain kingdom" first when Chang Tso-lin was murdered in the train explosion of 1928 and next with the blowing up of the railway line at Liu-t'iao-kou in the Manchurian Incident of 1931. Control over Manchuria, which extended to 40 million Chinese people, was known by the Japanese to be an extremely difficult matter. It was only natural that Gotō Shimpei's plan for the colonization of Manchuria had to await the assistance of military force. For, the realm could not be ruled solely by force of arms.

The Liu-t'iao-kou Incident was a planned scheme, although it occurred suddenly in the sense that it had not been foreseen even in the program of the "Tanaka Memorandum." Nonetheless, the political program advanced as a countermeasure to this plot was a confused mess that had to be carried out in an act of grandstanding. It was an inevitable course.

For the 40 million Chinese, the cosmetic cover of a "harmony of the five ethnic groups," pointed to by the 1911 Revolution, had to be borrowed. The political ideology of what the appropriate role of the Japanese was among the Japanese, Han Chinese, Manchurian, Mongolian, and Korean peoples clearly was the focus of the problem here. Looking at two groups generally known, the Manchurian Youth League and the Yūhōkai, we cannot ignore Kaneko Sessai, an ideologue of Manchurian-Mongolian control since the middle of the Taishō period. He owned the Chinese-language newspaper *T'ai-tung jih-pao* (T'ai-tung Daily News), and he ran the Shintōsha (Society for the Encouragement of the East) as an academy for young men. Among his contacts in the former were Abe Makoto, Nakano Seigō, Ogata Taketora, Kazami Akira, and Uetsuka Tsukasa. After Kaneko's death the journal *Shin tenchi* (New Universe), drawing mostly on SMR staff members, continued his line of thought. When you discuss political affiliations in Manchuria, whatever the political grouping of Japanese you mention, since SMR staffers were the intellectuals' cradle there, they played the central role. Also, many participated in the management of Manchuria after the Manchurian Incident as experts, without belonging to any particular group.

The Manchurian Youth League

As I pointed out above, in the early years of the changed circumstances in Manchuria, following the Liu-t'iao-kou Incident, the leadership of the SMR was completely ignored and subsequently became critical, even negative, with respect to the military's policy. The Manchurian Incident itself, however, could not have arisen without the assistance of the SMR structure, for the SMR controlled the lines of transportation. Furthermore, SMR researchers would have been unable to devise and implement a host of subsequent policies. Thus, whether they liked it or not, staff members employed particularly in on-site research organs followed the general unfolding of events and took a cooperative position while retaining a conscious attitude as SMR staffers. This was described in detail in the lengthy record published by the company, *Manshū jihen to Mantetsu* (The Manchurian Incident and the SMR). There were a great many SMR staffers who lost their lives in attacks by "bandits"—namely, guerrillas fighting against the Japanese in Manchuria—or in fighting against guerrillas' efforts to destroy rail lines, as well as in other hostile activities.

> Number of staff members called into action by the military at the time of the Manchurian Incident, about 1000
> Number of staff members who joined the military after the Manchurian Incident, about 16,000
> Number of staff members who died during the Manchurian Incident and the founding of Manchukuo, 179
> (among them, those later honored at the Yasukuni Shrine, 61)
> Number decorated with the order and/or the trophy presented by the emperor, 23,391

These were the figures formally indicating the relationship between the SMR and the Manchurian Incident. Among the staff, particularly the intellectuals, if there were those who expressed a common intellectually critical attitude toward the military, there were also many staffers who were unhappy with the negative, uncooperative stance of their leaders.

For the purposes of discussing the people who were inordinately enthusiastic about cooperating in the early actions of the Kwantung Army, let me speak of three groups. The first was the Manchurian Youth League. The second was the Yūhōkai or Majestic Peak Society of Kasagi Yoshiaki, and the Society for the

Encouragement of the East cooperated with this group. Among those who joined Kasagi's association were Matsuki Tamotsu [or Matsuki Kyō] and Arai Shizuo, experts in the Research Section of the SMR, and Yūki Seitarō, Araki Akira, Uemura Tetsumi, and Ueda Kōtarō who belonged to the Society for the Encouragement of the East. The third group belonged to Miyazaki Masayoshi's Russia clique. I mentioned briefly that Miyazaki with his anti-Communist beliefs had made approaches to Major Ishiwara Kanji of the Kwantung Army. Later I will discuss his subsequent activities, but here I would like first to look at the Manchurian Youth League and the Yūhōkai.

In 1928, well before the Incident, the Manchurian Youth League was formed by Japanese in Manchuria who resented the intensifying anti-Japanese atmosphere. The year 1928 was the one in which Chang Tso-lin was murdered aboard his train. That same year the Tanaka Cabinet dispatched troops to Shantung and began to enforce its earlier policy of activity on the mainland. The activities of Japanese in Manchuria were in response to all this.

Among the Japanese in Manchuria there was a group who reacted sharply to the rise of a national consciousness on the part of the Chinese and the economic pressures enforced in coordination with it. These were primarily middle-level and small Japanese merchants who for some time had been restrained in their activities in Manchuria. In most cases, they had little chance of winning in competition with Chinese merchants. An awareness of gradual pauperization became extremely strong among them, and they felt that they had to resort to something to reorganize in one fell swoop the circumstances in which they were living. At just this time the Tanaka Cabinet set forth its policy of activity on the mainland, and they greeted it with ecstasy. They also began to exert pressure on the government to go one step further in its activism. In Dairen they convened an "All-Manchurian Convention of Japanese," which sent fifty representatives to Tokyo. This occurred just before the second dispatching of troops to Shantung, and when it was reported at the convention, they issued a resolution of thanks.

As mentioned earlier, though, the activist policy of the Tanaka

Cabinet was not handled skillfully. With the murder of Chang Tso-lin, this policy was effectively finished insofar as Manchuria was concerned. But this caused a problem itself. At that very moment Japanese in Manchuria were forming a coalition and beginning to pursue their objectives back home in Japan. In November of that year (1928) the Manchurian Youth League was founded.

> At the present time our sacred territory of Manchuria is on the verge of a crisis. We face a critical moment for the existence or destruction of this nation. The government has offered no countermeasure, and the people have not roused public opinion. Should we sit by silently and watch the present state of affairs in silence, our homeland would inevitably be on the verge of national ruin. We have thus arisen to proclaim a movement for the establishment of a new policy for Manchuria and Mongolia.

This was one section of their founding prospectus. Among the league's founders were such purely nongovernmental types as Okada Takema, Ozawa Kaisaku (father of Ozawa Seiji [conductor of the Boston Philharmonic]), Ōba Tokio, and Yamaguchi Shigeji. As the group's organization grew, Kanai Shōji, head of the Hygiene Section of the SMR, set out to gain leadership status. Kanai was the manager of the doctors at the SMR. Other SMR affiliates who were not charter members of the league but who in fact worked for it would include Nakanishi Toshinori, head of the Regional Section (later a director), and Hirashima Toshio (later vice-president). The league claimed 5,000 members, but the number who actively participated in its activities was not that high. SMR employees made up the great majority of them, of course, and a small number were Japanese adventurers living in Manchuria.

The ultimate objective of the league's members was "the creation of an autonomous Manchurian-Mongolian state"—that is, Manchukuo. However, they did not call for this from the start. At the time of its founding, there had allegedly been voices among its members who said: "We've gathered here, but what would be best for us to do for the league?" They publicized the "crisis in

Manchuria and Mongolia" with pamphlets and the like both on the scene and back home in Japan. Among their activities in the four calendar years prior to the Manchurian Incident, they sent proselytizing speakers to Japan any number of times. But, for all their stumping the home territory, they found little support, for their cries of crisis did not evoke the sympathies of the masses back home.

Their propaganda pamphlets centered around the "anti-Japanese incident" of the Chang Hsüeh-liang regime, and to produce these pamphlets they carried out a detailed investigation as part of their normal activities. They worked extremely hard to rouse public opinion about this "anti-Japanese incident." Their investigative report might best be seen as a product of a movement for their own recognition with the aim of protecting concessions that Japan insisted on acquiring through treaties. The issue of the Sakakibara Farm, the incident involving the obstruction of SMR rail cars, and the Wan-pao-shan incident became their targets. In effect the league was working to find reasons for the Manchurian Incident before it ever occurred.

With a consciousness merely of protecting Japan's special interests, there was no way they could move from the enforcement of interests in Manchuria to the conception of founding a state there. For that reason the notion of ethnic harmony became necessary at this point. There were members of the Manchurian Youth League who believed in this ideology, but there were also those who held firmly anti-Chinese, colonialist views; thus, believers in Japan's special interests coexisted with ethnic harmonizers within the league. After the Manchurian Incident, the league became a base for the Concordia party and its movement. It would be difficult, though, to say that the people who collected in this group were all harmonizers.

Naturally, the league worked closely with the military at the time of the Incident. One cannot ignore the work of Koyama Sadatomo, who joined the league just before the Incident occurred. Since Koyama had contacts within both the SMR and the Kwantung Army, he volunteered to enable the league to participate in the Incident and the creation of Manchukuo, beyond any structural links it had within the SMR.

Among the league's leaders, Kanai Shōji joined the Fengtien provincial government; Yamaguchi Shigeji worked at taking over the Chinese-owned Shen-Hai rail line in Manchuria and at the reorganization of the Northeast Communications Committee; Koreyasu Masatoshi of the SMR was involved in seizing Chinese mines and factories; and Ōba Tokio and Nakanishi Toshinori, among others, were conspicuously active in the Self-Government Advisory Department.

At first this Self-Government Advisory Department was a product of Kasagi's ideology, organized for reasons of unity by leading members of the league and the Amakasu Masahiko group, with Yü Ch'ung-han, the "purest" of them, as its head. As a result of military actions by the Kwantung Army, their capacity to govern the Three Northeastern Provinces declined, and at a host of sites their military and other strategic organs established Public Security Committees and Self-Governing Committees in the form of a spontaneous autonomy movement on the part of the Chinese. But they threw these up in utter confusion, and it became very difficult for the military to control them, which necessitated a centralized guidance over these administrative organs. Thus, in October 1931 they were organized as the Self-Government Advisory Department. Altogether there were seventy to eighty persons in the department, and they were dispatched to the various provinces to oversee the establishment of Manchukuo in the spirit of ethnic harmony. This group comprised twenty-odd men linked to the Manchurian Youth League, and roughly the same number each from Kasagi's Yūhōkai and the group around Amakasu Masahiko, who was responsible for the Ōsugi Sakae affair.

Kasagi Yoshiaki and the Yūhōkai

It would be impossible to speak of the ideology of Manchurian autonomy separately from Kasagi Yoshiaki. Kasagi undoubtedly ranked alongside Kaneko Sessai and Tachibana Shiraki as an intellectual leader in Manchuria. He went to work for the East

Asian Economic Investigation Bureau in Tokyo one year before I did. Kuchida Yasunobu entered the company at the same time as well, but he transferred to Dairen the next year, and we worked together at the Research Section there. Until 1929 Kasagi was employed in Tokyo. I don't know what his job entailed during those years, but a look at his chronological biography reveals that among his many and varied activities he joined the Hinokai (Society of the Sun), run by Ōkawa Shūmei and Kuchida Yasunobu, while still a student at Tokyo University. It was an organization like the Kōkoku dōshi kai (Society for National Prosperity) and the Shinjinkai at the university. While an employee of the East Asian Economic Investigation Bureau, he became a member of the Yūsonsha (Continued Existence Society) and the Kōchisha (Society to Practice the Way of Heaven on Earth). After he left the last of these groups, he made contacts with the Tōkō renmei (Eastern Prosperity Federation) and the Daihōkai (Society of the Great Country), the latter created by Kuchida. Under section head Nakanishi Toshinori, who joined the company the same year as he had, Kasagi worked as head of the personnel office in Dairen until he entered Manchukuo.

Such Nichiren devotees as Watanabe Kaikyoku and Fujii Kōshō were like gurus to him. He served as chairman of the East Asian Society of Young Lay Buddhists, before forming the Yūhōkai or Daiyūhōkai as it was sometimes called. And it was he who guided the unification of the latter group in the tasks of building the state of Manchukuo. It seems to me that he planned to carry out the "Shōwa Restoration" from overseas.

He assumed a "behavior expecting nothing in return" and acted as an "ascetic on the path to Bodhisattvahood." Thus, although he became close with the likes of [such right-wing figures as] Ōkawa Shūmei and Kita Ikki, he was not as politically inclined as they were. I believe he adopted the same pose when he met with men in the army from Ishiwara Kanji on down. I do not believe he ever really confided in them. Yet, his leadership in attracting unknown and unselfish young men seems to have been sufficiently conspicuous to an extent unsurpassed even by the more famous right-wingers.

In the preparatory period before the establishment of the state
of Manchukuo, advisers were continually being sent to various
counties, and the preparations for self-rule were being put into
effect. Thereafter, when the Self-Government Advisory Department came into existence and these advisers were installed as
government counselors, he brought out Yü Ch'ung-han, who had
been in hiding, made him head of the department, and directed
him from below. This was surely Kasagi's political high point.
With the establishment of an administration in Manchukuo, the
Self-Government Advisory Department became the National
Council and should have been subordinate to the prime minister
(Cheng Hsiao-hsü, whom Kasagi had gotten to know in Tokyo).
However, faced with opposition from Komai Tokuzō, director-
general of administrative affairs in the State Council, and others
from the Manchurian Youth League, he was reduced to the posi-
tion of head of the National Affairs Bureau beneath the Office of
Administrative Affairs in the State Council.

The following three months culminating in the dissolution of
the National Affairs Bureau witnessed a constant struggle between the ideology of Manchurian autonomy and the view de-
manding retention of a Japanese capitalist colonial establishment
in the name of Japanese-Manchurian unity (advocated by Komai
with the support of the Kwantung Army, which had changed its
political direction). The victor in the battle between Komai Tokuzō, who had fully completed the adventurer's course of study, and
the "faintly religious" Kasagi Yoshiaki was clear.

Of the SMR employees who joined the Manchuria Youth
League, many held comparatively high posts in the company. By
contrast, the Yūhōkai comprised mainly young employees, college
graduates without positions. Men of the caliber of Takano Tadao
and Kai Masaji provided the backbone of the group. Although few
in number in comparison with the Manchurian Youth League,
they formed a highly coherent group ideologically. The Yūhōkai,
unlike the Manchurian Youth League, was not particularly active
in educational propaganda prior to the Manchurian Incident.
They had met from time to time in a study group on issues
concerning Manchuria and Mongolia and solidified their internal

cohesion. Men like Major Hanaya Tadashi of the staff of the Kwantung Army attended the meetings of the study group. Having established such relationships with the military, when the Manchurian Incident occurred they received a summons from Major Wachi Takaji, gathered under Lieutenant Colonel Ishiwara Kanji, and put their ideas into action. It seemed that Kasagi and Ishiwara, both being Nichiren believers, would be sympathetic to each other, but Kasagi was saying that "Ishiwara is also a warlord!" When the Self-Government Advisory Department emerged, Kasagi's clique became its advisers. To manipulate this department, the Kwantung Army founded a Control Department (later renamed the Special Affairs Department).

Manchukuo and Komai Tokuzō

The man brought by the military to head this department was Komai Tokuzō, and he would become the first director-general for administrative affairs of the State Council of Manchukuo. From an anonymous adventurer he was thrust onto the international stage in one leap, and at a glance he had all the characteristics of a hero in turbulent times. As I mentioned in introducing him earlier, he was also an agricultural technician who had worked for the SMR. Let me now say just a few words about his career.

Komai was a pan-Asianist who in his youth attended the Shōkō Academy of Sugiura Jūgō and yearned for Arao Sei, the model for adventurers on the Chinese mainland. When he graduated from middle school, he read *My Thirty-Three Years' Dream*, became an admirer of its author Miyazaki Tōten, dreamed of performing great deeds on the Asian mainland, and set his heart on being an adventurer in China. Upon making this decision he entered the Sapporo School of Agriculture. As he explained it in later years, the impetus to attend this school was that, because an adventurer of the Miyazaki Tōten sort had no profession, no matter how pure his mind, he was sure to fall into depravity. To set one's mind on great achievements on the mainland, he maintained, one had first to gain for oneself a particular skill. His graduation thesis was entitled "On the Manchurian Soy Bean." Introduced to

Dr. Thiess by Nitobe Inazō, Komai joined the East Asian Economic Investigation Bureau shortly after its founding, learned
from Thiess, and completed his course of study. He reputedly
earned high praise from Ōkawa Shūmei. After graduation he
entered the SMR Company, and he was highly regarded for his
achievement of having contributed to the creation of the agricultural experimentation station at Kung-chu-ling.

Be that as it may, he was not merely an agricultural technician.
After he had quit the SMR and become an adventurer, he was one
of a group concocting plans in the background of the Kuo Sung-
ling affair. He and his group intended to support Kuo and make
Manchuria and Mongolia independent. I have already pointed out
that one segment of the Japanese Army supported Kuo's rebellion in opposition to the directives of the Japanese government,
and Kuo's army was tragically destroyed.

Komai later traveled a number of times between Japan and
China, and for a while he was involved in the reform of the textile
industry in T'ung-chou (also known as Nan-t'ung, north of
Shanghai), Chang Chien's "kingdom." But he eventually left this,
too, and returned to Japan to live a comfortable life in retirement.
It was at this juncture, prior to the storm in Manchuria, that he
was called upon by the Army General Staff. He received the title
of adviser on financial matters to the Kwantung Army, and just
after the explosion of the Liu-t'iao-kou Incident he arrived in
Manchuria to begin work. The task assigned Komai was to come
up with a form for the state of Manchukuo. That he became the
head of the Control Department, which ran the Self-Government
Advisory Department, paralleled this line of action. Although the
Control Department soon had its name changed to the Special
Affairs Department, its responsibilities remained unchanged.

Vicissitudes in the Drama of Establishing the
State of Manchukuo

It is of course impossible to conclude that the ideology behind the
establishment of Manchukuo was ethnic harmony. Even if one
were to assert it as such, it underwent a variety of twists and

turns, large and small, making it extremely difficult to explain. First of all, although the Kwantung Army clearly played the lead in the Manchurian Incident, there was a sense of opposition on the part of the lower-level military men who believed implicitly that the militaristic spirit back home in Japan was being oppressed by capitalism. Thus, in the early period of Manchukuo an atmosphere opposed to the homeland, anti-capitalist, anti-Soviet, and anti-English, prevailed. During this period the Yūhōkai, the Manchurian Youth League, and the Kwantung Army staff all worked laboriously in concert. But, as they embarked on the course of founding a state, a nonharmonious feeling emerged as a result of their respective intentions and seemed naturally to lead to strife.

Before the establishment of Manchukuo, the principles that had attracted people as an ideology of state formation were the radical ideas on ethnic harmony as espoused by men such as Kasagi Yoshiaki. Although in the confusion of the moment the Kwantung Army had thrown together a state, the military did desire a moral course of action, and it was attracted to the freshness of Kasagi's ideas. Yet, when Manchukuo came into existence, Kasagi's Yūhōkai ran directly into conflict with the Kwantung Army. Kasagi was unsatisfied by the inconsistencies of Ishiwara Kanji's plan for an East Asian federation.

The state of Manchukuo commenced on 1 March 1932. Before this, the Self-Government Advisory Department was dissolved. Komai Tokuzō's role had thus far been quite large, and he reached the high post of the first director-general of administrative affairs of Manchukuo. Once again he held superficial power, this time in Manchukuo. This day also, however, marked the exit of Kasagi and his followers in the Yūhōkai, who had been based in the Self-Government Advisory Department. Kasagi began to be seen by the army as a nuisance. He and his followers burned with the desire to fulfill the spirit of ethnic harmony within the state that was newly risen in form only. At the time of its founding, Kasagi was busy trying to install a National Council opposed to Komai Tokuzō within the central bureaucracy, but he was unable to do so and was demoted into the National Affairs Bureau within the

Office of Administrative Affairs. He tried to distribute the members of the Yūhōkai with a simple central and local organization into the counties, to control civil government directly with counselors (later, counselor officials), and to solidify them around county councils. Kasagi aimed at linking these county-level councils to the State Council through the National Council. Had Kasagi been successful and another center of power emerged in addition to that of the Office of Administrative Affairs under Komai, a coexistence or antagonism would have emerged within the government.

Thus, Kasagi planned for the recovery of lost territory. If realized, the influence of Komai, who was responsible for leading the State Council, would have been greatly restricted. For the military, too, such a situation would have made it difficult to assert its leadership freely. The establishment of the National Affairs Bureau and Kasagi's assumption of leadership over it apparently occurred at a time when Komai was unaware, and this incident led to the issue surrounding Komai's resignation.

Komai negotiated with the military, but it was not easy for him to reach a settlement. Undoubtedly there was a difference of opinion between the military men supporting Kasagi and those who called on Komai. In any event, an adjustment was made in the Kwantung Army staff, and with the disbanding of the National Affairs Bureau and the purge of Kasagi, things calmed down at the center. However, the lack of talented men in Manchukuo could not extend as far as the local, county-level counselor officials. Thus, when Kasagi was out of power, he established the Kō-A juku (Rise Asia School) at the center and in the counties, taught county-level counselor officials, and continued to labor for the creation of his ideal state of Manchukuo.

From the period of the Self-Government Advisory Department, he had been working in close harmony with his righthand man, Kuchida Yasunobu. As mentioned above, Kuchida and Kasagi had left Tokyo University and entered the East Asian Economic Investigation Bureau at the same time. In the year after he entered the company, Kuchida moved to the Research Section in Dairen. He was a Kantian, and in the year after arriving in Dairen he showed scarcely any interest in "research work" but devoted his time solely to reading Kant. Then one day he casually turned in his resignation at the SMR and became a teacher at the Hiroshima Senior Normal School. Ten years later, after the Manchurian Incident and the establishment of Manchukuo, he was called on by Kasagi, and without the least regret dispensed with his teaching position to share life's joys and sorrows once again with Kasagi.

Kuchida was more of a hermit than even Kasagi. I have no idea what he intended to do with the plans drawn up by his leader. He had the character of a well-intentioned incarnation of Kasagi, and he clearly worked hard in his role as Kasagi's first lieutenant in organizing and conciliating the counselor officials. One element of the mystery of Kasagi's continued influence over his former co-workers—now counselor officials—even after he left government service, I believe, can be found in Kuchida pure personality as well as his religious beliefs.

Some historian in the future will probably hypothesize that had Kasagi held political power, Manchukuo might have been closer in form to his ideals. Insofar as he worked with the military, though, it was this completely illusory Manchukuo alone that was in fact realized. The interference of America and the coercion of the Soviet Union, which the military feared at first, together with the weakness of Chiang Kai-shek's Kuomintang and the Conservative Party in England, did not for the time being materialize. Interference by the League of Nations was weak, and the military was able to succeed in giving skeletal form to Manchukuo. However, the actual exclusion of monopoly capital came to a complete end in Kasagi's fantasies. The very biggest monopoly, the SMR, continued as it had to retain control of the transport trunk lines; and Manchurian Heavy Industry under Ayukawa Yoshisuke, who sneaked in along the sidelines, having moved there speading demagogy, was a Nissan concern.

Behind this rivalry between Komai and Kasagi lay the issue of excluding or welcoming monopolies. This was a difference of a basic nature in each's plans for the construction of Manchukuo. Furthermore, they had divergent opinions on the ideology of ethnic cooperation.

For example, Kasagi enthusiastically supported the exclusion of monopolies, and this was communicated back to Japan early on through the military, lowering the popularity of Manchukuo back home. At this time, Komai repeatedly welcomed the importation to Manchuria of domestic capital; the exclusion of monopolies was total demagogy, he politely explained. In other words, this was the direction that the Kwantung Army would naturally take. As for the issue of ethnic cooperation, the National Affairs Bureau suffered its own dismantling before three months were out; and a group of veterans among the counselor officials collected at the center either quit and returned to the SMR or, in certain cases, maintained their original aims, formed a "danger-defying volunteer corps," and set out for the Soviet-Manchukuo border.

Peasant Riots in I-lan

The well-known "I-lan Incident" erupted in 1934. It caused a revival of Gotō Shimpei's plan, from the founding years of the SMR, for 500,000 Japanese to emigrate to the mainland. Later, as the first attempt to commit Japanese agricultural emigrants to develop the SMR's pioneering efforts in this direction, immigrant farmers from Japan settled in the I-lan area. At this time the resident Chinese farmers opposed the move, and a peasant uprising ensued. The county-level counselor officials under Kasagi's wing, at the risk of their jobs and their lives, opposed the officials of the public development company and the Kwantung Army, based on their beliefs in the notion of ethnic harmony. Kasagi supported them strongly, claiming that it was the responsibility of the county-level counselor officials to protect the people. In addition, at the time that the issue of the military police came up, with the placing of a police structure for the Kwantung governor-general's office at the disposal of the secret police of the Kwantung Army, the counselor officials raised voices of opposition and were put down by the military, and remnants of the Yūhōkai continued the struggle.

In the cause of "saving the world and aiding the people,"

Kasagi put forth a last-ditch effort, but the general trend was against him, and in January 1933 he withdrew to Japan. He then organized the Great Asian Construction Company and, with its organ, *Dai Ajia* (Great Asia), shifted his attentions to the domestic movement. Later, though, he frequently traveled to Manchuria and put together a whole assortment of plans, such as aiding the activities of his comrades who had stayed there at the time of the reorganization of the Concordia Society. When earlier the Self-Government Advisory Department was reorganized into the National Affairs Bureau, he personally selected young Japanese, planned to train them as advisers (or counselors), and entered them in a training institute for the National Affairs Bureau. After the National Affairs Bureau was disbanded, however, he gave birth to the conception of a training institute in the Great Harmony Academy, moved all of his young men there, trained them to be heirs to the Kasagi ideology, and sent them off to Manchuria. The encouragement of these young men seems to have been his objective in going back to Manchuria. Until the end of the war, they got along well with the local Chinese, and it is worth mentioning for posterity that, during the difficult times after the war, Chinese peasants protected them devotedly. In this sense, Kasagi's spirit continued in part to live on.

Although in 1955 he sadly lost his life in a traffic accident at the age of sixty-three, through a nationwide pilgrimage in the postwar years he developed ties with like-minded men as well as with independent types from India and Vietnam, primarily at his "Imperial Capital Rise Asia Academy," and he became a major figure in the Japanese right wing. Despite this, his personal conduct was, as before, thoroughly imbued with that of an itinerant monk. The Salvation Society, for which he wrote only a general plan at New Year's time of the year in which he died, remained his lifelong desire. Nothing of the notion of reviving Asia in his ideology of ethnic harmony remains in systematic written form. Writing was not his forte. He was the very embodiment of action and initiative. The fact that in rallying his men he accepted all those who wished to join of their own accord, rather than through propaganda or persuasion, is well attested in the *Memories of Kasagi Yoshiaki*, edited by his followers.

The Demise of the Ideology of Harmony

The Manchurian Youth League experienced a similar fate to the blow Kasagi received. An opportunity to realize their ambitions never arrived, and a year after the Manchurian Incident they disbanded. Nakanishi Toshinori returned to the SMR Company. One group of men, including Yamaguchi Shigeji and Ozawa Kaisaku, continued their movement and together with Koyama Sadatomo participated in the organization of a Concordia Society. This movement, centering around Koyama, was started afresh with Tachibana Shiraki as its ideologue, but it ended by violating its original aims.

In my view, Tachibana had been through and through a career journalist, but after the Manchurian Incident he "changed directions" and jumped from being a commentator to organizing a movement. Just after the Manchurian Incident, he met with the principal military leaders of the Incident—Ishiwara Kanji, Itagaki Seishirō, and others—on the roof of the Fengtien branch of the East Asia Colonial Company. He was impressed by them and spoke first: "Irrespective of whether their aim—the establishment of a state built on the principle of the kingly way—can actually be realized, as a faithful fellow traveler to a certain point, my hopes for this new trend are exceedingly deep." He occasionally appeared at meetings of Kasagi's Yūhōkai. He also "made contact with the group of spirited young officers under the command of General Minami Jirō, commander-in-chief of the army, deliberately so as to prepare them for a later date." And, using his powerful pen in the pages of the *Manshū hyōron*, he became energetically active in the movement.

As a scholar as well Tachibana excelled, though it was as an original thinker that he was positively electrifying. One might also say that he was worthy of esteem as a political analyst. In this connection we should note that Koyama's efforts in creating the Concordia Society, which he patterned after the Kuomintang, borrowed Tachibana's notion of harmony with a foundation in the rich farmer class. In constructing political ideals for the government of Manchukuo, they met with merciless defeat. Nevertheless, for all their failed efforts, they cannot even be compared to the infantilism of the recent U.S. attempts to support such a man as Ngo Dinh Diem and carry on colonialist control in Vietnam. There is no reason to believe, though, that the plan for the crystallization of political power in the new regime, as Tachibana imagined it through the Concordia Society, was welcomed by the puppet regime as conceived by colonial bureaucrats from Japan and military officials, because they clearly regarded it as an inordinately devious strategy. When the central military authorities and the government, after the May 15th and February 26th Incidents, regained control over this group of spirited young officers upon whom Tachibana had placed his hopes, they became opportunistic or were exiled, all of which disappointed him.

He continued to concentrate his last efforts in the pages of *Manshū hyōron* on the theoretical formation of the Concordia Society and to be concerned about the future of Manchukuo. Yet, none of his plans—"Strict Observance of the Local Boundaries of Manchukuo," "Freedom for the Weaker Peoples of Korea and Mongolia to Unite," "Peaceful Introduction of Foreign Capital," "Public Management of Major Enterprises Through State, Provincial, and Self-Governing Units," and the like—ever were realized. The military's advance into North China proceeded steadily; special charter corporations, such as the Manchurian Heavy Industry Company, Ltd., in Manchuria were created; complete control over the railways of Manchukuo was handed over to the SMR; and gradually the materialization of colonial control became plain to see. The Concordia Society was reorganized and watered down in the face of an assault by Japanese officials and the local resident landlords. "I feel profoundly desolate," he grieved as these events took place, "for if we were once to bow down before all this, we would not be able to get up again." He eventually left the mainland, where he had resolved to be buried, and returned to Japan.

If I might turn the story back a bit, Komai Tokuzō, who had

followed Kasagi, did not enjoy a long fate either. However, Komai himself took the occasion of the Japanese government's recognition of the state of Manchukuo to tender his resignation. Missed as he was by so many people at home, he made a graceful return to Japan. This behavior on his part, though, only showed that compared to others Komai was a bit smarter in recognizing a situation unfavorable to himself. Endō Ryūsaku, the retired colonial official who had originally been in charge of policy affairs for Korea, took over his position. The war minister, General Minami, became army commander. Thereafter, top-flight bureaucrats from Tokyo, men such as Hoshino Naoki and Kishi Nobusuke, came to Manchukuo. From this time forward, slogans like eliminating monopolies, ethnic harmony, and a realm of peace and prosperity were advanced with great fanfare to unify Japan and Manchukuo.

When he saw the outbreak of the Liu-t'iao-kou Incident, Nakae Ushikichi predicted World War II; he then wrote, as it appears in one of his letters, to Lieutenant Imada Shintarō, one of the commanders at the scene, describing the general trend to come. When the Pacific War began, Nakae said that the Japanese military would come to violent misery and that the whole nation would become involved. We now realize, a quarter century after the Manchurian Incident, the grievous extent to which he was right.

Behind the Scenes at the Economic Research Association

Formation of the Economic Research Association

As noted earlier, just after the Manchurian Incident the leaders of the SMR did not immediately cooperate with the military's plans. Of course, there was considerable cooperation in military activities at the SMR field sites, such as military transport and the like. Also, one group of Company employees participated with the military in the creation of the state of Manchukuo, through the Manchurian Youth League and the Yūhōkai, from the time of the Incident. However, neither case points to a collaborative structure based on Company orders. For all the efforts exerted by the Kwantung Army in Manchuria, without the devoted cooperation of SMR mechanisms, constructive projects would have been impossible.

On 18 January 1932, prior to the actual formation of the state of Manchukuo but at a time when one could more or less foresee this coming in the wake of the Manchurian Incident, the army sent the following letter in the name of Major General Miyake Mitsuharu, chief of staff of the Kwantung Army, to SMR Vice-President Eguchi Teijō: "In conjunction with the establishment of a new state, I keenly feel that we must offer careful guidance concerning political, diplomatic, economic, and cultural issues if we expect a healthy development. We must build a powerful overall structure for research, planning, and guidance 'so that it can respond to the queries of and cooperate with the military in the investigation of various conditions in Manchuria and Mongolia and in the research toward the drafting of constructive plans.'" Two days later the board of directors of the SMR conferred on this matter and the Economic Research Association (ERA) was founded.

When Manchukuo came into being, the plan for its essential economic construction was clearly set. According to this plan, the economies of Japan and Manchukuo were to be unified, self-sufficiency between them was to be firmly established, a defense economy was to be built through promoting a planned economy, and thus the Japanese population in Manchuria was to be increased. The aim in founding the ERA lay in drafting plans for economic construction from an integrated perspective and, in conjunction with this, to lump together its research facilities.

The ERA was organizationally placed directly beneath the president of the SMR. It had one chairman and one vice-chairman, and beneath them the research structure was divided into six departments: Department No. 1 covered economics generally; No. 2 was for agriculture and forestry; No. 3 was communications; No. 4 dealt with commerce and finance; No. 5 handled law generally as well as labor and colonial settlements; and No. 6 had responsibility for the North Asian economy. A board of directors was formed from the six heads of these departments, the department heads or assistant heads of each of the departments of the SMR, the interim board, and the chairman and vice-chairman of the ERA. Final drafted plans on research followed an arrangement whereby they passed from this board through the president of the SMR to the Kwantung Army. However, a route was also carved out whereby plans went directly to the army without the intermediacy of the SMR. Stressing this point, the SMR itself boasted of its achievements in cooperating with the military: "The Economic Research Association is formally an internal organ of the SMR, but in actual fact it takes a national perspective as a national organ and serves in economic construction and planning for all of Manchuria."

From its inception through its reincorporation into the Industrial Department of the SMR in October 1936, the research and planning activities of the ERA can generally be divided into four eras.

1. January-June 1932. The creation of research plans concerned with the urgent issues following the Manchurian Incident and concrete plans for the economic construction of Manchuria.

2. July 1932-March 1933. Drafting plans for the first period of the economic development of Manchuria.

3. April 1933-July 1934. Drafting plans for basic research for the economic development of Manchuria, research on natural resources, and plans for the second period in the development of the Manchurian economy.

4. October 1933-September 1936. As the focus moved to North China, a reinvestigation of earlier plans concerning the Manchurian economy.

One might say that the role played by the ERA, which was responsible for all this, realized the dream that Gotō Shimpei had had for the research organs of the SMR in their early days, the implementation of a basis for colonial management through scientific research.

My Short Period as Head of the Research Section

I have described the external details of the founding of the ERA and outlined its workings over a four-year period. The most influential figure in the founding of the ERA was Miyazaki Masayoshi. He was on close terms with the Kwantung Army, especially Ishiwara Kanji, from even before the Manchurian Incident. I have already pointed out that at the time of the Incident the leaders of the SMR were not cooperative with the military and collaboration did not proceed smoothly. Inasmuch as the SMR leaders were utterly ignored in the matter of the founding of Manchukuo, the fear arose among the employees that the SMR would lose its autonomy. Seizing this prevailing atmosphere, Miyazaki induced the employees of the SMR and those connected with its research organs to cooperate with the Kwantung Army. He first tried to build among the employees association something that essentially became the forerunner of the ERA, and he tried to lead it toward voluntary cooperation with the military. Although immensely energetic in planning, Miyazaki was an unpopular man, and few followed in his footsteps. He basically put the structure in place, but it would have died out from inactivity.

Upon self-reflection Miyazaki, with Mr. Sōgō Shinji as figurehead, reached an understanding with the military; as a result, he received a letter from the Kwantung Army encouraging the establishment of a research organ. The board of directors consented, and so the ERA came into being. The ERA's chairman was Sōgō, its vice-chairman was Ishikawa Tetsuo; chief investigator of Department No. 1, Miyazaki Masayoshi; Department No. 2, Okumura Shinji; No. 3, Satō Toshihisa; No. 4, Nakajima Sōichi; No. 5, Okada Takuo; No. 6, Nonaka Tokio; and Kijima Katsumi served as manager. Thus emerged a collaborative structure between the Kwantung Army and the research organs of the SMR.

The main workers at the ERA at first were a small group around Miyazaki who had been working with the Kwantung Army. They moved en masse from the Research Section of the SMR to the ERA. The Research Section, however, was not about

THE ECONOMIC RESEARCH ASSOCIATION 155

to dissolve into the ERA, and for the time being it continued as a part of the SMR Company. I was the man in charge of the Research Section at that time.

The only thing I actually did during my tenure as head of the Research Section was the work on China for the IPR with the remaining staff members, and after the Manchurian Incident the preparation of materials for the Lytton Commission sent by the League of Nations. In addition, the East Asian Economic Investigation Bureau in Tokyo became at that time an independent corporation. Responsibility for its directorship fell as well to the head of the Research Section, and that meant me.

With this transfer of importance to the ERA, the Research Section subsequently became a mutilated wreck. Shortly after the visit of the Lytton Commission there was an organizational reform, we were crushed, and I was dispatched to the leisurely job of counselor. I should discuss the circumstances leading up to this first.

My first task as head of the Research Section was to provide the Lytton Commission with materials on the SMR's operations in Manchuria. In addition to publicizing the extent of economic and cultural development there, I was the chief manager of the SMR reception committee, headed by one of the executive directors, and these tasks involved worrisome links with a group from the Foreign Ministry in Japan (which was headed by an ambassador), the Kwantung Army, and a group of newspaper reporters. Let me describe one episode. The casualty figures for 18 September, the day of the explosion at Liu-t'iao-kou, were reported to be zero. When we were queried on this by the Lytton Commission, the railway man came up with the forced explanation that there had been an explosion and that trains that had passed through the site afterward had been leaning and swaying all along the way.

I concurrently held the position of director of the East Asian Economic Investigation Bureau. Although Ōkawa Shūmei had already left the bureau because of his wide activities in the political sphere at that time, the leading faction in the bureau looked upon me with critical eyes. From my perspective, the prevailing winds at the bureau were not good. I have already described the rivalry between the left and right wings within the bureau from its inception, but now the secret strife between the liberal group—Kaji Ryūichi, Tanaka Kyūichi, Matsukata Saburō, Mizuno Masanao, Edayoshi Isamu—and the Ōkawa clique was finally settled, with the left wing withdrawing as a group. I had to quit the directorship, and shortly thereafter the Research Section was placed outside the organization. I tend to think that this was an inevitable fate for the Research Section ever since the emergence of the ERA.

After the inauguration of the ERA, the leadership of the SMR (who until then had been fence-sitting) was reshuffled, and the tendency developed whereby the SMR as a whole under Vice-President Hatta Yoshiaki was to be reorganized into a collaborative structure with the Kwantung Army. Those elements who were seen as uncooperative with the military could not be protected by the SMR. The Research Section was dissolved, and I was cast off into the sinecure of counselor. Thus, the Research Section was thoroughly liquidated into the ERA. Originally the ERA had planned at the time of its founding to continue for about a year and was hence built as an interim body. When plans for the economic construction of Manchukuo were first drawn up, staff selected from the Research Section, which was to be dismantled, returned to their original jobs. Because the Research Section then ceased to exist, however, the ERA assumed the form of an enhanced or developed Research Section.

The Role of the Economic Research Association

When the SMR's cooperative structure with the military received the ERA in full, Miyazaki basked in the glory of being its actual creator. From mid-1932 until 1933—the period up to the Japanese recognition of Manchukuo—his popularity rose with the force of the sun. He had a special relationship with Ishiwara Kanji, and he became inordinately popular among the military and civilian populace. Having to launch economic construction in

Manchukuo, even if only in form, the military had no choice but to depend on Miyazaki with his staff at the Research Section of the SMR behind him. The SMR, for its part, needed a channel through which to absorb the military's wishes. Through Miyazaki the military was able to get its hands on intelligence rapidly and firmly. From this position, the executive directors indeed had a strong advantage over Miyazaki.

This, however, did not continue for long. With the structure of the ERA regularized, relations between the military and the SMR became smoother. Furthermore, when the drafting of plans preparatory to the emergence of the state of Manchukuo proceeded, with the cooperation of SMR researchers and others, suddenly officials with an economics background, with Ministry of Finance officials in the forefront, came flocking to Manchuria from Japan. They assumed the more important posts in the Manchukuo government and the military, which is to say Manchukuo, and as a result no longer required the advice of the ERA. From the very start Miyazaki's way of doing things was not admired within the SMR. When the issue of reorganizing the SMR came up, Miyazaki stood with the Kwantung Army and encouraged a plan to liquidate the SMR. When the employees became aware of this, Miyazaki, although an SMR employee himself, became a target of criticism for allegedly leading the way to sacrifice the SMR for his own gain, and he withdrew.

He was a masterful planner, and when he left Manchuria and returned to Tokyo, he created the Japan-Manchukuo Financial and Economic Research Association with the sponsorship of the Army General Staff. His patron Ishiwara Kanji apparently returned to Tokyo and worked with him in this endeavor. At the Japan-Manchukuo Financial and Economic Research Association, he studied such issues as the bloc economy of Japan-Manchukuo-China and the notion of an East Asian league. About eight men, including Kainō Michitaka and Uchigasaki Kenjirō, were for a time supported by this Research Association. As far as they were concerned, it seems, there was no choice but to work at such a place, given the situation at the time in Japan.

Elegy for the Economic Research Association

Near the end of 1933, the importance of the ERA vis-à-vis Manchukuo declined sharply. Originally, the ERA, with its duties completed, was to break up, but as I noted earlier, with the Research Section dissolving, the ERA could hardly start over again. It did continue in an inordinately bloated form to carry out the past duties of the Research Section. There was no need now, however, for them to draft concrete plans for economic construction in Manchukuo. Retreating one step, they worked on basic research for the overall economy of Manchuria. Although their actual work decreased, when the structure expanded miscellaneous business grew proportionately, so that although business declined, the number of staff members grew. At the very beginning when the ERA came into existence, it had about 100 staff members together with the Research Section, but in the fall of 1936 the ERA, having now been reorganized into the Industrial Department, expanded to approximately 350 employees. This rise was related to the Japanese invasion of North China, beginning in late 1934, and the concomitant rise in the number of staffers sent to North China to work for research-related organs.

The filling out of the structure accompanied the increase in staff members, and the rise in the quality of researchers followed suit. The expansion of SMR research organs, as seen through the example of the ERA, was indeed a major step toward the Enlarged Research Department that would be established at a later date.

Late in 1933, concrete plans for economic construction in Manchuria and a variety of research to this end were being worked on at the ERA. These were implemented by Japanese immigrant officials working for the administrative office of Manchukuo under the direct control of the military. After being active in the employees' association, I became the head of Department No. 5 of the ERA, concerned with legal matters, in July 1934. This was my comeback into the research field, but about three months later I became the director of research stationed in Hsinking (present-day Ch'ang-ch'un).

After the time had passed when Miyazaki undertook to serve as the ERA's sole liaison with the military and the contact was in full swing, the ERA seemed to fall dormant. Even though his ideology ceased to operate, there remained an inclination within the SMR to cooperate actively with the military. The army and the state of Manchukuo steadily pursued their business, and the SMR considered it an embarrassment to stray too far from their own proper affairs. Thus, the SMR aimed at establishing direct connections, bypassing the ERA, with planning and research work in Manchukuo, and in this way get a hold on some sort of hegemony. For this reason I was sent to Hsinking.

I spent about a year in Hsinking. During that time I put together a federation of research organizations there. I worked in concert with the various Manchukuo organs of state, the Second Section of the Kwantung Army General Staff (materials on military provisioning), the Fourth Section of same (economic matters), and the ERA of the SMR to rationalize contacts between the administrative offices of these outfits. The military offered facilities for intelligence or research, both necessary for the military, and the SMR's knowing this served to streamline business.

When relations between Miyazaki and the Kwantung Army broke off, contacts between the SMR research organs, the military, and Manchukuo, as outlined, were regularized. As I shall described it shortly, this served to provide the underpinning to the cooperation between the military and the SMR that accompanied the military's invasion of North China.

6

The Sino-Japanese
War Begins

In North China

Advances into North China

Late in 1935 I moved from being director of the ERA stationed in Hsinking to be director in Tientsin. My departure from Manchuria to North China was tied to the advances there by the SMR and the military. In 1933 when an imperial form of government was founded in Manchukuo, Manchuria settled down for a time, and attention was now drawn toward North China. At that time one group in the military was calling for a "war on two fronts." The direction pursued by the military to that point was the single-minded principle of waging a war with the Soviet Union. Ishiwara Kanji and others were advocates of this war, and they were fortifying Manchuria against the Soviets. For that reason they argued against moving into North China.

Another view became more influential within the Ministry of the Army and among the officers concerned with China at the Army General Staff: to propel further the momentum gained in Manchuria and to stabilize that region further, North China had to be brought within Japan's sphere of influence. This position gave rise to a wide variety of maneuvering in and around Tientsin. Initially Ishiwara was determined to check this line of thought. When the transfer of the Chinese Eastern Railway in

1935, which enhanced the tension vis-à-vis the Soviet Union, was consummated and anti-Soviet preparations were seen to, North China itself had to be fortified before any eventual commencement of hostilities with the Soviets. Thus, war with China was unavoidable, and a war on two fronts for Japan became a serious option. This was the position of those who advocated the "war on two fronts," and it was to become the general inclination of officers concerned with China.

The SMR played a part in the invasion of North China. For example, Sōgō Shinji, chairman of the ERA, began to turn his attention to North China when the work of the ERA slowed for a time. Japanese aspirations in China, specifically North China, were, it was said, a desire to absorb into the Japanese-Manchurian economic bloc the iron ore, coal, salt, and raw cotton of this region of China. At the end of 1935, Mr. Sōgō created the Rise China Company with SMR capital. Initially conceived as a Sino-Japanese joint venture, Chinese ran the business operations and Japanese assisted by taking care of the aspects related to technology and investment. The idea was to bring North China within Japan's sphere of influence indirectly, without a direct invasion of the area. However, the political reverberations on the Chinese side and the insufficiency of funds on the Japanese side meant that the entire venture barely got off the ground. The Japanese invasion of China actually erupted over a rather slow and laggard period of time.

The Tientsin Office

Following on the heels of the advances of the military and the Rise China Company, research institutes too moved into North China. Within the ERA structure of the SMR, the military organized Consultant Desks, and following military orders they began investigations into the natural resources of North China shortly after the conclusion of the battle in Jehol. There were actually three desks under the heading of the Consultant Desks of the China Army. Desk A finished its work with the invasion of North China in 1934. Desk B was organized in June 1935 and was responsible for research into money, finance, and trade. Desk C was organized in November 1935 and was divided into six departments: general affairs, railways, mines, harbors, general economic matters, and industry. Desk C mobilized a total staff of some 200 men. These consultant desks, even prior to the Marco Polo Bridge Incident, carried out research into railways and harbors, looked for ways to develop resources in mining and manufacturing, and photographed and surveyed strategic points.

My responsibilities upon being sent to Tientsin in 1935 did not directly concern the consultant desks, which were involved with the war. In North China the various organs of research and intelligence were rather confused and held to their own ground. For example, the Consultant Desks, insofar as was warranted, were responsible to the ERA, but because they were employees of the military, their reports went directly there and did not necessarily arrive at the ERA. Something had to be done, so I was sent to the scene. It seemed to me that the root cause of the problem was a divergence in conception over the invasion of North China among the military, the SMR, and Manchukuo. There was an assortment of groups within the military, particularly the Kwantung Army, including those who wanted to protect Manchuria, those who wanted to invade North China, and those who placed the emphasis on the Soviet Union. Even in the China Army there were differences of opinion. Furthermore, there was the added complexity of a difference of views between the occupying army and the Kwantung Army. All sorts of maneuverings went on in North China, but there was no unified, unitary notion of how to deal with North China within the military. In any event, my work was not directly concerned with these military matters.

Report on the Investigation into Village Conditions in the Thirteen Counties of Chi-tung

I had free time in Tientsin, and to put my leisure time to practical use I devised a plan to investigate rural conditions in the thirteen counties of Chi-tung. The Chi-tung area describes a corridor between Manchuria and North China, north of a line from the Shanhai Pass to Peking and bounded by the Great Wall. Since the Tangku Accord of 1933, the area had become a demilitarized zone. As a result of the Ho-Umezu Accord, control by the Japanese Army there had been strengthened; and the Chi-tung Anti-Communist Autonomous Government came into existence in a form semi-independent of the central government, with Yin Ju-keng, one of those defeated in the Kuo Sung-ling Incident, selected as head of this regime. The government was placed in T'ung-chou, to the east of Peking, and it had thirteen counties within its jurisdiction.

Although under the control of the military, this was a demilitarized zone. Villages were tranquil and peaceful, ideal conditions for research. Since we needed the approval of the military to begin work, I proposed a project to Major Idogaki, who was in charge of financial matters, and unexpectedly received approval. I rapidly organized a research team of men from the agriculture desk of the Tientsin office, those concerned with agriculture at the ERA in the main SMR office, and those from the temporary Industrial Bureau of the Manchukuo government. We set up one unit in each county and decided to carry out sample surveys of the overall county scene as well as in one or two villages within each county. I framed our research goals with Mad'iar's theories in mind, and the work of each unit was especially directed toward the production of unified statistics.

The research units wholeheartedly carried out their work unguarded, and they were able to conclude their surveys without giving rise on the surface to any trouble. Aside from the Chinese peasants' instinctive disinclination to cooperate with us foreigners, I flatter myself that we were quite successful. The analysis of classes in Mao Tse-tung's village investigation cannot compare with it. Not only the poor conditions of agriculture and the heavy tax burdens on the peasantry, but the weight of usury and other unprecedented burdens reached a rate far more than we had expected.

I compiled the field research of the thirteen units into thirteen volumes of materials and one summary volume: *Kitō chiku jūsan ken nōson jittai chōsa hōkokusho* (Report on the Investigation into Village Conditions in the Thirteen Counties of Chi-tung). It was the first work of village research done in China proper by Japanese researchers. Although published in the name of the military, its methodology was entirely our own. In no direct way whatsoever did our aims comply with the objectives of the military.

At the time that the report appeared, a young man by the name of Nakanishi Tsutomu [or Nakanishi Kō], who had worked on China for the Proletarian Science group in Japan, entered the SMR and was attached to the office in Tientsin. He was critical both of the report and in particular of our adopting Mad'iar's approach, and he wrote an article to that effect for the journal of the China Issue Institute, run by Funakoshi Hisao and others in Tientsin.

In line with village studies by SMR researchers, this investigation was an extension of our work in Manchuria; later, SMR researchers added to its actual working troops a group of first-rate scholars from Tokyo University, including Yamada Saburō, Suehiro Izutarō, Hirano Yoshitarō, Wagatsuma Sakae, and Tanaka Kōtarō. Their work, *Kita Shina nōgyō kankō chōsa* (An Investigation of Agricultural Practices in North China), followed our earlier work.

Methodologically our research was carried out in the spirit of scientific inquiry. But we cannot ignore lateral ties to the fact that it was pursued at the time of Japan's invasion of North China. Clearly it emerged in the process of a Japanese imperialist invasion. When I visited China after the war, Liao Ch'eng-chih laughingly said to me: "Before the war—and during it as well—my country was investigated many times, but now I'd really like you to investigate Japan." I should add that I had no particularly apt response for him.

The Marco Polo Bridge Incident, 7 July 1937

The year and a half during which I served as director of the ERA in Tientsin, adviser to the Tientsin Army, and head of the Tientsin office corresponded to the critical time just prior to the outbreak of the Sino-Japanese War. Other than the investigation of village conditions in Chi-tung, though, I did not do any real work.

After the founding of the state of Manchukuo, the army aimed the spearhead of its North China invasion in the direction of Jehol and Inner Mongolia and advanced their work of strategic agitation. Ishiwara Kanji, now returned to the army's General Staff, opposed the intrusion into North China. Ishiwara's authority to speak at the General Staff still retained its earlier influence there. When the war with China erupted and he again went to Manchuria, he lost in his conflict with Tōjō and idled away his time as a regimental commander in Sendai (Japan) as the war in China spread. [Translator's note: Itō has conflated several events here, and the result may be somewhat distorting. Ishiwara's transfer to Sendai represented a promotion. He subsequently rose to be vice-chief of staff of the Kwantung Army in Manchuria where he came into conflict with his chief of staff, Tōjō Hideki. In December he became commander of the Maizuru Fortress, effectively a demotion to an insignificant post.]

The inclination of the Japanese residents in Tientsin prior to the Sino-Japanese War, unlike at the time of the Chinan Incident and the dispatching of troops to Shantung, was not to wait in anticipation of the military taking decisive action.

By virtue of the Tangku Accord of 1933, the Chi-tung area was turned into a demilitarized zone in 1936. Establishing a demilitarized region right next to the Japanese Army with its great force was virtually identical with incorporating it into the Japanese sphere of influence. Effectively this area became a marketplace for contraband trade in Japanese goods. An atmosphere emerged in which fleets of vessels formed bands that sailed from the free port of Dairen and thronged to the Chi-tung sea coast. Contraband products then inundated North China from Chi-tung and seriously undermined Chinese markets. Bands of armed ships and trucks of adventuristic merchants, ignoring customs and checkpoints of the Nationalist government, unloaded in China large quantities of such items as narcotics, cotton thread, and cloth. Gradually the situation grew ever more precarious.

Aside from the temporary influx of Japanese (such as corrupt merchants involved in illicit trade, "China adventurers" ushered in by strategic military and other organs, and ruffians), long-term residents did not welcome the disorder. They hoped that the military would pacify Manchuria and not advance into North China and that the perilous atmosphere would calm down. Ordinary Japanese residents involved in the buying and selling of ordinary products were hurt by this secret trade, and their businesses suffered. The state of instability and disorder proved to be extremely problematic for the Chinese residential population as well. As a reaction to the domination of these arrogant and corrupt merchants, some Japanese in T'ung-chou were eventually murdered. The victims of the Nikolaevsky Incident, the Chinan Incident, the T'ung-chou Incident—all due to Japanese imperialism—were common people; and ravages were an inevitable product. Yin Ju-keng, head of the Chi-tung government, was questioned about responsibility in these events and was thrown in prison by the Japanese military. He was a typical puppet.

The Sian Incident occurred in the midst of all this, in December 1936. Japanese intelligence analyses at this point might be characterized as wishful thinking, and with the "downfall" of Chiang Kai-shek, Japan was seized by the illusion that the opportunity for an invasion of China was ripe. The SMR was at this time, together with the military, involved in negotiations with the North China Political Affairs Council over laying rail lines of a financed Ts'ang-Shih Line, linking Ts'ang-chou along the Tientsin-Pukow Line to Shih-chia-chuang along the Peking-Hankow Line, as well as over iron ore mining rights in Lung-yen. After the Sian Incident, the Chinese side became firmer, and the strategic forces of the military that had entered Inner Mongolia were met with merciless counterattacks and had to withdraw. We were unaware of all this at the time. In March 1937 the Chinese Communists announced their plan to cooperate with the Nationalists. In May of that year in Yenan, Mao Tse-tung issued his report, "Tasks in the Present Stage of the Chinese Popular United Front to Resist Japan." We, of course, knew nothing of this.

The Marco Polo Bridge Incident occurred on 7 July and was followed by several other incidents elsewhere, such as the Langfang Incident and later the Ōyama Incident, when a certain Captain Ōyama of the Japanese Marines was killed in Shanghai. On the basis of the second United Front, the Chinese set up liaison committees in various areas during this period and, at the Lushan Conference presided over by Chou En-lai, the decision was made to recover the Northeast and defend the homeland in North China. Preparations for commencing war with Japan were now complete. The Konoe government in Japan as usual proclaimed a "plan for nonexpansion" on 11 July, and General Hashimoto, chief of staff of the China Army, gained control over the activist clique on the scene and for a time held to this policy of "nonexpansion." Once the fire had been set and was about to spread, we were already rushing headlong into full-scale war.

The North China Development Corporation and the Rise China Company

While operations were not going terribly smoothly for Mr. Sōgō's Rise China Company, he was faced with the beginning of a war with China. Early in the war, the Japanese Army moved steadily into North China, and all the most important enterprises run by Chinese in the area that now became occupied territory were seized and came under military control. Aside from spinning and flour milling, the military decided to entrust the great majority of enterprises concerned with the development of North China's more important resources—coal, mining, electricity, iron manufacture, salt manufacture, and the like—to the Rise China Company. As the occupied territories expanded, however, all of this could not be entrusted to Rise China, which is to say to the SMR. The capital and technology for new development could no longer be provided by the SMR alone. Monopoly capital in Japan did not remain silent in this matter. Management was consigned to major Japanese capital firms: coal went to Kaijima, Mitsui, Mitsubishi, and Ōkura; electricity went to Tokyo Electric Lighting, Nihon denryoku, and Daidō denryoku; and iron went to Nihon seitetsu and Ōkura kōgyō. Furthermore, Tōyōbō, Kanebō, and Toyotabō received spinning, while Tō-A, Nittō, and Nis-Shin received flour milling.

At the time of the Marco Polo Bridge Incident, the enterprises that fell under the SMR's control gave it immense economic influence in Manchuria; after the Incident, these concerns only fattened. The purchase from Russia of the Chinese Eastern Railway in 1935 gave the SMR control over 10,000 kilometers of rail lines. As a result of military advances onto the Chinese mainland, the rail and transportation networks in the occupied territories were handed over to North China Transportation, a subsidiary of the SMR. The SMR ran the rail lines, and together with control over the Rise China Company, it planned for taking control over the mainland. In addition, as had been the case in Manchuria, the SMR's notion was widespread that if a parent company did not run its own business properly, full organizational activities were inconceivable. This was all occurring just at the time that both the government and the army were suffering due to the reorganization of the SMR. Thus, even if the parent company were able to gain control over the railways, as the SMR had been in Manchuria, it would be in trouble if it got too strong. So, the SMR's plan was not accepted. Finally, in November 1938 a national policy company, the North China Development Corporation, was created, and the Rise China Company was absorbed into it and set apart from the SMR.

The North China Development Corporation was a kind of holding company that embraced the principal transport lines of North China, the transport business, communications, telegraph, mineral products as well as salt and its derivative businesses. North China Transportation was incorporated into it as a subsidiary. It was confirmed as well that North China Transportation was in the hands of the SMR. This meant that as concerned the operation of the occupied railways on the Chinese mainland, depending on whether they used the Japanese Railways Ministry or the SMR, the standards of operation would be different, which caused a problem. This confusing matter was resolved in favor of following the SMR track. Of course, there were conditions at-

tached, and the rail lines of Central and South China were handled along the Railways Ministry track, and so it was decided to
run a "Central China Railway."

. As had been the case in North China, when the occupied lands
extended into Central China, a Central China Promotion Corporation was established, and it integrated Chinese enterprises
seized by the Japanese Army. Central China Railway, together
with Central China Hydroelectric and other companies, became
subsidiaries of it. The SMR and the Railways Ministry were
given spheres of influence extending to Chinese rail lines under
Japanese occupation along the coastal areas. However, from the
perspective of the Kwantung Army and the Japanese Army, the
transportation network on the Chinese mainland was to be best
served through a unification, and the view was espoused that the
controlling hand of the SMR need be extended to Central China in
the manner of North China Transportation. Although there was a
variety of infighting during the war, particularly between the
army and the navy, this sectarianism eventually settled down.

I Go to Run the Shanghai Office

If we can back up momentarily, when the Sino-Japanese War
began I went to Shanghai to head up the SMR office there, right
in the middle of all the confusion over whether the Railways
Ministry or the SMR would retain control over the rail lines of
Central China. When the question of my assuming this new position arose, the navy called in a temporary veto, for the navy was
in a commanding position in Central China. They said that since I
had been in Hsinking and in Tientsin, I was close to the Kwantung
Army, and the navy in Shanghai would not ratify my appointment. Rumor had it that, embroiled in the fight over rail line
spheres of influence in North and Central China, the Railways
Ministry had gone to work on the navy and interrupted my assuming this new job. After arriving in Shanghai, however, I met
with Satō Eisaku of the Railways Ministry (I have forgotten his
actual title within the ministry at that time) on this whole matter;
Satō's elder brother, Kishi Nobusuke, and I had been classmates,

and I remember the two of us grinning at one another when we met.

I received my transfer orders to the Shanghai office shortly after the Marco Polo Bridge Incident. Only about one-half year had passed as head of the Tientsin office, and I was transferred as part of the organization of personnel matters, principally in the SMR's Railway Department, in North China. Also, no one wanted to go to Shanghai for fear that the ravages of war might soon spread there. The position of head of the Shanghai office was an important post in which Mr. Ōbuchi Miki and Mr. Izawa Michio had served, and when their service ended they were made SMR directors. The war was clearly near at hand, though, and as a result Central China, unlike Manchuria and North China, was going to be full of trouble. That was why these two men had ceased working there.

Although it was a considerably troublesome affair, the SMR gained the navy's acquiescence for me. I arrived in Shanghai in October, and by then Shanghai had become a battlefield. The Concession area was an international neutral zone, and the war was fought along its perimeter. It was thus the best place from which to witness the fighting, and when severe fighting did break out, stray bullets at times flew my way. It was a strange place from which I was able to see in great detail.

Head of the Shanghai Office (1): War and the Enlarged Research Department

The Industrialization of SMR Research

Gradually the stage moves to Shanghai and the story moves to wartime Shanghai. Before I come to the various kinds of research I was in charge of there, let me just say a word about the reorganization of the ERA into the Industrial Department and then its reincorporation into the Research Department.

Founded at the time of the Manchurian Incident, the ERA was reshuffled into the Industrial Department in October 1936. I was in Tientsin at that time, so I had no involvement in the changeover, though I can say something about the general outline of the story. When Manchukuo came into existence, the need for the ERA to continue its work in economic planning for the state of Manchukuo came to an end. It was decided that the research organs of the SMR should assume the duties of drafting plans, and after the reorganization the SMR itself was to develop along these lines. At the same time, the Central Laboratory, the Geological Research Institute, and the like were integrated with agencies working in the natural sciences. As a result the SMR placed emphasis on business planning, and with the changed name of "Industrial Department" it began to investigate the development of new enterprises. The intrusion into North China as well as the establishment of the Rise China Company were linked to this "development of new enterprises." The department head was director Sakatani Kiichi; the two assistant heads were Okumura Shinji and Sera Shōichi. The Industrial Department was Mr. Okumura's conception.

Let me say a few words about the organization of the "business office" of this new Industrial Department. Under Mr. Oshikawa Ichirō, the head of the General Affairs Section of the Industrial Department, Mr. Ōgami Suehiro assumed the position as head of the business office, a post held by Hōjō Hidekazu in the days of the ERA. The "business office" of the General Affairs Section comprised a staff that carried out overall research plans within the research structure. Although by itself the staff lacked the power of final decision in drafting plans, since their superiors did not give instructions covering details, they effectively drew up research plans, sent them to their bosses, and these plans were then sent back to them. Hence, the business office was a kind of secretariat. Although the ranks within the SMR Company of the "business office" employees were low, a number of young prodigies were attached there, and Ōgami Suehiro was put in charge.

A graduate of the Economics Department of Kyoto University, he was reared as a researcher in the SMR, having learned his perspective on China from Tachibana Shiraki. The theoretical level of the SMR research staff at the time of the Manchurian Incident was not particularly high, and as an economic theorist among them he attracted some attention. Later, though, when a number of left-wingers shut off from Japan came flocking to the SMR, his reputation dropped a bit, but Ōgami remained very popular due to his extraordinary personality.

With Ōgami's arrival at this important position, the manner in which the SMR compiled its investigative reports became more theoretical and more elaborate than before. Some, attentive to this point, esteemed Ōgami for bringing science and rationalism to the research work of the SMR. Clearly he brought a theoretical appearance to the investigative reports, but it would take time before its integration within the overall organization could take form.

I had at this time come to the main office from a branch office, and what I noticed at every meeting was that the principle of "expertism," a kind of cottage industry among SMR researchers of past days, remained intact. I felt that, even if each of the research staff's individual reports (the product of individual expertise) were put together into a bunch, this would not mean we had created comprehensive research. In fact this could hardly be considered proper research work at all. Ōgami and others at the business office stressed theory, but their method remained expertism. He loved theory, but the research conducted according to his plans was unable methodologically to escape from the older SMR tradition.

Late in 1937, in conjunction with the regulation of affiliated business, the Industrial Department's room for activities grew considerably smaller—aside from the railways and coal mining of the SMR, its business was transferred to the Manchurian Heavy Industry Corporation—and it was reorganized. In April 1938 its name was changed to the Research Department. Then, in April 1939 this was in turn reorganized into the Enlarged Research Department. The roughly one and one-half years from late 1937 through April 1939 constituted a period of confusion, but I was then working in the Shanghai office and was not in a position to know all the details at the main office. This confusion arose for two reasons: the SMR, essentially the parent company, was scaling down with the establishment of the Manchurian Heavy Industry Company; and the SMR was unexpectedly slow in Japan's advance into North China. This was the period in which the role to be played by the Research Department of the SMR was being weighed in the balance, and there was a lively exchange of opinions over research methodology between myself and Ōgami group's of young commissioned officers.

So, in April 1939 the Enlarged Research Department was founded. I shall touch on its line-up and the importance of its creation a little later, but after it emerged plans were energetically pursued for "comprehensive research." As concerned the mobilization of resources, it produced reports on conditions for the location of Japanese-Manchurian-Chinese industry, principal resource supplies, the wartime Japanese-Manchurian-Chinese economy, and the impact of military operations in the South. For analyses of the contemporary situation, it produced reports on world conditions, the Japanese-Manchurian-Chinese inflation, and the resistance capacity of the Chinese. A huge number of personnel and a great quantity of money went into these long-term (three- to four-year) research projects. In form this alone seems to indicate "comprehensive research," but in actuality I could not help feeling that it was not. Until the end the Research Department of the SMR relied on its principle of expertise, and until its demise it never once implemented a true program of cumulative, integrated research.

The Formation of the Enlarged Research Department and the Left-wingers

When the Enlarged Research Department was founded in 1939, leftists from Japan were entering the SMR one after another. A number of them were quite well known: Horie Muraichi, Okazaki Jirō, Itō Kōdō, Yamaguchi Shōgo, Fujiwara Sadamu, Kawasaki Misaburō, Hiradate Toshio, Gushima Kenzaburō, Ishidō Kiyotomo, Ishida Seiichi, Motani Koichirō, Nonomura Kazuo, Andō Jirō, Toki Tsuyoshi, Satō Hiroshi, Ishikawa Masayoshi, Suzuki Shigetoshi, Nishi Masao, Hosokawa Karoku, Ozaki Hotsumi, and Itō Ritsu, among others. They entered the area of research at the main office in Dairen, and in the branch offices in Peking, Shanghai, and Tokyo as well. Some of them had been academics, some political activists, some publicists, as well as various and sundry other professions difficult to sum up in a word. Their channels into the Research Department, generally speaking, followed three courses.

One group were men who had traveled to Manchuria after coming under severe attack in Japan with their political movements back home crushed. A second group were men who escaped to Manchuria after being arrested any number of times by the police and having renounced in writing their left-wing political views; but the police did not trust them and continued to treat them as dangerous elements. A third group was those who were unable to find work because of their activities in the political movement and had accordingly come to Manchuria. Still different conditions pertained within the Research Department that hired these men, where in 1939 more than anything the major issue was the lack of capable talent to increase the ranks of the Research Department rapidly.

The expansion of the Research Department in 1939 aimed at creating a basis on which to strengthen its capacity for strategic conceptualizing in the stage of total war. There were in addition internal conditions within the SMR that made such an expansion inevitable. The president of the SMR at this time was Matsuoka Yōsuke, who wanted to be another Gotō Shimpei, the first SMR president. As we have seen, there was considerable discontent within the SMR with the lack of vigor in the reorganization and the invasion into North China. The Asia Development Board had already been established for the management of the mainland, and a Planning Board ran its resource mobilization planning. The position held by the SMR on the mainland was weakening.

To pacify the discontent within the organization, President Matsuoka recognized the need to demonstrate the position of the SMR on the mainland. He got the government to accept a whopping budget of 20 million yen, and he decided to expand the Research Department. As he envisioned it, Strategic Staff Headquarters would subsume the three areas of politics, the economy, and the military on the mainland. Thus, he invited Mr. Tanaka

Seijirō, a young SMR director from Mitsui Bussan in the days of Gotō Shimpei, to be head of the Research Department and made the position equivalent to a vice-president of the SMR. This immense budget of 20 million yen in the currency of those days would come to roughly 10 billion yen now. And, at its largest, the staff reached some two thousand workers, including the personnel in General Affairs. This even exceeded Gotō Shimpei's plans at the time that the Research Department was founded.

In any event, as this immense structure was swelling up, large numbers of men had to be brought in from the outside. They could not just bring in newcomers with degrees from economics departments of universities and assign them to jobs, because university graduates could not immediately be put to use. The personnel pool was to come from left-wingers who had been forced to renounce their political views, for they were competent to do this kind of work by virtue of the fact that they had gained a rudimentary training in social science. It was in line with the character of these men that the research at the Research Department would be carried out with a certain scientific demeanor. It was ironic that the people who had been struggling against the war were taken in at face value and became the assistants to the central figures in the period of total war.

I believe that certain of these left-wingers, such as Hosokawa Karoku and Horie Muraichi, entered the Research Department on the strength of their connection to Ozaki Hotsumi, a high-level consultant. Ozaki's father was a member of Gotō Shimpei's brain trust in the years of Gotō's administration on Taiwan, and Tanaka Seijirō, head of the Research Department, had worked for a time under President Gotō. Through this connection, Ozaki and Tanaka became close; and with Ozaki's introduction and Tanaka's authority, no one complained if someone had been a left-winger before coming to the SMR.

Investigation of the Resistance Capacity of the Chinese

There were as well a fair number of leftists at the Shanghai office where I was working. All sorts of people had come with introductions from acquaintances of mine from the Shinjinkai days. Altogether our office had over three hundred employees and a budget of over three million yen.

As the Research Department expanded, several large-scale research projects were carried out, and the Research Division of the Shanghai office bore its share of the responsibility. Shanghai played the most important role in three research projects: *Shina kōsenryoku chōsa* (Investigation of the Resistance Capacity of the Chinese), *Nichi-Man-Shi infure chōsa* (Investigation of Japanese-Manchurian-Chinese Inflation), and *Sekai jōsei bunseki* (An Analysis of International Conditions). The first of these occupied the attentions of the Shanghai Research Division for the three calendar years 1939–1941. Most prominently active in this project was Nakanishi Tsutomu.

The research theme was to analyze comprehensively the political and economic strength of the Nationalist regime in Chungking and the Communist bases of resistance and to determine their capacity to fight Japan. The materials used were primarily newspapers and magazines in Hong Kong, but documents transported by the military from war zones were also examined, and the analysis of them had to take place at our office. The research report was about ten volumes, but it seems that original full sets are no longer extant in Japan.

Nakanishi Tsutomu's report accurately captured the state of economic construction in Chungking and the economic work under way in Yenan. He recognized the achievement of the Anti-Japanese United Front and concluded that the resistance capacity of the Chinese against Japan was inordinately ferocious. At the time, materials of great utility for the military were appearing, and a request for a copy of the investigative report came to us from the Nanking Army. Nakanishi went to the Nanking Army and lectured on the subject. He was much admired by the military, and the Army General Staff in Tokyo, informed of this, requested his presence and arranged a plane for transportation. So he set off for Tokyo, where he delivered a speech. The reason the military was so interested in his report had to do with the logical and articulate presentation of his argument that if the

Japanese Army fought deep into Chinese territory, the supply lines would be stretched too thin, it would be an immense task to protect them, and ultimately they could not bring the Chungking government down. This understanding of things spelled a stage of protracted war from the military's perspective, and it was a conclusion fully consistent with Mao Tse-tung's "On Protracted War."

The time was one in which the military was seriously considering how to avoid a protracted war. The report thus served an extremely important purpose. The materials that Nakanishi provided the SMR and the military were one part of the book he compiled. The larger part of it was published in several volumes as a study of the Chinese Communists after the war, and it caused renewed excitement among scholars of China.

Although the military had thought highly of SMR research, the situation changed for the worse when there were growing signs of defeat in the air. Since this report did indeed present defeatist notions, the researchers became the object of military repression. The question was raised of the means by which Nakanishi had secured these Chinese documents. In March 1942 Nakanishi was arrested together with Ozaki Shōtarō, and the first step in the repression of the Research Department of the SMR began.

Ishihama Tomoyuki

Concerning the economy of the Nationalist regime, Ishihama Tomoyuki wrote *Jūkei senji keizai taisei ron* (On the Wartime Economic Structure in Chungking). We had been friends since the Shinjinkai days and had entered the Research Section together. Soon thereafter he left the SMR to become a professor at Kyūshū University. Later, he was driven from his teaching position at the time of the Popular Front Incident, and when the war began he was drafted and sent to Shanghai as a forty-two-year old veteran. It was a pitiful situation, so I helped arrange for my fellow provincial Mabuchi Toshio, head of intelligence for the Shanghai Army, to take Ishihama onto his staff. Work there was leisurely and relatively free, and a soldier in military garb had free access to the SMR office, could meet with the young research staff, and could make good use of the materials in our office. The product of his labors was *On the Wartime Economic Structure in Chungking*. In his introduction, Ishihama expressed his gratitude to Colonel Mabuchi for being able to work and write.

The Communists' New Fourth Army was involved in guerrilla activities around the perimeter of Shanghai. In response the Japanese Army was engaged in antiguerrilla, clean-up activities, as it had done in Manchuria and North China. (The U.S. Army is now doing the same thing in South Vietnam). They collected peasant families together in rural areas and worked in earnest to separate guerrillas from ordinary people. Since Ishihama now worked for intelligence, he had the responsibility of observing in the field and publicizing their successes. Although he had not gone to the scene of action with this specifically in mind, reports from the Pacification Desk mounted up in the Shanghai office. With these reports as source materials, Ishihama wrote a book entitled *Seikyō kōsaku* (Clean-up Activities). Although it is not the least bit interesting, it is rare as a work published during the war that touched on the activities of the New Fourth Army.

Formation of the Pacification Desk

Let me now say something about the Pacification Desk that appeared immediately after the occupation of Shanghai. Because civilians in military employ were not readily forthcoming for service in the military's occupation administration, the SMR, as the military demanded, provisionally dispatched fifty of its employees from the local administration and the labor relations departments. They were instructed to set up the Pacification Desk at the Shanghai office. Comprised from the excessive staff at the SMR, they were gathered in Shanghai and from there sent to the counties in the outskirts of Shanghai. Their job was to make contact with the local peace preservation committees and the Japanese Army, collect information concerning local public order, work closely on local issues of popular welfare, and generally pacify the occupied residential populace in many ways. A variety of things fell under the heading of pacification, and they were said generally to have done wicked things to the Chinese populace.

However, using SMR employees whose livelihood was secure was, I think, a brilliant way of proceeding. Many of them worked on behalf of the local residents under their charge, negotiated with the military, discharged food supplies, and implemented good government as conscientiously as possible. There were also men who paraded around under the shelter of the might of the military. At the Shanghai office, we were attentive to avoiding harm as well as we could by sending office staff members of the level of desk head to important areas. We took them back after one-year terms as agreed, and all expenses were taken care of by the military. This was extraordinary at that time. Since these were conscientious staffers who could not bear this pacification work, they left the office one by one and, as a result, not a person from the era of the "clean-ups" remained.

After the *Investigation of the Resistance Capacity of the Chinese*, the Shanghai office next cooperated in the *Investigation of Japanese-Manchurian-Chinese Inflation*. Manchurian economic problems could not be resolved solely in Manchuria but were best addressed from the perspective of an economic structure linking Japan, Manchuria, and China. Furthermore, the report concluded that inflationary aggravation would be difficult to avoid in the process of the rapid industrial construction that paralleled the war economy. At first, the report was not issued publicly. Since it was implied, however, that the report indicated a gloomy future in the war, it was not apparently too popular with the military.

In *An Analysis of International Conditions*, the Research Department offered the overall structure, and here the main roles were played by the Tokyo and Shanghai offices. I believe that Tokyo, principally Ozaki Hotsumi, directed the general plan. Hong Kong served as a vigorous source of materials. While work was in progress, employees of the Research Department who were of a liberal bent were all arrested in the SMR Incident. As a result the majority of capable research men were just rounded up in a wholesale arrest.

In the Research Department, other than the group that drew

up policy plans and political analysis, there was a group consisting of men such as Amano Motonosuke who worked closely on empirical investigations. This group did not take a conspicuous part in our integrated research but became engrossed particularly in agricultural problems. No one surpassed Amano in the collection of materials and documents. In this regard, Amano was a man with a distinctive style all his own. His articles for which he subsequently received the Academy Prize in Japan were assiduously compiled from work begun in this period.

As researchers at the SMR, if there were types like Ōkawa Shūmei, Kasagi Yoshiaki, and Miyazaki Masayoshi, there were also men like Ōgami Suehiro and Ozaki Hotsumi. We employed men like Nakanishi Tsutomu, Anzai Kuraji, and Ozaki Shōtarō as well as men like Amano Motonosuke. In a word, the talent at work for the Research Department was of a wide variety. It is hard to evaluate them all as a single group.

Head of the Shanghai Office (2): The Inside Story of Shanghai During the War

Head of the SMR's Shanghai Office

The basic job of the head of the Shanghai office, the position I held for five years from October 1937, did not involve research itself. As the representative of a national policy company (the SMR) in Shanghai and South and Central China, my responsibilities included not only dealing with the various military and civil organs. In addition I had agents under my management in Nanking, Hankow, Hong Kong, and Kwangtung; and I directed the subsidiary Dairen Steamship Company and a branch of the Nichiman Shōji Trading Company. I was in a position as well to establish ties with officials and with the people. For example, when the Pacific War began, the Japanese Army occupied the Municipal Council, which was the administrative organ of the International Concessions. Under the circumstances, the consul-general in Shanghai, who represented the Foreign Office of Japan, had to study how best to deal with the Shanghai municipal government, and to this end he held meetings with private citizens. As someone with experience in such matters, being head of the Shanghai office, I participated in these meetings. I also served as the head of the China office of the East Asian Research Institute. A word on my work in this last capacity: we planned and completed research for the work *Chūgoku ni okeru gaikoku tōshi* (Foreign Investment in China).

So, the head of the Shanghai office was a major Japanese position in Shanghai. When Diet members, high-level officials, newspapermen, representatives of the financial world, and big-shot adventurers came from Japan, they always showed up at my office, looking for information. Among them, I remember Kishi Nobusuke of Manchukuo and Mizutani Chōzaburō from Japan. On occasion there were visitors from other foreign nations. In any case, important figures from Japan usually paid their respects at the Shanghai office. The *North China Daily News* always carried my movements in the personals column. The significance of the position of an office head was due also to the responsibilities owed the SMR. He had an office staff and ran a place in which wide-ranging political and economic information was concentrated.

From my position, I was able to glean the general contours of the maneuverings among the special services agency, the strategic services agency, and the intelligence agency, all for a time competing in Shanghai. We obtained from its inception the secret moves made by such Japanese outfits to entice Wang Ching-wei into becoming the head of a central government in China.

Wang Ching-wei

I still remember the strange contact I had with Wang Ching-wei. On my return from Europe in 1929 just before assuming my position in Nanking, we met in Peking. This was not our first meeting, for in 1926 I had made his acquaintance in Canton on the podium at the first memorial in honor of the late Sun Yat-sen. I came to Peking and dropped in at our office there to catch up on news about China from the time I had been overseas and to see old friends. It was there by chance that I ran into Wang. At that time he was the leader of the reformist faction within the KMT, opposed to Chiang Kai-shek. He was living in Peking to collaborate with the anti-Chiang warlords, Feng Yü-hsiang and Yen Hsi-shan, and to strengthen the anti-Chiang movement. Yamada Junsaburō, an SMR consultant and former assistant to Sun Yat-sen, had worked with Wang; and, as the head of the Peking office at the time, he had arranged a dinner party in Wang's honor, and I happened to run into them dining and joined them.

From about 1938, when the Sino-Japanese War was on the verge of exploding into a major confrontation, while I was head of the Shanghai office, Wang Ching-wei's name hauntingly re-emerged. As is well known, before Kagesa Sadaaki's agency got off the ground, there was an SMR employee who offered his services in the preparatory work to enticing Wang Ching-wei. This was Nishi Yoshiaki, who was working under special orders from President Matsuoka Yōsuke. The case is chronicled in detail in his book *Higeki no shōnin* (Witness to Tragedy). Nishi was an SMR employee stationed in Nanking, attached to the Shanghai office, but for this affair he was transferred, I believe, to the East Asia Section. On business he used to visit Tokyo, Hong Kong, and Shanghai, and we often dined together, but he never once mentioned progress in his maneuverings with Wang or anything related to it. And I never asked. I never asked, but from other intelligence sources we became aware of overall shifts.

Soon thereafter, Major General Kagesa set to work, and the Wang Ching-wei affair reached its denouement. It was not as Nishi had conceived it at all. Wang flew out of Chungking alone, fully prepared for his role as traitor, and established the "Nanking Government."

It seemed to me that Wang Ching-wei was in a sorry state when he arrived in Nanking. As a matter of etiquette on behalf of the SMR, which had set up an office in Nanking (under Noma Kiyoshi), I had to go and pay our respects to Wang. Wang offered a simple greeting, assuming the pose of a very important man. Although he never showed his face in an unassuming and rather embarrassed state of mind, I remember that I left for home with the feeling that it was only natural that Wang now lacked his former luster.

Among Wang's followers there was Chou Fu-hai, who I happened to meet on a flight to Dairen when he was on his way to
Tokyo. It was our first meeting since my time in Nanking, and
after arriving in Dairen, we dined together and I saw him off to
Tokyo. Our intelligence knew the general contours surrounding
the villainous behavior of such characters as Li Shih-ch'un or Ting
Mei-ts'un at their residence at No. 75 Jessfield Road. They were
members of the special organ of Wang Ching-wei's group in
Shanghai.

Wartime Shanghai was like a breeding ground for strategic
scheming. Agencies of various countries were confusingly engaged in an assortment of intelligence-gathering activities. There
was England, America, and France, and on the Chinese side were
the Wang Ching-wei clique, the Nationalist regime in Chungking,
the Chinese Communists, the General Chamber of Commerce,
and the Green Gang. On the Japanese side, the Ministry of Foreign Affairs was not, of course, the sole line of action. There was
the army, the navy, the Ministry of Foreign Affairs, and great
commercial houses, in addition to the SMR. Sectarianism and
competition among the various Japanese agencies remained as it
had been before. Among them, however, the SMR's information
was collected as basic material for a cumulative investigation,
and thus took a holistic approach, achieving a rather high analytic
level.

The Pacific War Erupts

Amidst the information that we amassed in this manner, we generally gleaned the trend toward war with the United States and
England. I recall that this occurred at the time when Mr. Kurusu's trip to America was made public, despite the fact that Ambassador Nomura was stationed in the United States and involved in negotiations there. A piece of intelligence came to us
from Hong Kong: "Although Kurusu is going, this is total camou-
flage, a tactic. He is going to delay the commencement of war
with the United States."

As concerns intelligence about the Chinese Communists, we
learned from the very start that Hu Tsung-nan's troops were sent

to surround Yenan and not in any way to be party to a war with Japanese forces. While Japan was in negotiations with Chungking, a feeler went out to see if they might not compromise to counter the Communists. The Japanese military suffered from having stationed a great number of troops on the mainland and wanted to find a route for rapid troop evacuation. Since a protracted war would put them in an impossible situation, they were prepared to approach Chungking with a peace proposal. However, the Chungking operation never became an issue after Wang Ching-wei's escape, although this did set the stage for a united anti-Communist line and a variety of channels for this cropped up. Since the moronic Japanese military could not lose face, they never found an acceptable meeting point.

We received news of the New Fourth Army Incident very quickly, and, as I think back on it now, it was remarkably accurate. Even our understanding of the expansion and growth of the "liberated areas," when Yenan began its essential economic construction from 1941 through 1942, was accurate. This was due to the fact that captured documents were collected at the Research Department of the SMR, and we were able to analyze and understand them. When the Japanese Army began mopping up campaigns into the liberated areas and into the raided areas surrounding them of the Eighth Route Army and New Fourth Army, the Chinese Communists held out well and escaped, but on occasion documents left behind were brought to the SMR because the military could not understand them.

We well understood Chungking's impatience with the growth of the Chinese Communists, and we carried on a peace operation and a Chungking operation with the idea of an anti-Communist united front opposed to the popular United Front. The Chungking operation, though, was not solely implemented along these general lines.

Peace Talks Between Tsuda Shizue and Hu O-kung

During this period, Reserve Admiral Tsuda Shizue of the navy became engaged in peace talks with Hu O-kung, a retired scholar living in Shanghai. I had known Tsuda since my years in Peking, and because Hu O-kung was a patron of Suzue Gen'ichi, Suzue acted as interpreter and intermediary. Hu spoke Chinese with a thick Hupeh accent, so there was no one other than Suzue who could interpret. Tsuda was a well-mannered person, and he did not hesitate to talk freely as long as he was in a nonofficial capacity. After he became the head of the Asia Development Board in Central China, he cut off these discussions altogether. When he retired from public office, however, these talks continued as if reborn. Thus, although this was a "peace operation," in fact both sides were really trying to pry information out of the other.

What was interesting about these meetings was that Hu O-kung was well aware of the entire course of events in the peace operation from the Japanese side and of their lack of unity, and he clearly saw that the meetings would be of no avail. I was impressed by the acuity with which he understood the situation.

In any case, though, a stalemate in the conflict on the mainland as it entered a state of protracted war was not to be influenced by such an operation, and the stalemate developed toward the dangerous consequence of the explosion of the Pacific War. On 8 December 1941, I was away from Shanghai on a trip to Tokyo, and I returned to my post in a hurry.

7

The SMR Incident:
The Assault on Science

Point of Departure

Mr. Ozaki Hotsumi

I heard the news of Ozaki Hotsumi's arrest in the Sorge case just before the Pacific War began. It was quite a shock and difficult to believe at first. As a person he was not well suited for involvement in this incident. He was an open-hearted, magnanimous, extremely sociable man who often engaged in quiet gossip. Nakanishi Tsutomu's arrest in 1942 had been expected, but Ozaki's was quite a surprise.

My ties to Ozaki went far back. When I had returned from study overseas and was stationed in Nanking, he was working on the staff of Ōta Unosuke, special correspondent for the *Asahi shimbun* in Shanghai. At that time Ōkata Kōhei, a younger classmate of Ozaki from high school, was working at the Shanghai office of the SMR. Through this contact, he became one of my contributors to *Mantetsu Shina gesshi* at the Shanghai office, which I had been putting out under the name *Pekin Mantetsu geppō* while in Peking and had brought with me to Shanghai. I have already mentioned that this journal had the ambitious aim of nourishing the sprouts of Sino-Japanese scholarly cooperation, with essays from both Chinese and Japanese authors. On the Japanese side we had contributions by Suzue Gen'ichi and Nakae

Ushikichi. Nakae allowed us to publish the brilliant article he had printed himself: "Shina no hōken seido ni tsuite" (On the Chinese Feudal System). This was the only piece for which he gained any publicity during his lifetime. On the Chinese side, Hsü Te-shan submitted his "Chung-kuo she-hui shih" (A History of Chinese Society), and Ch'en Han-sheng and others served the journal well as advisers.

At this time Ozaki had not as yet established contact with Sorge, though he had wide ties with such people as student activists in the East Asian Common Culture Academy and theorists such as Wang Hsüeh-wen who participated in the "Debates on the History of Society." Although I have no memory of it, Kawai Teikichi, who was arrested together with Ozaki in the Sorge case, describes in a book his meeting me in Nanking. Inasmuch as Ozaki's associates and mine were a small group of scholars and Japanese friends, we shared a large area of overlap.

Ozaki and I became close friends. After he returned to Osaka, I visited him there every time I traveled to Tokyo, and we exchanged views on the state of Sino-Japanese relations. Shortly thereafter, he moved to the main office in Tokyo of the *Asahi shimbun*, where he belonged to the Research Association on East Asian Issues. Ozaki's popularity as a journalist resulted in his being invited by the SMR to be a high-level consultant, and accordingly he often visited the Research Department. Our relationship thus became even closer, as we cooperated at every meeting on comprehensive research, particularly on two projects, "Investigation of Japanese-Manchurian-Chinese Inflation" and "Analysis of International Condition" projects.

He was an old China hand, but because he was also well versed on the scene in Japan, the Research Department welcomed him with open arms. Nevertheless, since research-oriented meetings were occasions to discuss our research methods, I don't think he ever gained any top secret information involved with the Sorge case from us.

After Ozaki became a consultant, whenever there were research meetings in Shanghai concerning the resistance capacity of the Chinese, he came to Shanghai, and every time he met with friends and collected information. Suzue Gen'ichi was one of his best friends. He always worked enthusiastically in a cheerful mood with Nakanishi Tsutomu and other staff members of the Research Department.

The Cooperative Association Incident and the Nakanishi Incident

Nakanishi's arrest was unrelated to Ozaki Hotsumi's, although this was not known at the time Nakanishi was apprehended. In the Research Department, Gotō Kenshō, who worked on the Company's business statistics, and Kaieda Hisataka of the Tokyo branch office, among others, were implicated with Ozaki and arrested. Thereafter in November 1941 Suzuki Kohei, Satō Daishirō, Hanabusa Shigeru, Komatsu Shichirō, and others were arrested from the Research Department in the Cooperative Association (Gassakusha) Incident. These men were rounded up because they formed a group active in the agricultural cooperative movement in Manchuria, which had leftist overtones.

Nakanishi and others were arrested in March 1942, shortly after the outbreak of the Pacific War. Apprehended with him were Ozaki Shōtarō in North China and Anzai Kuraji in Pao-t'ou, both of whom had been acquaintances of his from the East Asian Common Culture Academy and the Proletarian Science group. There was a mass roundup of the *Manshū hyōron* group in Dairen early on, but it had not extended to the editor-in-chief, Tachibana Shiraki himself.

Ozaki Hotsumi's influence spread widely within the SMR, so when he was arrested everyone became alarmed. This feeling deepened in the Research Department with the Cooperative Association Incident and the arrest of Nakanishi Tsutomu; we were all on the lookout. It was assumed that Nakanishi's case was somehow tied in with Ozaki Hotsumi, for it was only later that we learned that Nakanishi had no contact with Ozaki's Sorge-Comintern link.

The Manshū Hyōron Incident

Although the arrest of Nakanishi and others seemed connected to the Sorge case, we did not think as much in the case of the *Manshū hyōron* group. I have already said a few words about the journal *Manshū hyōron*. It began under the editorship of Tachibana Shiraki and enjoyed the sponsorship of Koyama Sadatomo, who had close ties to the Kwantung Army and the SMR. Capable young writers in the Research Department published their ideas, often under pen names, concerning current events drawn from their research. From the Manchurian Incident through the founding of Manchukuo, these pieces mainly concerned the Concordia party and the notion of the Heavenly Way. After the beginning of the Sino-Japanese War, ideas about a Japanese-Manchurian-Chinese bloc economy, theories on the revival of Asia, East Asia as a "community," and the New Structure movement became more influential. At times, some of these articles indirectly criticized the policies of the military and the Manchukuo government, but some of them were also opportunistic. Why was this group rounded up? There was a group within the Research Department, some of whom were critical of the situation and some of whom were cooperating with the military, who sensed military pressures being brought to bear on the Research Department.

With the string of the Cooperative Association Incident, the *Manshū hyōron* Incident, and the Nakanishi Incident, preparations began at the upper echelons of the SMR (people who were in contact with the activities of the military and the military police) to find safe haven for those intellectuals in the Research Department who were concerned for their lives and were being watched by the military police, to be reassigned to coal mines or transferred to a subsidiary company. Thus, the capable research staff was completely dispersed. The organic assignment structure of the staff, supporting the system of integrated research begun in 1939, came tumbling down. In the end the Enlarged Research Department of the SMR vanished.

I became a counselor in February 1942 and moved to Dairen

from Shanghai. A fair number of SMR researchers had already been apprehended by that time. It is unclear whether my transfer was in fact tied up with the transposition of the research staff. Four years had passed since I had taken the Shanghai job, and it was a good time for a transfer.

The First Arrests in the SMR Incident

As the situation became increasingly frantic and staffers from the Research Department were being busily transferred, about six months after the Nakanishi Incident in the middle of September 1942 a large-scale arrest of Research Department employees was carried out on the orders of the Kwantung Army's military police in areas from Japan to the Asian mainland. In all twenty-nine men were arrested, including Horie Muraichi, Gushima Kenzaburō, Inaba Shirō, and Nonomura Kazuo in Dairen; Yokogawa Jirō, Watanabe Yūji, Matsuoka Mizuo, Yoshiue Satoru, and Yoshihara Jirō in Hsinking; Ishida Eiichirō and Ishii Toshiyuki in Peking; Nishi Masao, Suzue Gen'ichi, Ishikawa Masayoshi, and Noma Kiyoshi in Shanghai; Hazama Genzō in Tokyo; and, in Kyoto, Ōgami Suehiro who had settled at the Research Institute for Humanistic Sciences at Kyoto University, after having spent time at the East Asian Research Institute.

The reason for the arrests remains unclear, but at the time there were people who had a foreboding that they might be apprehended. Those who by virtue of their left-wing views had come to Manchuria in "exile" from repression heard in the fall of 1942, when the tides of the war looked rather discouraging, that their friends in Japan were being held in preventive detention, and so they seemed prepared for it. What remains unfathomable is that there were people arrested without such a background, who had kept up associations with the special services agency, and who had cooperated in a variety of ways with the military.

After the first round of arrests, when I look at it in retrospect, I heard the following story, which was not far off the mark. It was told to me by General Hasebe, a staff officer during the Siberian expedition who later became an SMR consultant.

Tōjō is aiming more and more toward defeat in the war, and if we are defeated, left-wing intellectuals will probably cause riots. He's arresting them all in advance as a defensive measure. It's not that they're left-wing but the fact that they're intellectuals that makes them dangerous. About 50,000 people over as wide an area as possible will be apprehended. In short, the plan is to arrest 50,000 intellectuals from Japan and overseas. He took aim from the outset at that den of left-wing intellectuals in the Research Department of the SMR.

When I first heard this story, it was unclear to me what the object of mass arrest was to be. When I was later arrested, I asked the military police but they did not know anything.

The Second Series of Arrests

Morning, 14 June 1943

I was arrested in the middle of June 1943, a fair amount of time after the first round of arrests and after I had returned to Dairen in February 1942 to serve as a counselor in the main SMR office. My position as counselor there was a kind of temporary waiting point until I would be appointed director of a subsidiary company. I had heard a rumor when I was still head of the Shanghai office to the effect that I might be appointed civil administrator of the island of Celebes, which was at that time at the center of the Japanese-occupied Southeast Asia. The rumor apparently emanated from the navy. Before coming to Shanghai, I had been on close terms with the army, particularly in North China, and the navy issued some complaint when I was appointed head of the Shanghai office. But, after I had taken up the Shanghai post, I became quite friendly with the ablest China hand in the navy, Mr. Tsuda Shizue. Tsuda later was put in charge of the Asia Development Board of Central China. Before two years had passed, though, he returned to the field once again. I got to know him when he was stationed in Peking, and we were together in Nanking as well. Among the many Japanese stationed in South China, Tsuda used to be teasingly called a "naval infantry commander."

Nonetheless, I thought that there was much in this fellow's views on China that was worthy of our attention. I remember hearing him once say that Japanese views of China had been extremely derisive; Japanese had attached importance to Manchuria and North China, while knowledge of the South was sparse, and, he said, it was all a major blunder.

Since I heard the story of my going to Celebes after moving to Dairen, I don't know how reliable the information was. Perhaps it was connected to the transfer of research personnel, for I had come to Dairen to be a counselor because conditions in Shanghai had become dangerous. Generally speaking, a counselor had nothing in particular to do, and for quite a while I did nothing but remain in my holding position until I would be transferred to a subsidiary company. I had heard that I might become head of the newspaper *Manshū nichinichi shimbun* (Manchurian Daily News). It was precisely at that moment, when I was doing my exercises one morning, that the military police came to arrest me.

It was a shock, though I had expected that they would come for me. I had known Ozaki Hotsumi well; Nakanishi Tsutomu had worked under me; and I was close with the *Manshū hyōron* group. In addition, the business office people in the first arrest had been my counterparts in debate. I was prepared for the authorities when they arrived and had put all my papers in order. The military police looked at my bookcases as if to say: "There's nothing there!" It was widely known that I would probably be arrested. In fact, the reason the navy had proposed my name as administrator of Celebes probably was out of concern that I not be arrested. I later learned that Prime Minister Tōjō had opposed the navy's proposal.

In all, ten of us were arrested in the second round of the SMR Incident. The nine others were Tanaka Kyūichi, Ishidō Kiyotomo, and Hotchi Zenjirō in Dairen; Hirano Shigeru, Daimoto Masashige, and Shuzui Hajime in Hsinking; Ishida Seiichi in Peking; one person in Fengtien; and Miwa Takeshi from the battlefield. Also, a number of men arrested earlier in the Cooperative Association Incident and the *Manshū hyōron* case—including Suzuki Kohei, Satō Daishirō, Hanabusa Shigeru, Satō Haruo, and Tanaka Takeo—were now implicated in the SMR Incident, but no one else was arrested. Nearly one hundred people were interrogated for involvement in the case and were purged from the Research Department into another department. In short, this was the SMR Incident. With almost one hundred research staff arrested or interrogated, the Enlarged Research Department was undermined and ultimately exhausted. Those involved were not arrested for having done anything particularly suspect, but the SMR's acquiescence in the aims of the military police ultimately served to destroy the Research Department.

Jail in Tun-hua

I was taken by the police to a military station in an extremely remote area in Chilin province known as Tun-hua. We were held in different places all over Manchuria, but since there was some indication that I was someone of importance, I was taken into the hinterland. My friend since our days in the Shinjinkai, Tanaka Kyūichi, was held in Dairen. Perhaps they decided these things by the respective conditions of our health.

The detention room of the military police in Tun-hua was in an old-fashioned jail, a solitary cell with thick wood lattice. Near the ceiling inside was one small window. Even at noon the room was dark, which made reading impossible. Outside remained invisible. Over the wooden floor were strewn three blankets. There were apparently five or six other cells, and I learned several days later that Hirano Shigeru was being held in one of them. Anti-Japanese guerrillas were very active in the Tun-hua region of Chilin until the end of the war, and among the Chinese prisoners were a number of peasants who were said to have had contacts with Communist guerrillas. I could hear their screams and the cracks of the whip as the military police tortured them for about an hour every single night.

I, however, was never tortured, nor did I undergo any harsh interrogation. I just had to squat in my cell. Once, after his interrogations were over, a provost sergeant in the military police paid me a visit by himself that I still remember. He led me to the interrogation room and told me to write down why I had been arrested. Essentially, I was forced to write a memo. I simply wrote that I felt strange being arrested in view of my enormous cooperation with the military. He seemed not to know what it was that I should be made to confess to.

From the start it was unclear where the military police of the Kwantung Army were heading. I later heard that the public prosecutor's office in Tokyo had unraveled the Ozaki Hotsumi case and had landed the Nakanishi affair as well. This was the territory of the military police because both were considered spy cases, but they seemed to have been outmaneuvered by the prosecutor's office. The SMR fell within the jurisdiction of the military police, and their territory had been trespassed on. Since there were many left-wing remnants in the Research Department of the SMR, the military police probably thought that if they investigated, something was bound to turn up. While the public prosecutor's office in Japan remained uninvolved, the military police rushed in to take over and grab all the credit for themselves.

The police apparently thought that they might get something out of those arrested in the first crackdown through beatings. But there were no central figures or leaders in that first group. In the second round of arrests, Tanaka Kyūichi and I were brought in as suspects because of our backgrounds in the Shinjinkai. Members of the left-wing intellectual movement, anticipating defeat for Japan in the war, were meeting within the Research Department, and it seemed to the military police that Tanaka and I were their ring-leaders. So they apparently fastened onto us and tried to concoct an incident. Among those arrested, Tanaka and I had held the highest positions in the Research Department, and we had both been active in the Shinjinkai. Also, I had been in charge of the journal *Pekin Mantetsu geppō* when it was seized in the Soviet Embassy at the time of Li Ta-chao's arrest. Because of the problems relating to the reorganization schemes for the SMR, I had long been under watch by the Kwantung Army. At that time I was serving as director of the employees' association and had opposed the Kwantung Army, as I described earlier. From that time there was evidence that the military police had been carrying out a thorough investigation by shadowing me in an effort to turn up my contacts. But the whole thing was for nought. They probably were waiting for an opportunity to take their revenge on me. My record since the Shinjinkai days was spotless. I was surrounded by left-wing researchers, and I think I was arrested because the police thought that if such people were meeting, I had to be their boss. What else could it have been? Because, actually, I had been very cooperative with the military.

I was questioned just once and induced into making a confession. The police told me something to the effect that I had made grievous errors in one section of an article I wrote for a journal. But it was so silly that I can't for the life of me remember what those "errors" were.

Tun-hua was in Manchuria and the climate was terrible, but I was there from summer through fall, so I did not suffer too much. Also, because I had committed an offense of dangerous thoughts, some of the police actually treated me with a kind of respect. This was, needless to say, not at all the case for the Chinese political prisoners.

Dietary conditions in Manchuria were rather good even late in the war. In Tun-hua we were given boiled rice and on occasion noodles. Although this was not nutritionally sufficient, the policeman in charge there was rather polite. Once during a walk, he took me to a vegetable garden in the military police compound, cut up a tomato, and gave me some of it to eat. In our detention cells, we were given a variety of things, including sweets. As far as they were concerned, they probably did not know what I had done to be arrested, but they did know my former position in the SMR, and they recognized that I had not committed some nefarious crime. So I was treated fairly well.

Prison in Fengtien

I was in Tun-hua for about six months before being transferred to the Manchukuo prison in Fengtien. That was in the wintertime prior to New Year's. This prison was entirely for Chinese. It was boasted of as the newest, most civilized prison in Manchuria. The cell in which I was held had a wooden floor about six feet by nine feet. Originally a solitary cell, five people were now crammed into it, so that nocturnal tossing and turning was impossible. Each of us was supposed to have an individual cell, but either there were not enough of them or they had some other reason for crowding us in, in view of the fact that we were frequently so poorly treated. On the first night of imprisonment, they made me exchange the clothes I had been wearing for prison khakis—I was being treated as if I had already been convicted.

Among the people in prison with me was a Japanese (a former SMR employee who had stolen some goods), a Korean morphine dealer, and an assortment of petty thieves. I had been all alone in Tun-hua, but in Fengtien the place was bustling with people. I chatted with these extremely interesting people all the time. In their eyes I was some sort of professor, so they treated me with respect. A prison guard in charge of watching us even asked me to help him get a better job.

The Korean morphine dealer was a cheerful fellow with enormous vitality. He had completely bought off the prison guards, and gradually more and more things were sent to us in prison. For example, since we were prisoners awaiting trials, we were held in a place where bedding was provided. On the pretext of having to resew the bedding he was given, the Korean had his bedding sent out and brought back once a week. All sorts of things would be crammed into it when it was brought back to him. Ordinarily these things would have been easily discernible, and they would have been confiscated, but since he had already greased the guards' palms, nothing was said.

During winter in the Fengtien prison there were specific hours of steam heat. Often it broke down and wouldn't work from five in the afternoon on. It was not rare for the temperature to plummet to -20C. or -30C., so the Korean had a pair of snow boots smuggled in, with tobacco and rice cakes stuffed inside them. When contraband arrived, the Korean would always come and offer me something first. Our prison food was sorghum—last year's sorghum which reeked—so my Korean friend's "flow of contraband" was welcome indeed. When I was transferred to the Fengtien prison, the food situation in Manchuria had become more and more strained. Aside from the cold, though, my life in prison was relatively comfortable.

Although I was never tortured, I did endure one painful experience. One day we were having a physical examination, and we were all standing next to one another in the medical office completely naked. Our "doctor," I later heard, was actually a veterinarian. Real doctors had been sent to the front lines, so prisons could only hang onto "doctors" of this sort. When I was standing before him, I had no particular reason to be embarrassed nor to show him a smiling face. I didn't smile, but it must have seemed to him as though I did. He became enraged: "Why are you laughing at me? It's rude to laugh!" he said. He then took a leather belt from his waist and flailed me with it. There was nothing I could do but remain there and be beaten. "What nerve!" he yelled. He put some water in a wash basin, but rather than pour the whole thing on my head all at once, he let it pour very slowly. The room was already several degrees below freezing, so my body became increasingly chilled. As I recall, this went on for some time until I was chilled to the bone, but I didn't say a thing. Such was my lone encounter with "torture" of a sort.

One time when I was in the Fengtien prison I had to appear at the Manchukuo court for an interrogation. Although our case had initially been handled by the military police, the suspicion of spying activities was unclear, and I was eventually taken to the Manchukuo prosecutor's office. We went to the courthouse, but there was no interrogation, so it was more of an annoyance. They handcuffed me, stuck a braided hat on my head, and marched me through the streets, which seemed to be the main aim of this whole business. In any case, they took all of us out in a truck, but they could only question a few of us that day. The majority just returned. We were able to talk freely on the truck and exchange things to eat. For the first time since my arrest, I met the faces of others implicated in the SMR Incident.

All sorts of stories came out aboard that truck, such as news of others arrested at the same time and changes in the case, but I never heard a story of torture. Of those arrested in the SMR Incident, the five men who died in prison—Nishi Masao, Ōgami Suehiro, Hotchi Zenjirō, Satō Haruo, and Shuzui Hajime—all died of typhoid fever, not from being tortured. Since we were still not allowed to bring things into the Fengtien prison from outside, my eating habits avoided the worst thanks to the Korean morphine dealer, but the others often made do with sorghum in salt water. Malnutrition and typhoid fever became severe, and some did die.

Four or five people were placed in detention cells originally built for one. We were at that time held together with Koreans (who were Japanese nationals), but while they were apparently invulnerable to lice, I went on a wholehearted crusade of extermination. They were all fine, so they didn't bother killing the lice. Meanwhile the lice propagated, and every day there were deaths from typhoid fever. Most confusing of all was the fact we had surrendered to the prison everything we owned, which was placed in a pan of boiling water for sterilization. We were walked through the halls stark naked, and they arranged for us to wash in baths of steaming hot water, but all with no effect. The middle-aged, they said, contracted typhoid fever even more easily than the young. But being held in such a prison as ours was hard on the lives of the young too. Older people naturally knew how to take care of themselves; they were more proficient at life itself. This is apparently the reason there were unexpectedly few deaths among the older people.

Arrested for Suspicion of a Scientific Approach

New Year's of My Fiftieth Year

Greeting New Year's of my fiftieth year in a prison cell in Fengtien caused me considerable sentimentality. I was thinner, but I felt healthy overall. It felt wonderful as I stretched my arms through the iron grating into the frigid air of –30C. and swam with my arms in the rays of the New Year's sun. Having concluded the first half of my life through my forty-ninth year in prison, I was reminded of the great Watanabe Kazan, who came from the same area of Japan as I and who passed away in his forty-ninth year. I was full of emotion, wondering what lay in store for me in the latter half of life from the age of fifty on.

Before the previous year was out, or perhaps it was after New Year's, I received permission for the first time to see my family, and my wife came to visit. As we spoke for ten or fifteen minutes through an iron mesh screen in the presence of a prison guard, I remembered thinking that I was being treated like a full-fledged criminal. My wife later told me that my shaggy unkempt hair left her with an impression of unrelenting pity. I had intended to be as strong as I could, but I was overcome by my circumstances. I also learned later that, unbeknownst to me at the time, another visitor before my wife had come once or twice to inquire about me and peered in at me from outside my cell. He told her that I just sat there all day and never relaxed. The prison guards said I had assumed the bearing of an old samurai, and since my wife had heard this she felt even greater sorrow for the unexpectedly haggard figure she confronted that day in the prison.

Released

In March there was another transfer from the detention center, this time to a prison in Hsinking (present day Ch'ang-ch'un). March in Ch'ang-ch'un is still 100 percent winter. The bumpy road we traveled in the horse-drawn carriage from the station to the prison outside the center of town was snowbound, and I remember feeling as though spring was still far away.

Here I was thrown into a cell all by myself, about nine feet by twelve feet, almost too expansive. A bright electric light shone radiantly from the ceiling. I wondered at first whether someone was waging some sort of war of nerves with me. Eventually I made out that my compatriots were in cells in front and next to mine. Ōgami Suehiro lay here on his death bed at this time. Several days later his young life came to an end, and his wife rushed to him from Kyoto. This can only be called a great tragedy. His final sorrow was the destruction of a beautiful, peaceful flow-er garden by which he had been living—the stable life of a university professor that he had enjoyed was his ideal—trampled over by one of the military policemen in full footgear. Hotchi Zenjirō passed away in his cell in Fengtien. Nishi Masao, who had in Shanghai unassumingly carried on his studies of Islam, was arrested for no reason, and he died in prison. These were the effects of the cruel atrocities committed by the military police.

For the first time I was allowed in Hsinking to bring in food and reading material, although the *Shih-ching* (Classic of Poetry) kindly sent by Suzue Gen'ichi did not reach me until I was released.

The people arrested in the SMR Incident were not kept in the same cells. During exercises outside the cells, though, we wrestled together, and we were together when we deposited the contents of our chamber pots outdoors. From these contacts I gradually learned of the fate of my friends, in general terms how prison life had been for those involved in the case, and the state of progress in the interrogations. On the basis of this information, it seemed to me that the military police who had arrested us were extremely embarrassed. Having now apprehended us, they had gone too far to retreat without doing something. Clear evidence was needed to concoct a spy case. If they changed this to an ideological problem, then it was considerably easier to make the story hang together. They passed the case to the public prosecutor, supplied a synopsis of their story that we were planning to use the activities going on at the Research Department of the SMR for some future revolution, and tried to pin this tale on those of us who had been arrested.

Although no physical torture was used on us when the outlines of this story appeared, all sorts of psychological pressures were applied, and we were enticed into voluntary confessions along their lines. There were those who stubbornly held out, but many groundless claims were also made. These false statements caused us considerable trouble.

Finally they decided on the charges against us, and in the fall of 1944 twenty-one of us were indicted, with the others receiving a stay of prosecution. The presiding judge was Iimori Shigetō of the Manchukuo court (at present a judge in the Tokyo district court), the younger brother of Tanaka Kōtarō, former chief justice of the Supreme Court. The verdict was handed down in May 1945. Watanabe Yūji and Matsuoka Mizuo received the longest terms: five years of penal servitude. Two men received three-year terms, and the rest received one-year suspended sentences.

Iimori Shigetō of the court of Manchukuo read the verdict, but he was no more than a marionette; the military police were pulling all the strings behind the indictment and the verdict. The guilty verdict was probably an indication that the court was under military police pressure. When Manchukuo collapsed, Iimori was taken off to the Soviet Union as a war criminal and later delivered over to the Chinese. I believe he was charged with responsibility for complicity in the fabrication of the SMR Incident. He underwent a personal conversion and issued a statement of his change of heart, but after returning to Japan he once again issued a statement of changed beliefs, and now he is well known as one of the most right-wing judges in the Tokyo district court.

In the summer of 1944, around the time of the indictment against Watanabe and others, people began to be released in dribs and drabs. After a formal inquisition by a Manchukuo judge (I forget his name) at the prison in Ch'ang-ch'un, on 27 May 1944 I was released, much to my surprise. The day after I had been wrestling with my frequent partner Horie Muraichi during exercise period outside the cells, he was freed, and the day after I was in the bath house with Matsuoka Mizuo, I was set free. The sentence was a suspension of prosecution. The ten months I had lived in detention, not knowing whether I was awaiting trial or had been convicted, finally came to an end.

I had tendered my resignation from the SMR in October 1943 during the time I was being held in Tun-hua, and I had been relieved of my position then. I was surely not going to return to work for the SMR. I now felt greatly refreshed with my new status as a "rōnin." I had never thought much about quitting, and I could not very well predict how long my life in prison would continue. It was time, I felt, to abandon the SMR.

Aimed at the Destruction of the Research Department

The majority of those persons released who had worked for the SMR had themselves transferred elsewhere. Many of the researchers who had not been arrested were reshuffled into the area of field work.

After the repression of the main research staff, the Research Department had its name changed in May 1943 to the Research Bureau, and headquarters were moved to Hsinking. Its work continued precisely the everyday business from the days of the Research Department. It could no longer carry out the kind of ambitious integrated research covering the areas of politics, the economy, and culture that had been the aim of the Enlarged Research Department, nor could it play a role for the army's General Staff in the administration of East Asia at the stage of total war. Amputated by the series of arrests of capable staff, the vitality that had dreamed up the Enlarged Research Department was thoroughly eviscerated. In the confusion over what to do, the corpse of the old Research Department continued to wriggle and greeted the fifteenth of August.

The Suppression of Science

Of the twenty-one indicted in the SMR Incident, Watanabe and Matsuoka received the longest sentences of five years in prison, but even these terms were suspended. In the final analysis the whole affair produced much ado about nothing.

The authorities treated the incident as ideological in nature, as a violation of the peace preservation law of Manchukuo, but this was simply not true about those who were arrested. As I mentioned in passing earlier, those who held power, in preparing for defeat in the war, were anticipating the postwar situation and struck first, as in the case of Tōjō's planned "arrest of fifty thousand intellectuals." Were defeat to have become a reality, people would surely concentrate their energies in that direction. Thus, some sort of action had to be considered. Those of us arrested at that time were not in that frame of mind. The prosecutor's office went to pains to resolve the case as an ideological one, but in the final analysis this was the reason they were left with no choice but to concoct such a fabrication. The major motive behind this case, I believe, was the dissolution of the Research Department. Other reasons pale by comparison.

During my time in the Fengtien and Ch'ang-ch'un prisons, as it became quiet in the evening, I used to hear voices singing the "Internationale." Anti-Japanese guerrillas had been active without stop in Manchuria since 18 September 1931, and these fighters when arrested were held in the same prisons as we were. They were a courageous group, and during exercise period they used to come together on the prison walking grounds. Although they had no expectation that it would help, they still vigorously exercised during that period. Without a trace of timidity, they spent what superficially seemed to be comfortable lives in prison. In addition, there were Korean Christians who lived in Chien-tao province at the "Korea-Manchuria" border and the eastern region of Manchuria who had been arrested and held in cells next to ours. They remained resolute in attitude and filled me with admiration. Although we were all linked by a common bond of military repression and arrest, there still remained a firm gap between them and us.

From the very beginning the military welcomed and made use of the results of our research activities, but as defeat in the war became more clearly ominous, the situation changed. They compelled intellectuals to provide all sorts of materials and to study them, but when the results of all this research pointed to defeat, it was extremely undesirable to them. Although the military realized that it would be defeated, they had to continue to fight, and to cover over this complex they abused their final authority and the Research Department of the SMR was liquidated.

The dissolution of the Research Department did not have to wait for the fifteenth of August—it had occurred in the arrests of 1942–1943. The real significance of the SMR Incident lay in *the fascist assault and repression by the military of our scientific work.*

8

Defeat and the Dissolution of the Enlarged SMR: Structure Destroyed but Personnel Remain

Defeat

To Tokyo Just Prior to Defeat in the War

I was freed on 27 May 1944. It was indeed strange to spend the next year away from the SMR, leading a rather "carefree" life in Dairen. The impasse Japan had reached in the war was pressing in on Dairen from all sides, and we soon began to see on frequent occasion the silvery wings of the B–29 planes flying leisurely high in the sky. More than a fearful sight, it was utterly spectacular. However, not a single anti-aircraft shot was fired at them, and when buildings in the city were destroyed by the one or two bombs that were dropped, people then became unnerved. That proved to be a great show of force.

In May 1945 I bid farewell to a Dairen now building shelters for air defense and training people in the use of bamboo spears, and I had no choice but to plunge into the chaos of Tokyo. Although unaffiliated with the company, I received a telegram from the Tokyo branch office through the main office in Dairen which urged me to return to the capital. They seemed to be intent on some peace move with China through plans for the establishment of a Sino-Japanese Association that would be realized by uniting all civil groups concerned with Chinese affairs. What a time for this, I thought. The government wanted to bring the war in China to an end at the earliest possible date, but despite having failed in every peace maneuver till then, they refused to learn from experience and tried once more. It was Mr. Tsuda Shizue of the navy who suggested this move for me. He must have been thinking of our links since the days of his talks with Hu O-kung in Shanghai.

For my own part, in any event, I decided to return to Tokyo because it was important for me to feel the approaching historical catastrophe directly. Realizing that I would probably not return to Dairen before the end of the war, I left word with my family and set off.

Since the sea route to Dairen had already been closed off, there was no way to return to Japan except via the the Japan Sea. So, I began by riding the SMR north and was able in Ch'ang-ch'un to meet my friends, recently freed from prison, Watanabe Yūji, Noma Kiyoshi (now professor at Aichi University), and Yokogawa Jirō (who is still living in China). Watanabe had just been drafted, and this was the last time I would see him. Later, around the fifteenth of August, he was missing in action in a battle with the Soviet Army in Hsing-an-ling, and all news from him ceased. In preparing a radio broadcast a year later, I got to know one of Watanabe's war buddies who had been with him until the last moment and had been to visit him in the city of Hikari (in Hiroshima prefecture). This fellow surmised that Watanabe probably fell from a cliff into the hands of the Soviet Army. His family suffered greatly. While he had been in prison, his wife died, and his father, who had been a town mayor during the war, was purged from his job during the Occupation after the war. Thus, Watanabe's father was unable to look after his granddaughter, who had lost both her parents, and she suffered no end until finally being adopted by a friend of his from the SMR. I believe she has now grown up and is an adult in her own right, but this was one example of the tragedies to which the war and the military police gave rise.

With the threat of American submarines, we sailed into the Japan Sea and reached land at the port of Niigata at the same time late in May that Tokyo was being dealt the final coup de grâce. All routes to Tokyo were closed off. I remained in the

North for awhile, and during that time I paid a visit with my companion Sudō Yūhei to Ishiwara Kanji who, having lost in his fight with Tōjō, was leading a secluded life in Tsuruoka. I remember him saying that the SMR Incident was a clear indication of our defeat in the war.

I gained a deep sense of the gloom of defeat after walking through a burnt out area in Tokyo. Rice had never been rationed, and people had to survive on soybean waste and raw soybeans. From the air raids some time in June, you could see in a straight line all the way from the Mamiana plateau in Azabu (Tokyo) that Kawasaki city was ablaze. I then went to my home town of Mikawa, traveling along the Tōkaidō. In Toyohashi I walked down streets still burning after a massive air attack the previous evening, and I made my way through the shells of incendiary bombs lying along the streets in bunches.

Although the smoke and fumes of the anti-aircraft guns rose up to the B–29's illuminating their silvery wings as they cut across the sky, not one anti-aircraft shot hit the mark. The "difference in scientific strength" could be hidden from no one's eyes, and after the dropping of the atomic bombs on Hiroshima and Nagasaki, we all greeted the arrival of 15 August.

The Sino-Japanese Association and the China Research Institute

I returned to Tokyo in order to participate in planning the formation of a Sino-Japanese Association. The plan was to form this organization by combining earlier groups concerned with China, but these groups each had their own histories, and the process was not necessarily going to proceed smoothly. Finally, though, under the direction of the Ministry for Greater East Asian Affairs, former Prime Minister Konoe was made president, Hosokawa Moritatsu vice-president, former Ambassador to Thailand Tsubogami chairman of the board, and I was put in charge of the General Affairs Bureau. In addition, Tsuda Shizue of the navy became head of the Advisory Bureau, which was to take administrative control over the integrated dormitory for Chinese students in Japan who had formerly been boarding at various independent dorms. Further, the board brought together executives of all the earlier groups. Thus, the new Sino-Japanese Association was formed as an immense line-up of all sorts of people "concerned with China."

In July we managed finally to have our inaugural general meeting, and President Konoe offered his salutations. Just at that time Konoe was preparing for negotiations with the Soviets to bring an end to the war. The notion that in this way we could approach the KMT in Chungking to attain peace through this Sino-Japanese Association was utterly ridiculous.

Thus, shortly after it was formed, this semigovernmental institution, the Sino-Japanese Association, went into immediate liquidation together with the end of the war, and without having done a single thing. What were we supposed to do? I argued that we should hand over our total assets to an institution concerned with Chinese issues that would be newly formed, and this view was accepted without any problem.

Iwamura Michio (formerly of the China Study Group of the Proletarian Science Research Institute), Nakanishi Tsutomu, and others planned and proposed the establishment of a China Research Institute. I became a sponsor together with Hirano Yoshitarō and Ishihama Tomoyuki, and we held an opening ceremony in the auditorium of the Asian Cultural Research Institute (an institute under the Ministry of Education, built with Boxer Indemnity funds) in the Ōtsuka section of Tokyo, the seat of the former Sino-Japanese Association. We moved forward with a program to hand over all the assets of the Sino-Japanese Association. However, the Ministry for Greater East Asian Affairs, the competent authorities in the case of the Sino-Japanese Association, and the Ministry of Foreign Affairs objected to this transfer of the total assets. In principle the liquidator's office held the real estate until a separate institute came into existence, and instead the China Research Institute was given 100,000 yen as funds for its establishment. A Sino-Japanese Study Society later emerged under the auspices of the Ministry of Foreign Affairs, and it was given the remaining assets once they had been put in order. But, as everyone knows, to this day it has not done a single thing that one can actually point to.

Final Scene of the Enlarged SMR

Whereabouts of the SMR's Research Materials

Although I no longer had any connection with the SMR, I lived as a freeloader in Tokyo at the residence of the SMR president in Mamiana. I thus witnessed the demise of the Tokyo branch office, one wing of the enlarged SMR. Compared to its initial feeling of vigor, how wretched was its collapse! What remains? What was born from this history of a generation of human suffering?

"Mr. Itō, right now the momentum of the Japanese is on the rise, but it won't last for a hundred years. This is a lesson from the history of my country." I remember Hu Shih saying this to me once in a calm tone of voice just as Japanese were raging violently through the Chi-tung area. Less than fifty years had passed since the laying of the Chinese Eastern Railway, and the history of the SMR since it had passed into Japanese hands was but forty years old.

I believe that it was in late September of that year (1945) that the SMR was designated as one of the organizations to be closed down. Although it had a fair amount of time to take care of business, communication from the Tokyo branch to the main offices in Dairen had been cut off, so neither the SMR office in Tokyo nor the Mamiana residence knew what to do about things like problems of severance pay. The sole exception to this was the revival of the Nichi-Man Warehouse at the Tōyō Pier.

I was primarily concerned with the enormous volume of research materials at the East Asian Economic Investigation Bureau at the Tokyo branch office. But, while I was hesitating to do something to protect these materials, a second generation Japanese with the American Occupation army, who had ridden on the SMR itself, arrived at the evacuation area in Fukushima and, startled by the bulk and great value of the materials, sent them hastily to the United States just as they had been packed for evacuation. He recognized the tremendous value of the Russian-language documents as well as the Japanese-language documents, principally the materials prepared by the Research Department. The collection of the East Asian Research Institute was evacuated to Nihonmatsu (Tokyo). Despite the fact that the East Asian Research Institute avoided an order to close down, its materials were sent in the same way to the United States. As chairman of the board of this institute, I applied to have them returned but was informed that their status was unclear and was ultimately compensated by the supply office in Japan.

These materials, without a doubt, are of great utility for American studies of the Far East, particularly research on Sino-Soviet relations and on Soviet policies and programs with respect to China. Though the materials for my own drafts and publications can no longer be found in Japan, they do exist in the Library of Congress in the United States.

As for the materials of the Research Department and those of the SMR's Dairen library, it is unclear just what size the collection held at the Dairen library was at the very end, but it was one of the major distinguished collections even in Japan. When the Soviet Army seized Port Arthur and Dairen, I heard that three freight cars full of documents were transported to the Soviet Union. Among them were over ten volumes of the *Yung-lo ta-tien* (Yung-lo Encyclopedia), painstakingly compiled by Mr. Matsuzaka Tsuruo, which reportedly were returned to China from the Soviet Union some time later. I believe the materials in Fengtien and Harbin had the same fate.

The materials at the Shanghai office, collected while I was head there, were considerable, and these were seized by the KMT. I have it from a reliable source that when Shanghai was liberated they were sent to Hong Kong. Perhaps these have now crossed the sea to Taiwan. I have heard nothing about what happened to the materials from the Research Division in Peking.

The facilities and papers of the Central Laboratory—the core of the SMR's natural science research—in Dairen were preserved amidst the chaos, owing to the painstaking management of Professor Marusawa Tsuneya, who was its head and a former adviser, as well as some of his staff who stayed behind in China and later were employed as consultants by the People's Republic of China. They prepared a complete list, put it in order, and, spurning the long-cherished desires of the Soviets, handed it over to the appropriate persons at the Chinese Academy of Sciences. This, I believe, was an exemplary achievement of the personal way Japanese handled matters after the end of the war. Professor Marusawa returned home to Japan after remaining in China for ten years, and he described this story in great detail in his book *Shin Chūgoku no omoide* (Memories of the New China). It is a precious chronicle in the history of Sino-Japanese relations.

The SMR Returned unto Caesar

In the journal *Shin tenchi*, published in Dairen during the Taishō period, I once wrote that the day would probably come when we would "return unto Caesar that which is Caesar's" and that such restitution would become an issue. In May 1961 I was invited to a meeting of the People's Overseas Cultural Association. It was my second trip to the new China, and I spent several days in Shen-yang (formerly, Fengtien) and An-shan. There I took a look at the traces of the dreams of the SMR.

The express train bound for Harbin left Peking station at 8:00 p.m. and arrived in Shen-yang station *just* in time, after 6:00 the next morning. I had bid my final farewell to the SMR rail lines seventeen years earlier, so this sight left me with an inestimable feeling. The morning sun glistened on the roadbed, and the sense of cleanliness at the station was stunning. I felt this sense of cleanliness again when I saw the Rail West Factory Area and when I visited a suburban commune. I had a strange feeling of self-reproach and a deep impression that this was a reborn visage of the "Chinamen" who Japanese had ridiculed as "filthy." The former waiting room for Chinese (which had been filthy) had a new sign over it reading "Waiting Room for Breast-Feeding Mothers and Their Infants." The sight of baby buggies and toys was heartening. The tram that used to run along Chiyoda Street by the station and the scene of swarming cars there had vanished, and a new trolley bus ran by. Promenade Avenue, which ran to the Northern Manchu Tombs, was now luxuriantly grown with fresh grass and trees along the roadside. The Yamato Hotel, which had been turned into a hotel for receiving foreign guests, was undergoing repairs, so we stayed at a different, eight-storey inn. The buildings of the former SMR lots remained just as in the past, but the houses were built side by side from this area all the way to the old Manchu Palace grounds. Over warlord Chang Tso-lin's old residence now hung the sign of the municipal library.

The Rail West Factory Area had swelled to ten times its former size and had become China's first machine industry town. Four-storey residential apartments for the workers stood in rows, and a savings bank and a store for the purchase of everyday necessities were situated at the appropriate places. City planning here had been splendid.

I was also overwhelmed by the "educational and cultural zone" constructed in an area linking the Northern Tombs to the South Gate of the old Manchu Palace. Schools and institutes stood side by side, and in the center the swamplands of South Lake had become a park. Also, the park at the Northern Tombs had been refurbished to accommodate as many as 500,000 people taking leisurely strolls.

I learned that after the war the An-shan Iron and Steel Works had been withdrawn and abandoned temporarily by the Soviet Army, and the Japanese technicians who remained behind predicted that it would take twenty years for it to return to its earlier working capacity. Nonetheless, ten blast furnaces were now in operation; the production lines for seamless steel tubing and the rolling mills had been strengthened; and with a work force of 100,000 it was now the centerpiece of the Chinese iron industry. Although before the war An-shan had occupied 89 percent of the pig iron and 95 percent of the steel of total Chinese production, it had now dropped 40 percent in pig iron and 50–60 percent in steel. This was a result of the fostering of three great steel foundries and their dispersed sites.

The main street of the city, Promenade Avenue, had a fragrant smell from the trees along either curb and the thick growth of lilacs along its sides. An-shan boasted that it was China's first city of cultural welfare, but my guess is that this applies to the recreational facilities including Ch'ien-shan and T'ang-kang-tzu.

Although I only had a few days to observe, I could well imagine the position that industry in the Northeast occupied in the heavy industrialization that China was undergoing. The oil liquefaction industry around Fu-shun, the automobile industry in Ch'ang-ch'un, and the chemical fertilizer and shipbuilding industries in Dairen were leading the way. In addition, the development of Harbin, Chia-mu-ssu, Chilin (the Sungari River dam is being reinforced), Liao-yang (the Rail West area is being reorganized), and Dairen was shocking to behold. When I saw the smoke emitted by the train bound for Chungking as it arrived in the Shenyang station, I felt within me that sweep of scenery of the Northeast beyond the Great Wall, merging completely into the huge system of Chinese industry and gradually increasing as its mainstay.

Despite all this activity, the city markets remained strangely quiet. The population of unemployed and semiemployed laborers had been absorbed into the suburban factories, and a process of differentiation between residential and production zones was clearly underway.

The Research Department's Personnel after Returning to Japan

The Japanese employees of the SMR during its demise numbered some 140,000. Employees at work in the Railway Department and in the coal mines might not have found it hard to gain employment back in Japan, but one can surmise that Company office workers, such as in the Research Department, may have been thrown out in the cold.

In fact, no one from the Research Department was turned adrift. All found appropriate employment beyond their expectations. Those that went into the government's planning area during the war became superb officials in the field of planning, an essential area after the war as well, and rose to the highest positions. The local self-governing bodies which had previously lacked research and planning divisions scrambled to welcome in these people from the Research Department for their research and planning divisions. Thus, these people were widely distributed into numerous self-governing bodies throughout Japan.

Previously established and newly founded university research institutes happily welcomed the former researchers as teachers, and as a result there is an extremely large number of former employees of the Research Department among university professors in Japan. Needless to say, the natural science area as well as the cultural field and particularly the field of economics contain a huge number of former SMR people. Superior staff members who had been imprisoned as leftists often became superior professors even in universities. A large number of researchers played a central role in the postwar reform parties, and their activities were heartening. The Research Department was aimed at the pursuit of scientific truth, and with certain differences of depth to their commitment, each researcher demonstrated his own capacities. In the reconstruction of Japan after the war, a firm basis in a scientific direction was perfectly natural.

When you look at all of this, you have to say how exceedingly pitiful it was that a number of exceptional researchers were sacrified to the politics of the military police or lost their lives in prison. I feel great sympathy for their descendents. Surviving the postwar turmoil without being reduced to beggary, they helped each other and have lived on till today.

I should say a word about the handful of Research Department staffers who stayed on after the end of the war and participated in the building of the People's Republic of China. After a period of five or ten years of cooperation, these people usually returned to Japan to universities or into businesses, and they contributed toward the normalization of Sino-Japanese relations. A fair number of them have stayed the entire eighteen years since the war's end and served a pivotal function between our two countries. To this day members of the Research Department are freely offering their experiences gained in the scientific pursuit of truth. Born from the complete destruction of the SMR, buds have sprouted again, and they are being nurtured by a group of people in a scientific spirit.

Creation of the Sino-Japanese Friendship Association

On 1 October 1949 the Chinese Communist Party established the People's Republic of China. Just as Suzue Gen'ichi had predicted in one of his writings, the CCP was born as it had to be, in the objective circumstances facing China then, and succeeded as it had to succeed.

The Sino-Japanese Friendship Association was created by people who accepted the fact that this new China was Japan's best companion with whom to link hands. A proposal of sorts was issued to the effect that Kazami Akira was to serve as chairman of the board of the association and I was to be managing director, but we both declined. Eventually, the association got started with Matsumoto Jiichirō as chairman and Uchiyama Kanzō as managing director. The proposal naming Kazami as chairman got so far that it was published in the *People's Daily* in Peking, but Mr. Kazami ultimately turned it down. Apparently he could not get over a feeling of personal responsibility during the war because of the fact that he had been a high official in the Konoe Cabinet. I turned down the position of managing director for the same reason, but after a year as a regular board member of the association, I breached my earlier resolve and had to take over the post from Uchiyama.

Among the business handled during my period as the managing director and later as secretary-general was the organized sending of groups to China in exchanges of friendship, such as the first scholarly cultural group (led by Abe Yoshishige), the first literary mission (led by Tanabe Hisao), and a kabuki group (led by Ichikawa Ennosuke). From the Chinese we received the first Red Cross mission (led by Li Te-ch'üan), the first scholarly mission (led by Kuo Mo-jo), the first commerce and trade mission (led by Lei Jen-min), and the first group to give a public performance of Peking opera (led by Mei Lan-fang). We took part in the first

Chinese industrial fair; we concluded the Tientsin pact on the release and acceptance of war criminals; and we concluded a second pact on their repatriation. By this last accord the Sino-Japanese Friendship Association agreed to take on the search for Chinese taken captive during the war and forcibly taken to Japan where their labor was exploited and where many died violently, their remains simply neglected. The association agreed also to arrange to have these remains sent back to China for memorial services. An executive committee to this end was immediately organized, and a first group of remains were returned to China.

On the domestic front, the premises of the Nisshinkan, a building constructed by Kai Masaji (a former SMR employee and member of the Yūhōkai), who had been an adviser during the war for the Chinese students from Shansi, was turned over to the Relief Society for Overseas Compatriots (I was its director) for Chinese returning home. When the Relief Society went into liquidation, this building was donated to the Sino-Japanese Friendship Association. Sasa Hiroo, a former member of the Social Thought Society, worked hard so that this building (which was actually Chinese property) played an important role in the work of the Friendship Association. That the Ministry of Foreign Affairs, the supervisory office of the Relief Society for Overseas Compatriots, recognized the donation of this building in the name of Yoshida Shigeru is simultaneously haphazard and very interesting.

9

Conclusion: A Statement of Introspection

I must say that I am more than a little concerned with how I should go about bringing this long story to a close. I hesitate at this point to add anything superfluous. Inasmuch as the great majority of the foregoing is a product of my memory, mistakes may abound, particularly, I fear, as concerns the personal names of individuals and conversations I had with them. Although this problem is inescapable even in careful historical investigations, I must beg the reader's forgiveness for my one-sided views. I used people's names as a way to grab hold of the stream of times and places that runs through this volume. Perhaps it is best at this point, as we come to the conclusion, to turn to my reflections, for which I can claim full responsibility.

Our defeat in the war, a major experience for our people, served as a serious turning point in the link between the Chinese and Japanese peoples. For me personally it was a milestone between the first and second halves of my life. I would like to offer a "Statement of Introspection," made public by myself and several sympathizers, in place of a conclusion.

I should first explain the process leading up to the issuance of this "Statement of Introspection." The People's Republic of China, from its founding in 1949, continually extended its hand in friendship to a Japan just defeated in war, as a part of its larger plan for peaceful coexistence. In May 1958, however, despite the signing of the fourth trade accords through private negotiations, the Kishi government ended the firm policy of separating politics and economics and, adhering to the bogus Sino-Japanese peace treaty (with the Republic of China), frankly expressed support for the Taiwan regime. It was at this time that the insult to the national flag of the People's Republic of China occurred in Nagasaki. It made me think of the repetitive history of numerous invasions that Japanese imperialism had launched on the pretext of an insult to its national flag. Since the Kishi government argued casuistically that the flag of an unrecognized state was not a national flag, the Chinese eventually returned to the wartime situation of a suspension of trade, with a stringent protest, arguing that Japan's hostile policy—a dagger in one hand and the profits from trade in the other—was intolerable (although they permitted a small quantity of trade out of humanistic considerations).

The Japanese people were shocked by this suspension of trade, and certain elements of public opinion held that the attitude of the Chinese was either obstinate or mysterious. This sort of opinion came from many people who forgot that, in spite of the Chinese position encouraging trade and offering enthusiastic friendship, Japan had not even carried out its end-of-the-war declaration and had continued to reject a revival of diplomatic relations. The Japanese government understood only superficially the true intentions of the Chinese and forgot its own status as a defeated nation with heavy responsibilities for the war; Japan further maintained the illusion that diplomatic relations could be revived without doing anything in particular. This shallow optimism was harshly criticized.

A group of us, centering around Kazami Akira, held discussions concerned with Sino-Japanese issues, and we thought it was necessary to appeal to the Japanese people that they reflect deeply on the true state of affairs. In response to the call of Ōyama Ryūko and others, four of us—Kazami Akira, Hosokawa Karoku, Nakajima Kenzō, and myself—decided to issue a "Statement of Introspection" at home and abroad. We four were strongly conscious of the fact that each of us, as individual Japanese, was assuredly not immune to personal responsibility for imperialist acts of aggression against China both before and during the war. At the same time, we recognized that in order to establish a moral solidarity as the groundwork for future Sino-Japanese relations, we Japanese had no choice but to begin to recognize that introspection and self-admonition were inescapable.

Statement of Introspection

The advice recently offered Japan by the 600,000,000 people of China has great importance not only for breaking open Sino-Japanese relations but also for the future of our people. We find, however, that the attitude of our government and of people in the private sector has tended to consider only countermeasures to the events that occur before their eyes, without any insight into the importance such advice will have in the long run. As individuals who feel a deep responsibility to face this problem, we wish to make a broad appeal that the results of this self-reflection be made known to similarly unhappy persons.

1. Friendly relations between Japan and China have developed beyond many difficulties, and one reason they now face such a serious crisis is the attitude of the Japanese government.

We cannot forget the immense pains and agonies brought on the Chinese people by invasion and war in the past. Without a profound self-reflection concerning our moral responsibility, the Japanese people can have no future growth. The Chinese people have abandoned their enmity and extended their hand to us, despite the fact that relations between our two nations remain formally in the wartime situation.

Our government, however, ignoring the will of the 600 million Chinese who are burning with a spirit stirred up by great sufferings, recognizes Chiang Kai-shek and his coterie as representatives of China, men who were exiled from the mainland and who, depending on foreign might, confine themselves in Taiwan where they are violently repressing the people. This is indeed an insult to the Chinese people. In particular, since the establishment of the Kishi Cabinet, on the one hand we have heard them speaking of the expansion of trade beyond all calculations, while on the other hand they deepen our relations with Taiwan, look with hostility on China, and move forward in conjunction with Okinawa and Korea in planning to encircle China with nuclear coercion.

One can only say that the Chinese people are indignant, and this has necessitated their switching to an inflexible stand.

2. Today the situation in the world has completely changed. The era has passed in which those people with armed force and wealth held sway and in which they could attain strength and prosperity through control over other peoples. We now live in a time in which people who *band together on moral grounds*, who concentrate their efforts on autonomy and independence, and who struggle with other people for peaceful coexistence are not only gaining international respect; they are achieving prosperity and growth. The rise of China and India as well as other nations of Asia and Africa is the new beacon for the world, the powerful bearer of mankind's peace. These nations, in the "spirit of Bandung," are building new bonds of mutual cooperation and cohesion.

At this time our government remains servile to the policies of American might, deepens its ties to Taiwan and Korea, and moves toward destroying Asian unity and along a path that can lead to war.

Insofar as we follow this path, we not only run the risk of war; the future of our nation will be in a critical position morally, politically, and economically. This should remind us that the dream of prosperity through some cunning plan or an invasion will only destroy one's own nation.

3. We must recognize *the need for deep introspection into popular attitudes*, including our own. Even if one can appreciate certain results from our good intentions, one cannot deny that Japan has sought to take advantage of the new overall situation in the world, while presuming the good will and positive intentions of China and ignoring efforts at profound moral and political reconstruction of our people. Although numerous exchanges have transpired, it was often the case that once the government interfered, we did not make an effort to press it into changing its attitude, expected the Chinese to compromise, and emerged speaking as intermediaries between the Chinese people and our own government. As a result there has been a lively exchange on the surface, but behind the words "one constituency in Asia," Japan's role grows as the base of operations for the *encirclement of China* and the fragmentation of Asia. We Japanese have created a foundation for being deluded by the deceitful expressions of the present government, such as "politics is politics and trade is trade."

Our responsibility is particularly great in that we should be leading this movement.

4. While we speak of friendly relations with China and Asia and of economic exchange, policies that deepen our ties with states such as Taiwan are impossible. If we are to seek friendship with China and peace in Asia, we must work to sever our ties with Taiwan, which regards China with hostility and threatens Asia.

It is a misguided illusion to try and take advantage of the new situation in the world through cunning means, forsaking our own rebuilding, with a notion of oppressing other nations and seeking profit from them by means of force.

We must put our energies into domestic political and moral recontruction. To seek peace and prosperity, it is most important that we dispense with mean ambition and rise up from the depths of deep personal reflection. Sino-Japanese relations will unfold, and the future of our people will open brightly once our efforts and movements in all fields have been penetrated by this basic introspection and moved toward a great unity.

14 July 1958
Kazami Akira
Hosokawa Karoku
Nakajima Kenzō
Itō Takeo

By the time this statement appeared, we had worked hard to enlist the support of public organizations and to get as many names of well-known people as we could, but we settled for these four. Once again we realized just how difficult it was to gain a thorough awareness of responsibility in the war.

The statement was formally distributed to the press, but aside from the Kyōdō News Agency, all the major newspapers ignored it. Oddly enough, the Hsin-hua News Agency in China carried it, and the *People's Daily* in Peking gave it considerable play, which made its treatment in Japan appear even more surprising. The *People's Daily* carried the entire text of the statement a second time that October when a mission led by Kazami Akira was visiting Peking.

Thus, our "Statement of Introspection" ultimately had the

unlikely fate of receiving greater praise in China than at home where we had intended it. Such was the atmosphere just after its publication, but as the years passed, gradually it permeated a variety of spheres in Japan.

Years later a delegation of people in the literature field met with Deputy Prime Minister Ch'en I in Peking. When Ch'en I urged the delegation to forget the unhappy memories of the past on both sides, the delegation claimed that they would most assuredly not forget Japan's responsibility. Ch'en responded: "You say Japan would not forget. We say that we will forget. Perhaps true communication between us will be formed on this basis." I think his remarks were loaded with implications.

In September of that year, the four of us who had written the "Statement of Introspection" received invitations from the Chinese People's Institute of Foreign Affairs to visit China to attend the ceremonies in celebration of their National Day. A National Council for the Revival of Sino-Japanese Relations, headed by Kazami Akira and including Hosokawa and myself, organized a group for travel to China of ten members including Okada Haruo (a Socialist party dietman in the Lower House), Sakamoto Akira (a Socialist party dietman in the Upper House), and Sugimoto Fumio (a member of the Japan Communist Party). We went to Peking where we held wide-ranging talks with Chang Hsi-jo, head of the Institute of Foreign Affairs, concerning international affairs and Sino-Japanese relations. On the basis of these talks, we issued a declaration of resolve in the form of a joint statement, and the Institute of Foreign Affairs supported us fully.

Joint Statement of the Delegation to China of the National Council for the Revival of Sino-Japanese Relations and the Chinese People's Institute of Foreign Affairs

At the invitation of the Chinese People's Institute of Foreign Affairs, a delegation of the National Council for the Revival of Sino-Japanese Relations visited China to attend the celebration of China's National Day. The delegation was deeply moved by the pride of the Chinese, as socialist construction has accomplished in China a great leap which has surpassed imagination in all areas; and while the Chinese people are firming up their intent to defend their territory against imperialist incursions, they are uniting with the peace-loving peoples of the world to break through to a new era of peaceful coexistence.

The delegation keenly felt the need to establish a fresh and legitimate union of our two peoples on the basis of face-to-face Sino-Japanese diplomatic relations. The delegation expressed its views to this end, and the Chinese People's Institute of Foreign Affairs supported them in full.

The anti-imperialist struggle of both the Chinese and the Japanese peoples is the basis for the unity of our two nations. Our delegation expresses its deepest regret to the Chinese people that the Japanese were unable to prevent the invasion and war brought on the Chinese by Japanese imperialism. We resolutely oppose the present Kishi government's following along with American imperialism, its hostile posture with respect to the Chinese people, and its movement along the path toward the revival of imperialism.

The struggle to oppose colonialism and protect peace, which the peoples of Asia and Africa are at present carrying out in the spirit of Bandung, and the support of the socialist nations in this effort will destroy imperialist ambitions that seek to incite war and repress the freedom of these peoples. This struggle propels the tasks of the liberation of the peoples of the world and carves out a new age in which a permanent international peace may be realized with freedom and equality. It will fight the reactionary policies of American imperialism and the Kishi Cabinet, and it will fight to win the independence of a democratic Japan and our peaceful coexistence with the peoples of Asia. This is the only route that can guarantee the prosperity of the Japanese people living in this new age. The solidarity of the Chinese and Japanese peoples, which will be built upon such efforts by the Japanese people, will not only contribute to the normalization of relations between our two nations. It is a contribution to Asian and even world peace.

In taking this position, this delegation has discussed with the Chinese People's Institute of Foreign Affairs the situation concerning the Taiwan Straits and various problems facing both China and Japan. We are completely in agreement on the following points.

1. The war crisis surrounding the Taiwan Straits at present is due entirely to the aggressive, instigatory actions of American imperialism. America has bound its massive military strength to the

territory of Taiwan, linked up with Chiang Kai-shek and his followers (betrayers of the Chinese people), occupied Taiwan and the
P'eng-hu Islands, China's inseparable territory, sought to expand
further its sphere of aggression to such offshore islands as Quemoy
and Matsu, and effected military incitement against the People's
Republic of China. The liberation of Taiwan, the P'eng-hu Islands,
Quemoy, and Matsu is entirely a domestic political issue for China,
and the Chinese people have the right to liberate them freely without the intervention of other countries. America's attempt to main-
tain the present state in these regions and the effort to bring the
question of jurisdiction over Taiwan and these other islands to the
United Nations constitute an infringement of China's territorial
integrity and sovereignty. These are actions in violation of the United Nations Charter. The plan to make Taiwan "independent" or to
place it under the trusteeship of the United Nations and the design
to annex Taiwan as a part of Japan are both vain efforts to turn back
the wheels of history.

Our delegation supports completely the just struggle of the Chinese people, and we call for the immediate withdrawal of American
troops from Taiwan and the Taiwan Straits.

2. American bases in Okinawa and elsewhere in Japan are being
used for bellicose activities by the United States against China. The
Kishi government simply follows America's warlike policies, pushes
ahead with the nuclear arming of Japan, an ever more blatant policy
of hostility toward China, and aims at destroying Asian unity by
aligning with decadent forces in Asia—Chiang Kai-shek and Syngman Rhee—in an attempt to forge an anti-Communist military alliance.

In view of the fact that the American bases stationed in Japan are
not only violations of Japanese sovereignty and a repression of the
Japanese people but also the root of a threat to Asian peace, this
delegation calls for the abrogation of the U.S.-Japan Security Treaty and the withdrawal of American troops from Japanese soil, including Okinawa. Furthermore, this delegation calls for the immediate abrogation of the "Sino-Japanese Treaty," which links Japan
with the traitors of China, the Chiang Kai-shek regime, which is the
immediate hindrance to the normalization of diplomatic relations
between China and Japan.

The Chinese People's Institute of Foreign Affairs supports in full
the struggle of the Japanese people for independence and peace.

3. Threatening the peace not only of Asia but of the entire world, *American imperialism is the common enemy of the Chinese and the Japanese peoples.* The struggle of the Chinese people to liberate Taiwan is in the interest of the Japanese people, and the struggle of the Japanese people for independence and peace is in the interest of the Chinese people. The Chinese and Japanese peoples must strengthen their mutual support in opposition to imperialism. We must eliminate all artificial impediments, resolutely oppose the stratagem of "two Chinas," strengthen friendship and cooperation, and firmly support the revival of diplomatic relations between Japan and the People's Republic of China.

At present the might of imperialism is speeding toward its own ruin. Compelled to retreat step by step because of the united force of the peace-loving nations and peoples of the world, American imperialism stands completely alone. The determined struggle of the Chinese and Japanese peoples will be victorious.

11 October 1958
Delegation to China of the National Council for
the Revival of Sino-Japanese Relations
Chinese People's Institute of Foreign Affairs

A delegation of the Socialist Party led by Secretary-General Asanuma Inejirō went to China the following year. Under the name of the "Asanuma Statement," this delegation issued a declaration that followed the main points of our joint statement in 1958.

Postscript

All was gloomy in Asia in the decade or more after these memoirs were first published in the autumn of 1964. The revision of the U.S.-Japan Security Treaty and the opposition to it, the Vietnam invasion and war, the Great Proletarian Cultural Revolution, and the defeat of American imperialism in Asia all preceded President Nixon's visit to China. In September 1972 Tanaka Kakuei, prime minister of Japan, issued a joint statement together with Chairman Mao Tse-tung and Premier Chou En-lai on the revival of Sino-Japanese relations. The hallmark of this statement, the

wording "we have caused you troubles," reflected deep introspection on the part of the Japanese. This introspection indicated
a decisive stand to abandon derisive ideas about the Chinese that
had been current in Japan since 1895; and the Japanese people
commenced a new era, freed of this contempt. Over the next six
years from 1972, the Ōhira Cabinet signed a peace and friendship
treaty, focused on the item of antihegemonism, and this brought
to a conclusion our statement on introspection.

Two of my collaborators, Kazami Akira and Hosokawa Karoku,
died without having witnessed this glorious event. My two
friends Suda Teiichi and Nakajima Kenzō, both firm supporters
and expounders of the statement of introspection, are no longer
alive. Although I feel unbearably lonely, a stability unprecedented in this century can now be expected for the future of Asia.
While descendants of the Chinese and Japanese peoples will enjoy the blessings of history, they will spiritedly pose new chal-
lenges in the tasks facing the new century to come.

20 March 1982

Addendum to the New Edition

Twenty years have now passed since the first edition of my book
appeared in 1964. The transition from the 1960s into the 1980s has
seen major changes in world history. The defeat of American
imperialism's encirclement of Asia provided an impetus for the
advance of the Soviets into Vietnam and encouraged the stagnant
Japanese government to press with a treaty of peace and friendship with China. Now that the Cultural Revolution has failed,
China has opened up economic construction, and science, technology, and the capitalist managerial system have been included in
China's study program. The U.S.-Japan security structure has
expanded its depth toward a more equitable system from its
earlier hierarchical structure for developing the Japanese economy.

The year 1982, when the first printing of the new edition of this
book appeared, corresponded with the tenth anniversary of the
Sino-Japanese joint communique. Conclusion of the peace treaty

on antihegemonism by the Ōhira Cabinet carried through the spirit of introspection. However, that "sleeve of a suit of armor that cannot be hidden" has hauntingly flickered again in the recent textbook case and the war orphans issue.

Last winter my friends invited me to participate in a three-man panel discussion (with my former classmates Okazaki Kaheita and Matsumoto Shigeharu), and it was recorded and published as *Warera no shōgai ni okeru Chūgoku* (China in Our Careers)—a sixty-year retrospective. In that discussion what I wanted to advocate was that we release ourselves, through adherence to the spirit of introspection, from our past filled with contempt for other peoples, difficult as it is to eradicate, and call for cooperation in Asia toward the establishment of a new era. This was the reason I put my personal feelings aside and explained again the "seeking truth through facts" in our four-man statement of 1958, which was quoted in this book. Although the two editor-collaborators on this book (Sakatani Yoshinao and Tai Kuo-hui) as well as the great majority of reviewers of the book did not lay particularly great emphasis on this point, for me it was absolutely essential.

I believe that this point—the elimination of our contempt for other peoples and cooperation between Asian nations—will be vital in the basic directions toward which Asia will head in the twenty-first century (and which I will not witness). It is the essence of national ethics. In particular, although the Japanese people under the capitalist system can hardly recognize this point as a condition for cooperation, this is the key point to which all people must direct their attention. And even if "mutual trust" between our two peoples (Mr. Nakasone's idea, apparently) is advocated, failure to rely upon this condition will mean that this "mutual trust" will without a doubt be eviscerated. If we confront the risks of nuclear war in the twenty-first century, bearing in mind a firm belief in the everlasting friendship between the descendents of our two nations, this humility I am calling for will, needless to say, be a necessary and logical precondition.

15 May 1984

Index

Abe Makoto, 134
Abe Yoshishige, 214
Administrative Bureau (SMR), 98
Agricultural Experiment Stations, 15, 16, 27
Aichi University, 205
Akamatsu Katsumaro, 37
All-China Student Alliance, 92, 97
Alliance of Workers' Corps, 78
Amakai Kenzaburō, 19
Amakasu Masahiko, 42, 139
Amano Motonosuke, *xxvii*, 104, 112, 180
Andō Jirō, 173
An-shan, 27, 131, 210, 211, 212
An-shan Iron Works, 27, 118, 124, 130, 211
An-tung, 128
Anzai Kuraji, *xxii*, 180, 188
Aoki Residence, 62, 115
Arai Shizuo, 136
Araki Akira, 136
Arao Sei, 106, 142
Ariga Nagao, 64
Asahi Glass Company, 26
Asahi shimbun, 46, 62, 75, 129, 186, 187
Asanuma Inejirō, 224
Asia Development Board, 174, 185, 191
Asiatic mode of production, 112
Asō Hisashi, 37, 45
Audit Department (Manchukuo), 50
Aufzeichnungen eines chinesischen Revolutionärs, 104
Ayukawa Yoshisuke, 126, 131, 146

Bandung, 219, 222

Banzai Residence, 62, 115
Baumfeld, 25
Behrendt, 25
Belgium, 77
Berkeley, 100
Berlin, 24, 45
Boxer Indemnity, 113–14
Buck, John Lossing, *xv*
Bunsō teki bubi (military preparedness in civil garb), *viii, ix*

Canton, *xvii, xx*, 72–74, 92–93, 181
Capital, xiv, 67, 70
Celebes, 191, 192
Central China Hydroelectric, 169
Central China Promotion Corporation, 169
Central China Railway, 169
Central Laboratory, *viii*, 13, 14, 15, 16, 25, 26, 27, 171, 209
Chang Chien, 143
Chang Hsüeh-liang, 122, 123, 138
Chang Tso-lin: described, 54–55; murder of, 42, 121, 133, 136, 137; and Peking Raid, 82, 100–101; and railways, 98; revolt against, 90–91
Chang-chia-k'ou, *xxi*, 29, 31, 32
Ch'ang-ch'un, 27, 129, 130, 158, 201, 203, 205, 212. *See also* Hsinking
Ch'ang-hsin-tien Railway Factory, 75
Ch'en Ch'i-hsiu, 71
Ch'en Han-sheng, 110, 187
Ch'en I, 221
Ch'eng Heng, 69
Cheng Hsiao-hsü, 141
Cheng-chia-ch'un, 27, 56

Cheng-chih sheng-huo (Political Life), 70, 97
Cheng-chou, 75, 78
Chi Shih (Hsü Shou-ch'ang), 86
Chia-mu-ssu, 212
Chiang Hai-shih, 78, 101
Chiang Kai-shek, 81, 82; assumes power, 96; and *Chung-shan* incident, 94–95, 96; and Manchukuo, 146; resistance to, *xx*; and Sian incident, 166; Shanghai coup of, 92, 94, 101, 102; on Taiwan, 218, 223; and Wang Ching-wei, 182
Chiao-min-hsiang, 62
Chiao-t'ung University, 76
Chichihar, 56, 116
Ch'ien-shan, 212
Chien-tao, 203
Chihli, 78, 87, 91
Chilin, 32, 50, 56, 87, 116, 193, 212
China Army (Japan), 161–62, 167
China Issue Institute, 164
China Research Institute, 207
China Study Group, 207
China Today, 102
Chinan Incident, 165, 166
Chin-chou, *xxii*, 90
Chinese Academy of Sciences, 84, 210
Chinese Communist Party, 70, 96, 103, 214; beginnings of, 30, 63, 72, 110; documents on, 111; and Japan, 105, 176; and Kuomintang, *xix*, *xx*, 94–95, 166, 183–84; and labor, 74; and Nakanishi, *xviii*, 177; New Fourth Army, 178; Peking raid, 82; Second Congress, 88; in Shanghai, 183; suppressed, 102; and student movement, 98
Chinese Eastern Railway, 5, 6, 7, 10, 13, 53, 116, 133, 160, 168, 208
Chinese Labor Union, 74
Chinese People's Institute of Foreign Affairs, 224
Chinese Students Association, 91
Ch'in-huang-tao, 90
Chin-p'u, 73
Ch'i-shan Cement Factory, 76
Chi-tung (Kitō), *xiv*, *xvii*, *xviii*, 162, 165, 166, 208

Chi-tung Anti-Communist Autonomous Government, 163
Chōsa jihō (Research Review), 80
Chōshuntei, 64
Chou En-lai, 167, 224
Chou Fu-hai, 183
Chou Shu-jen, 86
Chu Tsao-wu, 86
Ch'uan Li-yü, 89
Ch'ü-fu, 29, 31
Chūgoku kodai seiji shisō (Ancient Chinese Political Thought), 111
Chūgoku musan kaikyū undō shi (History of the Chinese Proletarian Movement), 70
Chūgoku ni okeru gaikoku tōshi (Foreign Investment in China), 181
Chungking, 113, 176, 177, 182, 183, 184, 207, 212
Chung-kuo ch'an-yeh ko-ming shih (A History of the Chinese Industrial Revolution), 104
Chung-shan incident, 94, 96, 101
Chung-tung, 32
Columbia University, 43, 103
Comintern, 72
Commercial Affairs Department, 130
Communications Clique, 61, 63
Communist Manifesto, 93
Concordia Society, 12, 119, 138, 148, 149, 150, 189
Consultant Desks, China Army, 161–62
Control Department, 142, 143
Cooperative Association (Gassakusha) Incident, 188, 189, 192
Cordier, Henri, 84
Council of Japanese Labor Unions, 88
Crédit Lyonnais, 24
Cultural Revolution, 224, 225

Dai Ajia (Great Asia), 148
Daidō denryoku, 167
Daihōkai (Society of the Great Country), 140
Daimoto Masashige, 192
Dairen, 183, 210; arrests in, 189, 190,

191, 193; contraband trade, 165; convention, 136; coolies, 47, 77; Kempeitai in, *xxii*, Kuchida Yasunobu in, 145; library, 54, 209; postwar development, 212; Shimano Saburō in, 57; SMR research office, *viii*, *xvii*, 16, 46, 48–49, 54, 56, 118, 174; Tachibani Shiraki in, 110–11, 118–19, 188; transfer to, 45, 189–90, 191, 192; visit to, 29, 31, 32, 90; wartime, 204, 208
Dairen Steamship Company, 180
Daitō gappō ron (On the Confederation of the Great East), 107
Daiyūhōkai (Majestic Peak Society) (*See* Yūhōkai)
Das erwachende Chinas: ein Abriss der Geschichte und der gegenwärtigen Probleme Chinas, 104
Demokurashii (Democracy), 38
Dōhō (Brethren), 38
Doihara Kenji, 33
Dokushokai zasshi (Magazine of the Readers' Association), 127
Dōshisha University, 45, 68
Duara, Prasenjit, *xvii*

East Asia Colonial Company, 149
East Asia Section, 117, 182
East Asian Common Culture Academy, *xvii*, 39, 49, 52, 106, 187, 188
East Asian Economic Investigation Bureau (EEB): established, *viii*, 16, 23–24; expansion, *x*; foreigners in, 23–25; Ishikawa in, 48, 50; Itō's role in, 46, 155–56; Kasagi in, 11, 139–40; Komai in, 143; Kuchida in, 145; managerial role of, 44; Ōkawa in, *xi*; research materials, 208–209; staff of, 37, 39, 43, 57; strife in, 155–56
East Asian Institute, Columbia University, 103
East Asian Research Institute, 181, 190, 209
East Asian Society of Young Lay Buddhists, 140
East India Company, 10
Economic Research Association

(ERA): agricultural studies, *xiii*, *xiv*, *xv*, 163; and Consultant Desks, 161, 162; decline of, 158, 159; established, *xii-xiii*, 151–53; expansion of, 156; Itō's role in, 159, 160, 163–64; and Kwantung Army, *xiii*, 152, 153, 154, 156–57; Miyazaki in, 154, 156, 157; Ōgami in, *xiii-xiv*; reorganized, 158, 170–71; research and planning, 153, 158; role of, 156–57; Sōgō in, 161; staff, 154–55
Edayoshi Isamu, 45, 156
Eguchi Teijō, *xii*, 152
Eighth Route Army, 184
Encyclopedia Sinica, 43
Endō Moritoshi, 54
Endō Ryūsaku, 151
Enlarged Research Department, 158, 170, 172, 173, 189, 202, 208
Executive Department, 49

Feng Yü-hsiang, 87, 88, 90, 91, 182
Fengtien, 50, 55, 139; arrests in, 192; fate of research materials in, 209; Japanese Army in, 56; Kempeitai in, *xxii*; and Kuo Sung-lin, 91; and labor, 77, 78; and Manchurian Incident, 149; medical college, 14; prison, 195–98, 200, 203; revolutionary movement in, 90; SMR offices in, 116
Fengtien-Chihli War, 74
Foreign Affairs Section, 41
France, 62, 65, 97, 99, 183
Fu-ch'ang Company, 47
Fujii Kōshō, 140
Fujiwara Sadamu, 173
Fukuda Tokuzō, 45
Fukunichi (*Nishi Nihon shimbun*), 62
Fukushima, 208
Funakoshi Hisao, 164
Fu-shun, 7, 26, 27, 31, 47, 77, 128, 212

Gakuren, 68, 69, 88
Gakushūin (College of Peers), 116
Gate of Heavenly Peace (T'ien-anmen), 75
Gendai Shina shakai kenkyū (A

Study of Contemporary Chinese Society), 103
General Affairs Department, 66, 123, 129, 171, 175
General Chamber of Commerce, 183
General Labor Union, 78, 93, 94
General Staff Headquarters, xx, 106, 115
Geographical Society of Tokyo, 107
Geological Research Institute, 15, 16, 26, 27, 171
Geological Section, Mining Department, 26
Germany, 17, 24, 25, 30, 44, 64, 111
Gotō Kenshō, 188
Gotō Shimpei: evaluation of, 8, 9–10, 13; governor of Taiwan, 17, 18, 24; interest in research, vii, 9–10, 16–17, 20–21, 22, 24, 51, 117, 153; and Manchurian management, 12, 13, 17, 23, 53, 58, 132, 134, 147, 153; president of SMR, 5, 6, 7–8, 28, 174, 175
Great Asian Construction Company, 148
Great Britain, 5, 10, 72, 77, 89–91, 93, 144, 146, 183
Great Harmony Society, 148
Great Wall, 31, 163, 212
Green Gang, 183
Gushima Kenzaburō, xvi, xx, 173, 190

Hama Masao, x
Hamamatsu, 68
Hamburg, 24
Han Shu-yeh, 30, 31, 32, 33
Hanabusa Shigeru, 188, 192
Hanaya Tadashi, 142
Hankow, xvii, xx, 78, 180
Hara Kakuten, ix, xv, xxvii
Harbin, xxii, 18, 29, 32, 53, 54, 56, 57, 115, 116, 209, 210, 212
Harriman incident, 6–7
Hasabe, (General), 190
Hasegawa Nyozekan, 37
Hashimoto, (General), 167
Hatada Takashi, xxvii
Hatanaka Masaharu, 129
Hatano Kanae, 37, 39, 43, 45, 68

Hatano Ken'ichi, 107
Hatta Yoshiaki, 123, 156
Hayashi Daihachi, 91
Hayashi Hirotarō, 8, 123
Hayashi Kaname, 35, 39
Hazama Genzō, 190
Heilungkiang, 91
Hidaka Matsushirō, 89
Higeki no shōnin (Witness to Tragedy), 182
Hikari, 205
Hikasa Yoshitarō, 43
Himori Torao, 111
Hiradate Toshio, 173
Hirano Shigeru, 192, 193
Hirano Yoshitarō, 207
Hirashima Toshio, 137
Hiroshima, 205, 206
Hishikari Takashi, 130
Hitotsubashi University, 40
Ho-Umezu Accord, 163
Hōjō Hidekazu, 128, 171
Hong Kong, xvii, 72–74, 77, 78, 92–94, 176, 179–80, 182, 209
Hopeh, 113
Horie Muraichi, 43, 173, 175, 190, 201
Hoshijima Niro, 39
Hoshino Naoki, 151
Hosokawa Katoku, xvi, 4, 43, 104–105, 107, 173, 175, 217, 220–21, 225
Hosokawa Moritatsu, 206
Hotchi Zenjirō, 192, 198, 200
Hsiang-tao (Guide), 70, 110
Hsieh Lien-ch'ing, 69, 92, 97
Hsieh Ying-po, 74
Hsien Chen, 49, 50
Hsin ch'ing-nien (New Youth), 71, 110
Hsing-an-ling, 205
Hsin-hua News Agency, 220
Hsinking, xxii, 158–60, 169, 190, 192, 199, 200, 202. See also Ch'ang-ch'un
Hsin-min-ch'un, 56, 90
Hsiung Te-shan, 110, 187
Hsiung-yüeh, 27
Hsü Shih-ch'ang, 55
Hu O-kung, 184, 185, 205
Hu Shih, 85, 86, 208

Hu Tsung-nan, 183
Huang Chung-hui, 41
Huang Hsing, 37
Huang Jih-k'uei, 69
Huang, Philip, *xvii, xxv*
Hunan, 100
Hun-ch'un, 56
Hung-lou meng (Dream of the Red Chamber), 107
Hupeh, 100, 185
Hygiene Section, 137

Iashinov, 112
Ichikawa Ennosuke, 214
Idogaki, (Major), 163
Iimori Shigetō, 200, 201
I-lan Incident, 147
Imada Shintarō, 118, 151
Imai Yoshiyuki, 107
Inaba Shirō, 190
India, *xi*, 47, 87, 219
Industrial Department, *xv*, 153, 158, 170, 171, 172
Information Section, 111, 117, 119
Inoue Nisshō, 43
Institute of Foreign Affairs, 221, 222, 223
Institute of Pacific Relations (IPR), 111, 155
Intelligence Section, 42
Interim Industrial Research Bureau, 112
International Settlement (Shanghai), 73, 170, 180
Isaka Hideo, 19
Ishida Eiichirō, 68, 69, 88, 190
Ishida Kiyotomo, *xxiii*, 173, 192
Ishida Seiichi, 173, 192
Ishihama Tomoyuki, *xvi*, 39, 43, 45, 52, 177, 178, 207
Ishii Toshiyuki, 190
Ishikawa Masayoshi, 173, 190
Ishikawa Tetsuo, 25, 48, 51, 56, 58, 59, 60, 117, 154
Ishimoto Kenji, 66, 117
Ishimoto Shinroku, 117
Ishiwara Kanji, 118; demotion of, 165, 206; and Kasagi, 140, 142, 144; and Manchurian Incident, 149; and Miyazaki, *v*, 120, 154,

156; on North China policy, 160, 165; on SMR Incident, 206
Istanbul, 61
Itagaki Seishirō, 33, 149
Italy, 62
Itō Kōdō, 43, 173
Itō Miyoji, 46
Itō Ritsu, *xvi*, 43, 173
Iwamura Michio, 297
Izawa Michio, 170

Japan Communist Party (JCP), *xvii, xviii, xxi, xxii*, 66, 67, 221
Japan-Manchukuo Financial and Economic Research Association, 157
Japan Times, 43
Jehol, 161, 165
Jellinek, Georg, 64
Jena, Rudolph, 25
Jiji shimbun, 62
Jimbun toshokan (Humanities Library) (Peking), 114
Jinmin fuku nikki (A Diary of Serving the People), 20
Johnson, Chalmers, *x*
Jūkei senji keizai taisei ron (On the Wartime Economic Structure in Chungking), 177

Kadota Hiroshi, 37
Kagesa Sadaaki, 182
Kagoshima, 66
Kai Masaji, 141, 215
Kaieda Hisataka, 188
Kaijima, 167
Kailan, 75, 76, 77
Kainō Michitaka, 157
Kaizō (Reconstruction), 86, 103
Kaji Ryūichi, 37, 43, 45, 46, 103, 104, 156
Kakkoku musan kaikyū seitō shi (A History of Proletarian Parties in Various Countries), 105
Kamebuchi Ryūchō, 19
Kan Shu-te, 92, 95
Kanagawa, 67
Kanai Shōji, 137, 139
Kanda Masao, 107
Kaneko Sessai, 134, 139

Kano Kōkichi, 106
Kant, Immanuel, 145, 146
Kao I-han, 85
Kasagi Yoshiaki: decline of, 141, 144–45, 148; and ethnic harmony, 11–12, 144, 147; and Komai, 146–47; and Kuchida, 145–46; later career of, 148–49; leads Conscience Clique, 132; leads Yūhōkai, 135–36, 139–42, 145; and Ōkawa, 45; organizes Kōchisha, 44; SMR researcher, 180
Katakura Tadashi, 118
Katayama Sen, 67, 68
Katayama Tetsu, 37, 39
Katayama Yasuko, 68
Kawai Teikichi, 187
Kawai Yoshitora, 37
Kawakami Hajime, xiv, 45
Kawakami Kiyoshi, 43
Kawamura Chūjirō, 18, 19, 49
Kawanishi Taichirō, 35, 39
Kawasaki, 203
Kawasaki Misaburō, 173
Kawashima Naniwa, 50
Kawashima Yoshiko, 49
Kazami Akira, xx, 134, 214, 217, 220, 221, 225
Keiō University, 40
Kei-Shin nichinichi shimbun (Peking-Tientsin Daily News), 110–11, 118
Kempeitai, xxi, xxii
Kiangsi, 100
Kido Chūtarō, 27
Kido Kōin, 27
Kijima Katsumi, 154
Kimura Eiichi, 122–23
Kinney, (Bishop), 25
Kishi Nobusuke, 151, 169, 181
Kita Ikki, xi, 107, 140
Kita Shina nōgyō kankō chōsa (An Investigation of Agricultural Practices in North China), 164
Kitō chiku jūsan ken nōson jittai chōsa hōkokusho (Report on the Investigation into Village Conditions in the Thirteen Counties of Chi-tung), 163–64
Kō-A juku (Rise Asia School), 145

Kōchisha (Society to Practice the Way of Heaven on Earth), 11, 44, 140
Kodama Gentarō, 8
Koiso Kuniaki, 54
Kōkoku dōshi kai (Society for National Prosperity), 140
Kokuryūka, 35
Kokusai tsūshin, 62
Komai Tokuzō, 27, 91, 141–47, 150
Komatsu Shichirō, 188
Kōmoto Daisaku, 42, 121
Konoe Fumimaro, 167, 206, 207, 214
Koreans, 3, 4, 11, 42, 49, 196, 198
Korea, 5, 9, 22, 29, 89, 150, 151, 218–19
Koreeda Kyōji, 88
Koreyasu Masatoshi, 139
Koyama Sadatomo, 118, 119, 138, 149, 189
Kōzuma Mountains, 35
Kropotkin, Peter, 36
Krupp Company, 25
Ku Chieh-kang, 85
Kuan-ch'eng-tzu, 32
Ku-chin t'u-shu chi-ch'eng, 83
Kuchida Yasunobu, 140, 146
Kumamoto City, 197
Kung-chu-ling, 27, 55, 143
Kuo Mo-jo, 214
Kuo Sung-ling, 90, 91, 143, 163
Kuomintang (KMT), 149, 176, 209; administrative reforms, 72; alliance with CCP, xix-xx, 95, 166; in Canton, 93; conflict within, 102, 182, 183; economy of, 177; and Japanese, 73–74, 92, 95–96, 207; reorganization, 88; weakness, 146, 165–66. See also Chiang Kaishek
Kuraishi Takeshirō, 33
Kuroda Reiji, 37, 38, 44, 45
Kurohime, 35
Kwangtung, 75, 92, 95–98, 110, 180
Kwantung Army: and Chang Hsüeh-liang, 90–91; and Chang Tso-lin, 42, 121–22; and China Army, 162; cooperation with, 135–36; criticized, 113; headquarters, 55; and Ishiwara, 165; and Komai, 143,

145, 147; and Koyama, 138, 189; and Manchurian Incident, 141, 142, 144; and *Manshū hyōron*, 118; and Miyazaki, 57, 154, 157, 159; and Nakanishi, *xviii-xix, xx-xxii*; and police, 132; and Research Section, *xi, xii-xiii, xvi, xxiii*, 119–20, 123, 126, 128, 129–31, 152, 153, 155–56; scope of, 124–26; and transportation, 169

Kwantung Leased Territory, 5, 6, 55–56

Kyōdō News Agency, 46, 62, 220

Kyoto, *xxii*, 190, 199

Kyoto University, *xiii, xiv, xxii*, 18, 20, 39, 45, 49, 68, 106, 171, 190

Kyōwa (Harmony), 11

Kyōwakai. *See* Concordia Society

Kyūshū, 55

Kyūshū University, 177

Lang-fang Incident, 167

Lao-tung nien-chien (Laborers' Yearbook), 85, 104

Le Coq, A., 107

League of Nations, 145, 155

Lei Jen-min, 214

Li Te-ch'üan, 214

Li Chih-lung, 94

Li Sen, 94

Li Ta, 104

Li Ta-chao, 71, 75, 76, 78, 79, 85–88, 101, 119, 194

Liaison Section, 49

Liao Ch'eng-chih, 164

Liao-yang, 27, 212

Lin Ch'ang-min, 63, 91

Lin Hsiang-ch'ien, 78

Lin Po-ch'ü. *See* Lin Tsu-han

Lin Tsu-han, 82, 95, 96

Lin-hsi, 76

Liu Shao-ch'i, 94

Liu-t'iao-kou, 133, 134, 143, 151, 155

Local Section, 16

London, 7, 47

Lu Hsün, 86, 87

Lu Yüan-shan, 49–50

Lung-yen, 166

Lu-shan Conference, 167

Lytton Commission, 155

Ma Chan-shan, 32, 33

Mabuchi Toshio, 177, 178

Macao, 92

Ma-chia, 76

Mad'iar, Liudvig I., *xiv, xv*, 110, 113, 163, 164

Maeda Tamon, 48

Mainichi shimbun, 62

Manchukuo, 140, 202; court, 200–202; economic construction, 156–59, 171; establishment of, *xiii*, 12, 125, 137, 138–39, 141, 143–47, 160; and invasion of North China, 162, 165; leadership, 27, 42, 50, 61, 91, 132, 181; opinions on, 119; prison, 195–98; and SMR research, *xii*, 46, 112, 113, 124, 150, 151, 154, 156–59, 163, 171, 189

Manchurian Communist Party Incident, 127

Manchurian Film Company, 42

Manchurian Heavy Industry Company, 52, 146, 172–73

Manchurian Incident, 25, 53, 114, 118, 120, 146, 151; aftermath of, 46, 119, 125, 131, 133–34, 152, 153; Chinese actions in, 32–33; Kwantung Army role in, *xi*, 42, 122–23, 142, 144; and Manchurian Youth League, 136, 138, 149; reasons for, *xii*; and SMR research, 112, 117, 124, 126, 135, 154, 155, 170, 171, 189; and Yūhōkai, 141–42

Manchurian Youth League, *xii, xiii*, 124, 129, 134–35, 137–39, 141, 144, 149, 152

Man-Mō zenshō (Comprehensive Collection on Manchuria and Mongolia), 48, 50, 51, 52, 53, 56, 59, 106

Manshū hyōron (Manchurian Critique), 118, 119, 149, 188, 189, 192

Manshū jihen to Mantetsu (The Manchurian Incident and the SMR), 135

Manshū keizai nempō (The Manchurian Annual Economic Report), 112, 113

Manshū nichinichi shimbun (Manchurian Daily News), 42, 130, 192

Manshū nippō (Manchurian Daily News), 128, 129
Manshū nōgyō kikō (The Structure of Manchurian Agriculture), *xxi*
Mantetsu chōsa geppō (SMR Research Review), *xvii*, 80
Mantetsu Shina gesshi (SMR China Monthly), 81, 110, 186
Mao Tse-tung, *xx*, 163, 166, 177, 224
Marco Polo Bridge Incident, 162, 164, 167, 168, 170
Married Love (Stopes), 68
Marusawa Tsuneya, 209
Marx, Karl, 67, 109, 111
Marxism, *xiii*, *xiv*, *xv*, *xvi*, *xviii*, *xix*, *xxiii*, *xxvi*, 45, 72, 109, 110, 112, 119
Marxism Study Group, 86
Materials Section, 44
Matsu, 223
Matsukata Saburō, 45, 46, 156
Matsuki Tamotsu, 136
Matsumoto Jiichirō, 214
Matsumoto Jōji, 39
Matsumoto Shigeharu, 226
Matsuoka Mizuo, 190, 201, 202
Matsuoka Yōsuke, 11, 15, 174, 182
Matsuzaki Tsuruo, 42, 209
May Fourth Movement, 30, 38, 63, 65, 74, 75, 86, 89, 97, 104
May Thirtieth Incident, 68, 79, 81–82, 87–88, 90, 92–93, 97–98, 104
Mei Lan-fang, 214
Meiji Emperor, *xiii*
Memories of Kasagi Yoshiaki, 149
Mikawa, 206
Minami Jirō, 149, 151
Minehata Yoshimitsu, 86, 87
Ming Tombs, 31
Ministry for Greater East Asian Affairs, 206, 207
Ministry of Agriculture and Forestry, 112
Ministry of Education, 20, 86, 207
Ministry of Finance, 61, 62, 157
Ministry of Foreign Affairs, 107, 113, 115, 122, 123, 183, 207, 215
Ministry of Home Affairs, 69, 87
Ministry of the Army, 124, 160
Mitamura Shirō, 68, 88

Mitani Tōru, 82, 83
Mitsubishi Corporation, 44, 45, 62, 131, 167
Mitsui Company, 62, 74, 107, 116, 131, 167, 175
Miura Yoshitomi, 19
Miwa Jusō, 35, 38
Miwa Takeshi, 192
Miyake Mitsuharu, 152
Miyamoto Michiharu, 81, 84, 109
Miyazaki Masayoshi, *xi*, *xiii*, 57, 58, 120, 154, 156, 157, 159, 180
Miyazaki Ryūsuke, 37
Miyazaki Tōten, 37, 107, 142
Mizuno Masanao, 45, 46, 156
Mizutani Chōzaburō, 181
Mongolia, 4, 42, 134, 150; crisis in, 121, 122; Japanese advance into, 13, 165, 166; and Manchukuo, 137–38, 143; railways in, 98; research on, 23, 50, 54, 56, 106, 141, 152
Mori Mikage, 18
Mori Shigeru, 18–19
Moscow, *xi*, *xii*, 24, 57, 123
Motani Koichirō, 173
Municipal Council, 180
Musfeldt, 25
Myers, Ramon, *xvii*

Nagano prefecture, 35
Nagai Ryūtarō, 121
Nagao Sakurō, 10, 44, 45
Nagasaki, 206, 217
Naitō Konan, 106, 107
Nakae Chōmin, 64
Nakae Ushikichi, 4, 42, 64–67, 69, 70, 83, 99–100, 111, 151, 186–87
Nakajima Kenzō, 217, 220, 225
Nakajima Sōichi, 154
Nakanishi Kō. *See* Nakanishi Tsutomo
Nakanishi Toshinori, 137, 139, 140, 149
Nakanishi Tsutomu, *xvii-xxi*, *xxii*, *xxiii*, 164, 176–77, 180, 186, 188–90, 192, 194, 207
Nakano Seigō, 134
Nan-ch'ang, 102
Nanking, *xvii*, 73, 81, 98, 114, 118,

180–83, 186–87, 191
Nanking Army, *xx*, 176
Nan-t'ung. *See* T'ung-chou
Narōdo (The People), 38
National Affairs Bureau, 141, 144, 145, 147, 148
National Council, 141, 144, 145
National Council for the Revival of Sino-Japanese Relations, 221, 224
National Revolutionary Army, 91
Nationalists. *See* Kuomintang
Natural Sciences Agency, 16, 26, 27
New Culture Movement, 71
New Fourth Army, 178, 184
Nichi-Man-Shi infure chōsa (Investigation of Japanese-Manchurian-Chinese Inflation), 176, 179
Nichiman Shōji Trading Company, 180
Nichiren, 140
Nihon denryoku, 167
Niida Noboru, *xxvii*
Niigata, 205
Nikolaevsky Incident, 166
1911 Revolution, 34, 37, 55, 61, 88, 133, 134
Nippon Musical Instrument Company, 68
Nissan Corporation, 126, 146
Nishi Masao, 43, 173, 190, 198, 200
Nishi Yoshiaki, 182
Nishizato Tatsuo, *xxii*
Nis-Shin, 168
Nis-Shin bōeki kenkyūjo (Institute on Sino-Japanese Commercial Research), 106
Nisshin Kisen Lines, 74, 107
Nitobe Inazō, 48, 143
Nixon, Richard M., 224
Noda Ranzō, 82, 117, 119
Noma Kiyoshi, 182, 190, 205
Nomura Kiyoki, 19
Nonaka Tokio, 154
Nonomura Kazuo, 173, 190
North China College of Law and Government, 34
North China Daily News, 181
North China Development Corporation, 167, 168
North China Political Affairs Council, 166
North-China Standard, 63
North China Transportation, 168, 169
Northeast Communications Committee, 139
Northern Expedition, 96, 100, 104, 105, 109, 114
Nosaka Sanzō, *xxi*
Nu-li (Endeavor), 85
Numata Takezō, 128
Nung-min yüeh-k'an (Farmers' Monthly), 96

Ōba Tokio, 137, 139
Oberlin College, 66
Ōbuchi Miki, 170
Oda Yorozu, 17
Office of Administrative Affairs, 141, 145
Ōgami Suehiro, *xiii, xvi, xviii, xxi, xxii,* 119, 171–73, 180, 190, 198, 199
Ogata Taketora, 134
Ōhara Institute, 104
Ōhira Cabinet, 225, 226
Ojima Sukema, 106
Okada Haruo, 221
Okada Takema, 137
Okada Takuo, 154
Okamatsu Santarō, 17, 18, 20, 21, 24
Okamura Yasuji, 130
Okanoe Morimichi, 37, 38, 44, 45
Okata Kōhei, 186
Ōkawa Shūmei, *xi,* 10–12, 43, 45, 46, 143, 155, 156, 180
Okazaki Jirō, 173
Okazaki Kaheita, 226
Okinawa, 218, 223
Okuma, 30
Okumura Shinji, 52, 154, 171
Ōkura, 62, 167
Ōkura Kimmochi, 99
Ōkura Kōgyō, 168
On the Wartime Economic Structure in Chungking, 178
Osaka, 187
Ōsaka mainichi shimbun, 45
Oshikawa Ichirō, 171
Ōsugi Incident, 42

Ōsugi Sakae, 139
Ōta Unosuke, 186
Ōtani exploration party, 107
Ōtsuka, 207
Ōuchi Hyōe, 61
Ōuchi Ushinosuke, 17, 18
Ōya Nobuhiko, 73
Ōyama Ryūko, 217
Ōyama Incident, 167
Ozaki Hotsumi, 103; arrested, xxi, 186, 194; connections of, 175, 186–87, 192; in Shinjinkai, x; SMR consultant, xvi, xvii, 4, 43, 107, 108, 173, 179, 180, 187–88
Ozaki Shōtarō, xxii, 177, 180, 188
Ozaki Yukio, 107
Ozawa Kaisaku, 137, 149
Ozawa Seiji, 137

Pacification Desk, 178
Pak Sok-yun, 89
Paris, 24, 69
Pearl River, 73, 74
Pekin Mantetsu geppō (SMR Monthly of Peking), 80–85, 103, 108, 109, 119, 186, 194
Peking, xxi, 29, 33, 73, 74, 86, 88; described, 61–62, 210; foreigners in, 77; government, 30, 41, 115; Humanities Library, 114; Japanese in, 62–63, 64–70, 87, 118; Li Ta-chao in, 71–72, 82, 101, 119; SMR branch, 56, 59, 60–63, 71, 79–85, 103, 105, 108, 174, 190, 191, 209; student movement, 91–92, 97; visit to, 31; Wang Ching-wei in, 181–82
Peking-Hankow Railway, 15, 75, 76, 78, 87, 166
Peking Hotel, 84, 89
Peking Institute, 79, 82, 83, 84, 98
Peking Raid, 82, 100–101, 119, 194
Peking University, 68, 69, 71, 75, 82, 84, 85, 92, 97, 110
Pelliot, Paul, 107
P'eng-hu Islands, 223
People's Daily, 214, 220
Persian Gulf, 15
Planning Board, 174
Police Administration Bureau, 131, 132
Police Affairs Bureau, 55
Portsmouth Manchurian Relief Treaty, 5, 55
Pratap, Raja Mahendra, 89
Progressive Party, 63
Proletarian Scientific Institute, 109, 164, 188, 207
Public Security Committees, 139
Publication Committee for Materials on East Asia, 113
P'u-k'ou, 73

Quemoy, 223

Railway Department, 16, 42, 170
Railways Ministry, 62, 168, 169
Regional Section, 137
Relief Society for Overseas Compatriots, 215
Research Association on East Asian Issues, 187
Research Bureau for the Study of the Geography and History of Manchuria and Korea, 16, 21, 22, 23, 26
Research Committee on Chinese Customs, 113
Research Department: arrests, x, 12, 177, 189–93, 200; branches, xvii, 57, 60, 175–76; dissolution, 158, 202, 203; established, vii, xv; expansion, x, xv, 16, 49, 56, 170, 172, 173, 176; factions, 44, 46, 136; leadership, 18, 20, 44, 48, 154–56; leftists in, xvi, xxi, 12, 44, 46, 173–75, 194; and military, xii, xxii, xxiv, 54, 57, 106, 114, 116, 119–20, 157; publications, 80–81, 105, 106, 113, 187, 209; scope of, 23, 26, 48, 51–52, 58, 79, 113, 117, 176, 184, 188; staff, 4, 25, 33, 43, 49–50, 84, 111, 118–20, 145, 179–80, 212–13; studies of, xxvii
Research Materials Section, 54, 117, 119, 123
Rhee, Syngman, 223
Richtofen, 84, 113
Rise China Company, 161, 167, 168, 171

Ro-Wa jiten (Russian-Japanese Dictionary), 57
Rōnō Rokoku kenkyū sōsho (Research Series on Workers' and Peasants' Russia), 57
Roshia keizai sōsho (Series on the Russian Economy), 57
Russian Revolution, *xi*, 57
Russians, 4, 42, 49
Russell, Bertrand, 36
Russo-Japanese War, *vii*, 5, 6, 7, 8, 15, 21, 54, 132, 133

Saburi, (Minister), 114–15
Sada Kōjirō, *xii*, *xiii*, 116
Safarov, Georgii I., 104
Saigo Takamori, 54
Saionji Kimmochi, 8, 65
Saipan, 29
Sakakibara Farm, 138
Sakamoto Akira, 221
Sakatani Kiichi, 171
Sakatani Yoshinao, *xxvii*, 226
Sakura Shigeo, 45
Sakuragi Shun'ichi, 60, 73
Salvation Society, 148
Sanjūsan nen no yume (My Thirty-three Years' Dream), 37
Sano Manabu, *x*, 37, 38, 44, 45, 47, 65, 67
Sapporo School of Agriculture, 142
Sarakura Masao, *xxvi*
Sasa Hiroo, 215
Satō Daishirō, *xxi*, 188, 192
Satō Eisaku, 169
Satō Haruo, 192, 198
Satō Hiroshi, 173
Satō Teijirō, 52, 53
Satō Toshihisa, 154
Sawara Tokusuke, 43
Sendai School of Agronomy, 49
Second International, 70
Secretariat for Manchurian Affairs, *xiii*, 124, 128
Sekai jōsei bunseki (An Analysis of International Conditions), 176, 179
Seikyō jihō (Sheng-ching Times), 43
Seikyō kōsaku (Clean-up Activities), 178

Self-Governing Committees, 139
Self-Government Advisory Department, 139, 141, 142, 144, 148
Sendai, 165
Sengoku Mitsugu, 65
Senku—La Pioniro (The Pioneer), 38
Series on Social Thought, 103, 105
Seta Shōichi, 171
Sha-chi (Shakee), 93
Sha-ho-k'ou, 127
Shakai kagaku jiten (Dictionary of the Social Sciences), 110
Shakai shisō (Social Thought), 88, 92, 103, 105
Shakai shisō sha (Social Thought Society), 88
Shakai shisō sōsho (Series on Social Thought), 103, 105
Shameen, 74, 93
Shanghai, 67, 77, 109, 114; Chiang Kai-shek coup, 101, 102; CCP in, 72, 88; impressions of, 89, 183, 192; Itō in, 73, 96–97, 113, 170–85, 189–90, 191, 205; Kwangtung Army in, *xix*; labor movement, 110; May Thirtieth Incident, 82; Ōyama Incident, 167; Ozaki in, 187–88; SMR branch, *xvii*, 60, 81, 170–83, 209
Shanghai Army, 177
Shanghai Incident, 123
Shanghai Merchants' Association, 97–98
Shanhai o chūshin to suru Shina no rōdō undō (The Chinese Labor Movement, Centering in Shanghai), 110
Shan-hai Pass, 90, 163
Shansi, 215
Shantung, 30, 31, 114, 165
Shen-Hai, 139
Shenyang, 210, 212. *See also* Fengtien
Shidehara, 114, 122
Shigemitsu Mamoru, 86, 87
Shih-chia-chuang, 166
Shih-ching (Classic of Poetry), 200
Shimano Saburō, 57
Shimizu Yasuzō, 66

Shimmei Masamichi, 37
Shin Chūgoku no omoide (Memories of the New China), 210
Shin tenchi (New Universe), 11, 134, 210
Shina bunkatsu ron (On the Partition of China), 107
Shina kakumei ni okeru kaikyū tairitsu (Class Conflict in the Chinese Revolution), 110
Shina kakumei no kaikyū tairitsu (Class Conflict in the Chinese Revolution), 70
Shina kakumei ron (On the Chinese Revolution), 107
Shina kakumei shi ron (On the History of the Chinese Revolution), 111
Shina kakumei shōshi (A Short History of the Chinese Revolution), 107
Shina kakumei to sekai no asu (The Chinese Communist Party and the World Tomorrow), 104
Shina keizai zensho (Compendium on the Chinese Economy), 106
Shina kenkyū (Chinese Studies), 111
Shina kokusaihō ron (On International Law in China), 107
Shina kōsenryoku chōsa (Investigation of the Resistance Capacity of the Chinese), 176, 179
Shina musan kaikyū undō shi (A History of the Proletarian Movement in China), 110
Shina shisō kenkyū (Studies in Chinese Thought), 111
Shina shōbetsu zenshi (Complete Compendia of China by Provinces), 106
Shina zeikan ron (On the Customs Duty in China), 107
Shinjinkai (New Man Society), 63, 140, 195; aims of, 37–38; connections to, xvi, xxii, 88, 176, 177, 193, 194; established, x, 34–35; journal, 105; members of, xxi, xxiii, 29, 37, 39, 43, 44
Shintōsha (Society for the Encouragement of the East), 134, 135–36

Shiomi Tomonosuke, 112
Shionoya On, 33
Shiraiwa Ryūhei, 106–107
Shirokogorov, 113
Shiratori Kurakichi, ix, 21, 22, 23, 106
Shizen kagaku kenkyūjo (Institute of Natural Sciences), 114
Shōkō Academy, 142
Shōwa Restoration, 140
Shuang-ch'eng-pao, 32, 33
Shun-t'ien shih-pao, 63
Shuzui Hajime, 192, 198
Sian Incident, 166
Siberia, 33, 36, 38, 42, 53, 56, 57, 115, 133, 190
Sino-Japanese Friendship Association, xxvi, 204, 206, 207, 214, 215
Sino-Japanese Manchurian Relief Treaty, 55
Sino-Japanese Study Society, 207
Sino-Japanese War, xv, 11, 17, 113, 165, 169, 182, 189
Smith, Henry, x
SMR Incident, xxiii, xxiv, 179, 190, 193, 197, 200–203, 206
Social Thought Society, 215
Society for the Encouragement of the East, 134, 135–36
Soejima Michimasa, 46
Soejima Taneomi, 46
Sogō Shinji, 129, 161, 167
Son Bun den (Biography of Sun Yatsen), 70
Soochow, 110
Sorge, Richard, xxi, 186, 187, 189
South Manchurian Medical College, 14
Soviet Union. *See* Union of Soviet Socialist Republics (USSR)
Special Affairs Department, 142
Special Services Unit, 115, 116
State Council, 141, 142, 145
Stopes, Marie, 68
Su Chao-cheng, 70, 74, 92, 93, 94
Su, (Prince), 49
Suda Teiichi, 225
Sudō Yūhei, 206
Suehiro Izutarō, 113
Sugimoto Fumio, 221

Sugimura, (Mr.), 47
Sugiura Jūgō, 142
Sumitomo Company, 131
Sun K'o, 73
Sun Yat-sen, 34, 37, 72, 74, 88, 104, 181, 182
Sung Chiao-jen, *xi*
Sungari River, 212
Suzue Gen'ichi, 64, 68, 74, 200, 214; arrested, 190; discussed, 69–70; and *Hsiang-tao*, 110; and Hu O-kung, 185; and Ozaki, 188; and Peking Raid, 82; SMR consultant, 4, 42, 84, 186; and Su Chao-cheng, 92, 93
Suzuki Kohei, *xxi*, 188, 192
Suzuki Shigetoshi, 173
Suzuki Tatsuo, 112

Tachibana Shiraki, 4, 42–43, 197, 110–11, 117–19, 139, 149–50, 171, 188–89
Taguchi Unzō, 88
Taguchi Yasunobu, 44
Tai Kuo-hui, 226
Taihei, 62
Taira Teizō, 37
T'ai-shan, 29, 31
T'ai-tung jih-pao (T'ai-tung Daily News), 134
Taiwan, 17, 18, 24, 175, 209, 219, 220, 222–24
Taiyō-maru, 100
Takano Tadao, 141
Takayama Gizō, 37
Takayama Jintarō, 26
Takayanagi Ken'ichirō, 107
Takayanagi Yasutarō, 42
Takenaka Masakazu, 98, 99
Takigawa Masajirō, 30
T'an P'ing-shan, 74
Tanabe Hisao, 214
Tanahashi Kotara, 37
Tanaka Giichi, 121, 134, 136
Tanaka Kakuei, 224
Tanaka Kōtarō, 201
Tanaka Kyūichi, 39, 45, 46, 156, 192, 193, 194
Tanaka Seijirō, 174–75
Tanaka Takeo, 193

T'ang Shao-i, 55
T'ang-kang-tzu, 212
Tangku Accord, 163, 165
T'ang-shan, 75, 76
T'ao Meng-ho, 84, 85
Taoism, 111
Taoka Masaki, 43
Taoka Reiun, 43
Tarui Tōkichi, 107
Ta-shih-ch'iao, 27
Tatsuta Kiyotatsu, 69, 86, 87
Thiess, (Dr.), *xxvii*, 24, 41, 143
Third International, 70
Three Section system, 16
Thursday Club, 37
T'ieh-ling, 27
Tientsin: foreign settlement, 89; Itō in, 29, 31, 169, 170; Japanese in, 34, 71, 118; repression, 77; SMR branch, *xiv*, 161–65; war criminals pact, 215
Tientsin-Pukow Railway, 166
Ting Mei-ts'un, 183
Ting Shih-yüan, 61
Tō-A, 168
Tō-A dōbun shoin (East Asian Common Culture Academy), *xvii*, 39, 49, 52, 106, 187, 188
Tō-A kōgyō, 62
Togakushi Mountain, 35, 36, 37
Tōjō Hideki, 119, 165, 191, 192, 202, 206
Tōkaidō, 26
Toki Tsuyoshi, 173
Tōkō renmei (Eastern Prosperity Federation), 140
Tokutomi Sohō, *vii*
Tokyo, *xx*, *xxvii*, 30, 93, 136, 157, 194; China studies in, 85, 114; Itō in, *xxiii*, 60, 71, 100, 185, 187, 204, 205, 206, 207, 208, 209; Nakanishi in, 176; Shinjinkai in, 37; SMR branch, *viii*, *xvii*, 16, 22, 43–44, 140, 155, 174, 179, 188, 190, 208, 209; stockholders' meeting, 129, 130; Wang Ching-wei in, 182, 183
Tokyo Electric Lighting, 167
Tokyo Industrial Laboratory, 26
Tōkyō nichinichi shimbun (Tokyo Daily News), 45

Tokyo University, *ix, x, xxi*, 21, 29, 33, 34, 36, 38, 39, 44, 45, 61, 64, 106, 140, 145, 164
Tōyō bunka kenkyūjo (Institute of East Asian Culture), 114
Tōyō jiyū shimbun, 65
Tōyō Kisen Lines, 60
Tōyōbō, 168
Toyohashi, 206
Toyotabō, 168
Truk Islands, 29
Ts'ang-chou, 166
Ts'ang-Shih Line, 166
Ts'ao Ju-lin, 65
Tsinan, 29
Tsinghua University, 114
Tsingtao, 25, 29, 30, 31, 70, 88, 93
Tsubogami, (Ambassador), 206
Tsuda Shizue, 184, 185, 191, 205
Tsuji Jirō, 30
Tsurumi Yūsuke, 48
Tsuruoka, 206
Tuan Ch'i-jui, 30
Tun-hua, 193, 195, 196, 201
T'ung-chou, 143, 163, 166
Twenty-One Demands, 30

Uchida Kōsai, *xii*, 122
Uchigasaki Kenjirō, 157
Uchiyama Kanzō, 86, 214
Uemura Tetsumi, 136
Uetsuka Tsukasa, 134
Union of Soviet Socialist Republics (USSR): and An-shan Iron Works, 210; and Central Laboratory, 210; and Chiang Kai-shek, 94–95; economists, 112–13; Li Ta-chao and, 79, 82; and Manchukuo, 144, 146, 147; sale of Chinese Eastern Railway, 210; Sano trip to, 66; SMR research on, 18, 57, 58, 117, 120, 209; support for China, *xx*, and Vietnam, 225; and war with Japan, 160–61, 162, 201, 205, 207. *See also* Peking raid
United Nations, 223
United States, 81; Boxer Indemnity, 114; China studies in, 102, 110; Chinese in, 25, 41, 66; imperialism, 222, 223, 224, 225; intelligence gathering activities, 183; and Japan, 183, 219; and Manchuria, 5, 53, 126, 131, 146; materials sent to, 208–209; and Peking, 62; study in, 3, 99–100, 104; and Vietnam, *xxiv*, 150, 224
University of California, 100, 102, 103
Ushijima Yoshirō, 82, 83, 98
Ussuri River, 133
Usuki, 19

Vietnam, *xxiv, xxv*, 150, 178, 224, 225
Voitinsky, Grigori, 72

Wachi Takaji, 142
Wagner, Wilhelm, *xv*, 104
Wang Ching-wei, *xx*, 95, 181–84
Wang Hsüeh-wen, 197
Wang Shu-chih (*see* Suzue Gen'ichi)
Wang Tzu-yen (*see* Suzue Gen'ichi)
Wan-pao-shan, 138
Warera, 66
Warera no shōgai ni okeru Chūgoku (China in Our Careers), 226
Waseda University, 45, 65, 81
Watanabe Kaikyoku, 140
Watanabe Kazan, 199
Watanabe Yūji, 190, 201, 202, 205
Westmoreland, William, *xxv*
Whampoa Bund, 73
Whampoa Military Academy, 94
Whitman, Walt, 36
Wiedfeldt, Otto, *xxvii*, 24, 41
Williams, (Professor), 100, 102, 103, 104
Wittfogel, Karl A., *xiv, xv*, 104, 110
World War I, 25, 35, 38, 44, 45, 50, 56
Wu Chün-sheng, 91
Wu P'ei-fu, 78, 79, 87, 91
Wuhan, 102
Wusih, 113

Yagi Shōzaburō, 42
Yamada Gōichi, *xv*
Yamada Junsaburō, 182
Yamada Seitarō, 113
Yamagata, (General), 8
Yamaguchi Shigeji, 137, 139, 149

Yamaguchi Shōgo, 173
Yamaguchi Susumu, *xvi*
Yamakawa Kikue, 103
Yamamoto Jōtarō, 46
Yamamoto Senji, 68
Yamana Yoshitsuru, 37
Yanaihara Tadao, 103
Yang Pao-an, 92, 95
Yen Ch'uan-yüan, 49, 50
Yen Hsi-shan, 182
Yenan, *xxi*, 166, 176, 184
Yen-t'ai, 7
Yin Ju-keng, 91, 163, 166
Ying-k'ou, 90, 127
Yokogawa Jirō, *xxvi*, 190, 205
Yokohama Specie Bank, 62
Yoshida Shigeru, 215
Yoshihara Jirō, 190
Yoshino Sakuzō, *xi*, 29, 33–35, 38, 71, 87, 105, 107

Yoshiue Satoru, 190
Yü Ch'ung-han, 139, 141
Yüan Shih-k'ai, 30, 34, 64
Yūhōkai (Majestic Peak Association), 12, 124, 132, 134–35, 139, 144–45, 147, 149, 152, 215
Yūki Seitarō, 136
Yule, 84
Yung-lo ta-tien (Yung-lo Encyclopedia), 209
Yūsonsha (Continued Existence Society), 140

Zai-Man Nikkei kyōsanshugi undō (The Communist Movement of Japanese in Manchuria), *xxii*, *xxiii*
Zen'ei, 67
Zumoto Motosada, 43